4-7-15
$29.95
BqT

AS

A Million Years of Music

A Million Years of Music

The Emergence of Human Modernity

Gary Tomlinson

ZONE BOOKS · NEW YORK

2015

© 2015 Gary Tomlinson
ZONE BOOKS
633 Vanderbilt Street
Brooklyn, NY 11218

Printed in the United States of America.

Distributed by The MIT Press,
Cambridge, Massachusetts, and London, England

Library of Congress Cataloging-in-Publication Data
Tomlinson, Gary.
    A Million years of music : the emergence of human
modernity / by Gary Tomlinson.—First edition.
        pages   cm
    Includes bibliographical references and index.
    ISBN 978-1-935408-65-9
    1. Music—History and criticism. 2. Musicology.
I. Title. II. Title: A million years of music.
    ML160.T635 2015
    780.9'01—dc23

                                        2014024072

For Juliet

Contents

Concepts, Models, Machines

Musical expression is today a universal and characteristic trait of our species. But how did it come to be? More specifically, how did the capacities and behaviors comprised in music-making (or *musicking*) emerge across the long history of our evolution and the evolutions of our ancestors and closest relatives? In this book, I propose a set of answers to this question.

It is a venerable question, posed in one form or another in countless cultures, framed often in myths, and discussed in learned fashion repeatedly across the last three centuries in the West. I have tried to put the question on a footing different from what it has had in the past, even in the recent past, in such discussion. This has meant gaining distance from what has seemed, in accounts from Vico and Rousseau on down through Darwin to Pinker and beyond, a self-evident truth about the case: the close relation of the origins of musicking and language. This connection has been conceived in numerous ways, which fall into two camps differing in the lines of dependency they propose. Sometimes language has been seen to give rise to music, as an outgrowth or aftereffect; much more often musicking has been understood as a kind of Ur-language of emotion, resulting only later in rational, propositional language. The two camps are united in searching for such priority, either for language or musicking, and they have attempted again and again to trace the lines of descent and causal ties extending between them.

There are grains of truth in both of these positions, but in emphasizing the priority of either musical or linguistic developments they have always obscured what they have tried to explain. In *A Million Years of Music*, I account for the developments of the capacities for musicking and language along parallel but independent tracks, with a meeting and coalescence of those capacities only very late in hominin evolution. The tracks were not formed by goals waiting at their endpoints—the goals of full-fledged speech or musicking. Instead, they arose from the necessities facing groups of nonmusical, nonlinguistic hominins as they together sought subsistence or survival in the material ecologies around them. Modern musicking and language, in a real sense, did not develop at all. Instead they fell out, as belated emergences, from patterns of sociality and communication neither musical nor linguistic that can be traced to periods long before *Homo sapiens* existed. As they coalesced, they formed not only the modern connections between them that most accounts have displaced back onto their origins but also other aspects definitive of our human modernity.

Following such developments may seem to pose intractable problems, even imponderable ones; for what kind of evidence can be brought to bear on the case? The question is pressing for musicking since, whatever else it is, it is an evanescent act or set of acts that fades as it sounds. Its product does not have the staying power of mammoths painted on cave walls or the heft of carved "Venus" figurines. When Jacques Chailley published his *40,000 ans de musique* in 1961, the joke made the rounds that he had dispensed with the first 39,000 years in the first two or three pages. My title suggests ambitions that make his overreaching chronological scope seem modest.

Much has changed, however, across the last half-century, and evidence today turns out to be plentiful—indeed, more plentiful than could be adduced in a single book, though I have tried to make my account cover all the areas I have deemed to be central. It is evidence, to be sure, of a certain kind: fragmentary, circumstantial, indirect, and requiring for its reading more-than-usual turns of inference, interpretation, and even speculation. It comes from fields in which such challenges are commonplace, especially archaeology, paleoanthropology, and human evolutionary studies on one hand and music cognition and music psychology on the other. (Other fields also have much to contribute: ethology and primatology, linguistics, semiotics, and more.) From the vantage of these primary fields, my project might be summed up this way: I have extended the new knowledge amassed in recent years in music cognition and psychology back across a deep history, but this is feasible only because of the effort that has taken shape in the same years among archaeologists to deduce the cognitive attributes and behavioral patterns of our ancestors and sibling species, an effort that can now be extended in the direction of musicking. Indeed, I believe that our deepening understanding of musical production and perception reflects back on this "cognitive archaeology," casting it in a somewhat different and brighter light. For this reason, my subtitle suggests that understanding the appearance of musicking will help us better to understand the emergence of our modernity in general.

The story told here includes capacities closely tied to our biological nature and the natures of our ancestors, but it attends also to cultural behaviors that express themselves at some greater distance from biology, however deeply they are rooted in it. It must do both, since unreconstructed nature/nurture dichotomies prove to be at best misleading, at worst utterly distorting in the analysis of just about everything interesting that humans are up to. From the historical vantage I have adopted, our most comprehensive accounts of human attainment need always to hold in balance our biological heritage and our cultural one. What must be described is a coevolution of biology and culture—a *biocultural* coevolution.

From this historical vantage, also, it can readily be seen that narratives of complex modern human attainments, musicking among them, must fulfill two requirements. They must trace a long path of incremental additions to our ancestors' capacities that were preconditions of a final emergence; and they must describe that final emergence, occurring so late in hominin evolution as to have involved, in some of its aspects, only *Homo sapiens*. I fulfill these requirements in chronological fashion. After the introduction of Chapter 1, Chapters 2–5 trace incremental additions before music or *Homo sapiens* existed. Chapters 6–8 (with a forecast in Chapter 5) describe the gathering of these increments, under new conditions, into the musicking that characterizes modern humanity. *A Million Years of Music* emphasizes first incrementalism, and then coalescence.

Humanistic forays into our evolution are many these days, and there are several recent accounts even of the "origins of music," as the usual phrase has it. In this context, it seems wise at the start to name one or two things this book is not.

It is not, first, an exercise in evolutionary psychology, a field that has provided the starting point for many humanistic accounts. This approach has devoted itself to speculating on the ways in which the modern human brain, mind, or psyche is an outcome of selective pressures and organismal adaptations to them. It has tended, however, to adopt an overly simple model of Darwinian variation and selection, a shortcoming prominent in many of those humanistic outgrowths of it. Darwinian selection-with-variation forms a foundation for my account, as it must for any deep-historical account of the emergence of humanity. But it is foundation only, and I recognize that the story cannot usefully be told from a narrowly adaptationist vantage. My alternative, coevolutionary model, neo-Darwinian or, more accurately, post-neo-Darwinian, represents something close to a consensus these days among evolutionary theorists, with changes of emphasis and one or two features added here. It will be presented across the chapters that follow.

One feature of this model can be introduced immediately and will help to identify another thing this book is not. If, on one hand,

I avoid the simple adaptive models often advanced in evolutionary accounts, on the other hand I do not fight my way into the thickets of recent evolutionary genetics and molecular evolution. Intracellular mechanisms—genetic, epigenetic, and extragenetic—have come to play a central role in recent discussions of evolutionary interactions between the genome and organisms embodying it (between, that is, genotype and phenotype), yet my account explores a different realm, extending *out* from the organism to its environment and social context rather than *in* from the organism-as-a-whole to the genome. This is not to assert any radical discontinuity between these realms; in fact, we are beginning to understand, at least in outline, a continuous network of intermeshed mechanisms that, in some hypothetical full picture of all the forces that have acted in our evolution, would extend from the molecular level out to such things as mind, society, and culture.

Positing such continuities, however, does not entail the assumption of a uniformity of the mechanisms involved. Indeed evolutionary theorists discern more and more clearly qualitatively different mechanisms that emerge at different levels of scale, marking or disrupting the continuities. Describing some of these mechanisms at higher levels of scale—moving outward, again, from the level of the individual organism—and tracing their history in regard to the formation of capacities for music and a few related aspects of our humanity are central goals of the book that follows. *A Million Years of Music* develops models of overlapping, biocultural mechanisms that emerged in the late evolution of hominins (and finally *Homo sapiens*) and that resulted in fundamental features of human behavior today. Its chronological, historical narrative aims at codifying these mechanisms of organismal and environmental interaction.

Beneath this narrative there is a specific and deeper structure at work in *A Million Years of Music*, which may be approached through a series of key words or concepts that are featured.

Together these form a network with implications well beyond the particulars of my topic, a network interlacing concepts that have been central in humanistic discourse of the late twentieth century with others that have taken hold there only in the last decade or two. There is good reason to think that something akin to this amalgam of concepts, old and new, familiar and not, will prove to be important as humanists recast their disciplines and reimagine the relations of them to sciences and social sciences in the twenty-first century.

Chapter 1: Neo-Darwinian theories of evolution depend on mechanisms of **feedback**. In the most schematic case, an organism's lifeways alter its environment, thereby altering the selective pressures on it and its descendants and changing the lifeways of future generations. Feedback defines coevolutionary theories, which replace models of selection that emphasize environmental causality on varying organisms with loops of mutual interaction, thereby substituting spiraling, nonlinear evolutionary trajectories for linear ones. The redoubling and interplay of such feedback loops is a prime generator of emergent qualities in nonliving, living, and cultural systems alike. It leads in unexpected directions and results in unanticipated systemic complexities. This theme of **emergence** recurs throughout the book and refers to the bottom-up construction of complex systems through feedback interrelations involving simpler components and more basic algorithms. Such construction characterizes culture in special ways, giving rise to self-organized systematizations or **epicycles** that achieve some independence of operation from evolutionary feedback cycles. Epicycle, in the sense it is developed here, names the unique potential of cultural sedimentation to produce feedforward elements in the broader cycles of biocultural coevolution.

Chapter 2: Without a model of emergent, bottom-up **complexity**, early hominin technologies unearthed by archaeologists are puzzling indeed, for they show design symmetries that could not have been envisaged by their creators. Feedback loops of cultural accumulation appear in these technologies, not yet deeply sedimented, to be sure, but operating through evident mimetic capacities. This **mimesis** defined a rhythmicization of interactions with the environment and conspecifics that characterized the taskscapes of these hominins—and that would, a million years later, have much to do with music. The **taskscapes**, however, did not involve **agency** as humanists usually think of it, and partly for this reason these hominins' behaviors settled into a cultural stasis across huge periods that has challenged archaeological presumptions of self-consciously fashioned artifacts. The technologies, in other words, are not instances of the *techne* analyzed by Heidegger in the mid-twentieth century and elaborated by Bernard Steigler and others fifty years later. To understand them we need a **poiesis** distanced from these conceptions and a model of emergent design prior to agency.

Chapter 3 and Excursus: Questions of the earliest hominin mimesis and culture cannot be raised without also asking when, finally, a recognizable agency began to take shape. This was initially a purposive, emotive, and manipulative expression born of face-to-face interaction, **copresence**. It was thus a primordial model of the conformation of interacting agents—of, in a language more familiar to humanists, **intersubjectivity**. From Wittgenstein down to Lacan and Benveniste and beyond, however, humanists have conceived intersubjectivity first and foremost through the medium of language and linguistic discourse. This will not do for our ancestors 500,000 years ago—long before language could have existed in its modern form—any more than it suffices for the complexities of social interaction in the nonhuman animal world today. Ancient hominin sociality raises the question of a **protodiscourse**, of the negotiation of intersubjectivity through vocalization and gesture but without language; in doing so, it problematizes the expressive antecedents of both language and music. It brings to center stage the nature of copresent interactions among these creatures and the rudiments of reciprocal understanding or **theory of mind**, and it suggests the rootedness of these interactions in connectionist neural models building complexity from simple foundations. This ancient sociality, at the same time, glimpses its own **transcendence** and that of the situation that spawned it, pointing forward to a later moment when copresence would begin to be transformed by other modes of cultural formation.

Chapter 4: These other modes involve structures of **hierarchy** in thought and behavior and, beneath them, the general cognitive capacity for hierarchization. None of the fundamental markers of human modernity—language, music, religion, elaborate kinship structures, complex social formations of all sorts—could exist without cognition capable of constructing hierarchies; this cognition is prominent in the organizing of musical information. An expressive sociality of complex, emotive, but still protolinguistic interactions might therefore, in taking on hierarchic organization, move a decisive step closer to modern music and language alike. At the same time, hierarchy forms a step away from copresence toward a cognized, formal **abstraction** of interaction in and with the world, writ large everywhere in modern human life but only modestly manifested beyond it. Hierarchy names a foundational structure for the transcendence of copresence indicated before. So it is all the more striking that we can trace hierarchization of behavior—and behind it of cognition—beyond our own direct ancestors and especially, in highly elaborated forms, to our cousins, the Neandertals.

Chapter 5: In numerous recent accounts by archaeologists and others, the idea of **symbolism** forms a paramount criterion for the final appearance of human modernity. Time and again, however, it is a particularly vexed and ill-defined criterion—and no wonder, since this terrain is a treacherous one. When **symbolic cognition** is clearly defined, we can follow in it an outgrowth of the abstraction already represented in the hierarchization of Neandertal culture; but even with this clarity the emphasis of symbolism has the unfortunate effect of narrowing our vantage as we look out on the last 100,000 years of our history. A corrective, however, can be fashioned from a neo-Peircean **semiotics** revived in the last few years by theorists such as Terrence Deacon and elaborated by a few of the most attentive analysts of archaeological symbolism. Using this approach, we can discern not only the symbol but also other semiotic modes in our phylogeny; we can describe, especially through Peirce's concepts of **interpretant** and **index**, the opening-out of both ancient and contemporary human semiosis toward broader realms of animal signification. This broadening points to the fact that hierarchical abstraction and systematic organization, while requirements for symbolic cognition, extend also to indexes. The extension yields important insights concerning both the expressive capacities of our ancestors and the early systematizing of musical pitch.

Chapters 6 and 7: The deep history of *Homo sapiens* does not trace a course of gradual but steadfast progress. The ever more complex pattern we reconstruct of human migrations out of Africa over the last 100,000 years, recently discovered complexities of sapient history within Africa, and the patchwork, start-and-stop, irregularly dispersed attainments of sapient humans across this period—all these require not merely new explanations of our heritage but new *kinds* of explanations. They call for **nonlinear histories** that forgo straight-line causality in order to accommodate the formative forces identified in Chapter 1: spiraling feedback loops and loops-upon-loops, and burgeoning complexity from simple structures and actions. New feedback cycles that archaeologists have explored for recent hominin evolution involve climate, ecology, and demography as well as human culture. And culture itself, sedimenting its bodies of transmitted knowledge more deeply than before, gives rise to systems that take on significant powers to redirect human biocultural coevolution. These systems, feeding forward into coevolutionary cycles, are the **cultural epicycles** introduced in Chapter 1 and elaborated here. They are mechanisms of nonlinearity that loom larger by far in *Homo sapiens* than in any previous lineage on earth. In them we can trace the interconnected coalescings that shaped fundamental modern human behaviors and capacities, including musical ones.

Chapter 8: In these behaviors and capacities, finally, we see two things: evidence of continuities reaching far back in our species' history, and dramatic changes that cut across it, marking our difference from our predecessors. Mounting archaeological analysis, often of stunning nuance, elongates the continuities ever farther back into our history; but as it does so it brings to light also momentous facts of change. This conclusion draws out both this sameness and this difference as they regard musicking.

Recently, Andrew Shryock, Daniel Lord Smail, and a team of coauthors identified **scale** as a conceptual ground for understanding these elongated continuities. They note that graphs against time of many issues in our deep history—population size, information and material exchange, technical innovations, and more—yield a particular curve: a "J-graph," in which the plotted line remains flat over a long period only to shoot steeply upward in the most recent millennia or centuries. They rightly caution that the flat-line portion of such graphs is deceptive, hiding at smaller levels of scale kinds of movement and disjunction similar to those amplified in the steeper part of the curve. Thus they perceive, reaching at least 50,000 years back into our history, fractal reproductions of patterns at different scalar levels rather than decisive breaks and revolutions at the Paleolithic/Neolithic border or the Middle/Upper Paleolithic border.

Through this fractal model they challenge us to rethink many aspects of human history, recasting, for example, the domestication of plants and animals not as a revolutionary Neolithic moment but as a series of multiple accretions starting far back in the Paleolithic era. These ideas form an important corrective issued against models of prehistory that picture it as eons of boredom, only cut short by the revolutionary excitement of the last three, six, ten, or even forty thousand years. They extend our history of dynamic change farther back than conventional views do—an extension certainly warranted also, as we will see, by new archaeological evidence from many locales.

What needs to be added to their corrective is an additional level of modeling, a metalevel, so to speak, for the production of change. At this level we encounter the fact that *processes of change themselves change*, functioning in different ways, at different rates, and with varying efficacies at the different fractal levels of Shryock and colleagues. Thus, for example, an innovation may play itself out in vastly divergent fashions depending upon the size of the population in which it occurs or the nature of relations of that population to others—to the extent that it might spawn new, sweeping innovations in one circumstance while disappearing without issue in another. Accumulations and transmissions of cultural knowledge may rush headlong at one scalar level or be short-circuited at another; sedimentations of population-wide behaviors may pile up in one locale while eroding elsewhere; epicyclic amplification may take over or never gain a foothold. All these varying patterns will feed back or forward into the loops of biocultural coevolution.

The key concepts I have previewed here gesture toward the production of these kinds of difference and metadifference at the same time as they extend the continuities of many aspects of our humanity into a past deep enough to outreach easily the lifetime of our species. These concepts together offer analytic tools to discern the mechanisms deep at work in our biocultural phylogeny. We can call the mechanisms thus identified **abstract machines**, in the sense in which Gilles Deleuze, Felix Guattari, and Manuel de Landa have borrowed the term from computational and information sciences. These are patterns immanent to the flows of matter/energy and information, bottom-up creations without controls guiding from above, self-generated schemata emerging from the nature of the arrays in which they function. Abstract machines point to no predictable outcome or telos, and the heuristic value of describing them is not predictive but retrospective. In deep history they help us to generalize from fragments of evidence to form outlines of a coherent, nonlinear narrative. Considering such mechanisms may well create a path to the best understanding we can presently achieve of how we came to be what we are today.

In any case, an account such as this cannot avoid abstract machines for, though recently and productively theorized, they are not new to our conceptual panoply concerning evolution. Long before they were first described in computational and information science, the most sublime instance of all had been detailed, richly and presciently, by Darwin: **selection with variation**. It is here that we begin.

CHAPTER ONE

Some First Principles

Listening Back

Humans today make music. Think beyond all the qualifications that might trail after this bald statement: that only certain
humans make music, that extensive training is involved, that
many societies distinguish musical specialists from nonmusicians,
that in today's societies most listen to music rather than making
it, and so forth. These qualifications, whatever their local merit,
are moot in the face of the overarching truth that making music,
considered from a cognitive and psychological vantage, is the
province of all those who perceive and experience what is made.
We are, almost all of us, musicians—everyone who can entrain
(not necessarily dance) to a beat, who can recognize a repeated
tune (not necessarily sing it), who can distinguish one instrument
or one singing voice from another. I will often use an antique
word, recently revived, to name this broader musical experience.
Humans are *musicking* creatures.[1]

The set of capacities that enables musicking is a principal
marker of modern humanity. There is nothing polemical in this
assertion except a certain insistence, which will figure often
in what follows, that musicking be included in our thinking
about fundamental human commonalities. Capacities involved
in musicking are many and take shape in complicated ways, arising from innate dispositions, from the ontogenetic development
of them, and from the acculturating circumstances in which
this development occurs. Most of these capacities overlap with

nonmusical ones, though a few may be distinct and dedicated to musical perception and production. In the area of overlap, linguistic capacities seem to be particularly important, and humans are (in principle) language-makers in addition to music-makers— speaking creatures as well as musicking ones.

Humans are symbol-makers too, a feature tightly bound up with language, not so tightly with music. The species Cassirer dubbed *Homo symbolicus* cannot help but tangle musicking in webs of symbolic thought and expression, habitually making it a component of behavioral complexes that form such expression. But in fundamental features musicking is neither language-like nor symbol-like, and from these differences come many clues to its ancient emergence.

If musicking is a primary, shared trait of modern humans, then to describe its emergence must be to detail the coalescing of that modernity. This took place, archaeologists are clear, over a very long *durée*: at least 50,000 years or so, more likely something closer to 200,000, depending in part on what that coalescence is taken to comprise. If we look back 20,000 years, a small portion of this long period, we reach the lives of humans whose musical capacities were probably little different from our own. As we look farther back we reach horizons where this similarity can no longer hold—perhaps 40,000 years ago, perhaps 70,000, perhaps 100,000. But we never cross a line before which all the cognitive capacities recruited in modern musicking abruptly disappear. Unless we embrace the incredible notion that music sprang forth in full-blown glory, its emergence will have to be tracked in gradualist terms across a long period.

This is one general feature of a history of music's emergence; others that will be considered at length later may be briefly noted here. The history was at once sociocultural and biological; hominin evolution always joined these two.[2] The capacities recruited in musicking are many, so describing its emergence involves following several or many separate strands. Since these capacities are for the most part not recruited solely in musicking, and were

24

not adaptations for it, the history reaches well beyond discussion of music alone and back to a period long before it existed. In fact, the history of human musicking cannot be seen in any reasonably comprehensive view without ranging back long before our species; this is why I have signaled in my title a full million-year span, even though it is implausible to think that anything like modern musicking existed before the last tenth or so of this span. Finally, musicking recruited capacities achieved across distinct, mostly pre- and nonmusical evolutionary histories, and that makes the story of its emergence one of incremental accumulation and ultimate synergy.

I have already employed three keywords of this account—music, the human, and emergence. Today these wander in search of definition across the pages of writings from many disciplines, and here such meanings will take shape slowly—as an accumulation across the chapters that follow. These chapters will offer, in chronological order, distinct vignettes in the long, divagating history of premusical, protomusical, and musical development. This chronological sedimentation of distinct histories aims to illuminate a certain *course* of the appearance of traits and capacities in the hominin line, the coalescing of these into a recognizably modern but still ancient *humanity*, and a specific set of activities involving intently organized, complexly perceived sound that is a product of the one and a feature of the other. Music and humanity were both defined by the history from which they emerged, while their crystallizing traits turned back at every point along the way to shape the further nature of their emergence.

The starting point for such a narrative will be in some measure arbitrary. Thinking history—and certainly thinking the long-term emergence of complex phenomena, among which the advent of human modernity must rank high—does not discern beginnings so much as movements of difference, each revising the formation that came before it. Fixing an "origin" for music, with all the pernicious border implications this would carry, is neither possible nor interesting. And pernicious is almost too mild a word: Are we to think of music as an innovation before which came absence and savagery, in the Enlightenment version? Or a lapse before which came purity and wholeness, in the scriptural? Instead the coming chapters will take snapshots of evolutionary processes in perpetual motion—"stills," to be sure, but stills composed so as to give a sense of the motion they freeze.

At all events there must be a first snapshot, a narrative that begins. It might start at the first signs in the biosphere of sound-perceiving and sound-producing organs, hundreds of millions of years ago. It might begin, still far back in geological time, with the first mammals, or the earliest primates. Or it might take a far shorter, more direct route, picking up the thread at the relatively recent coalescing of capacities into recognizable musicking, and thus remaining within the species-lifespan of *Homo sapiens* and evading the very question asked: How did musicking fall out of capacities and behaviors with long developmental histories in the hominin clade?

Beginning at about the million-year mark, 800,000 years before the advent of sapient humans, works well for several reasons. The early end of this span comes in a period when novel patterns arose in the social and technological lives of hominin species that preceded us, and both the archaeological and paleontological records, for all their fragmentary nature, convey enough evidence to describe these patterns. We can, moreover, discern a link between these patterns and certain musical capacities that took shape only much later. The patterns are, in other words, specific enough in their formation to enable such an interpretive connection. One million years back places us at a moment when behaviors and capacities that ultimately would underlie modern musicking do not so much appear for the first time, as become *legible*.

Incrementalism

Music processing in the human brain, as students of cognition have proclaimed more and more loudly in recent years, is a matter of mind-beggaring complexity. This holds true not only for evidently intricate musics—a Balinese gamelan in full swing, for instance, or a four-part Bach fugue, or a post-bop jazz ensemble—but for all musics. Indeed, in any ecumenical view of musicking a truth quickly emerges analogous to one that long ago dawned on comparative linguists: Just as there is no such thing as a simple human language, so there is no simple music.

The importance of this principle can hardly be overstated. All musicking easily surpasses a threshold of complexity of perception and processing that is high enough to continue to thwart, in some good measure, our efforts to see over it. The plainest song or drum cadence marshals neural circuitry of great complication for its production or perception; a crowd of football fans chanting in synchrony to urge on their team offers cognitive mysteries. The differences among musics—between a Mahlerian orchestra and a lullaby hummed to a nodding child—are real enough, but they are epiphenomenal relative to that high threshold, wrinkles on the surface of the stark immensity of brain resources required for musicking to happen at all. Most of my narrative will be devoted to illuminating the appearance of these resources.

There is no single, discrete neural network dedicated to this complex production and processing. There is, in other words, no dedicated music *module* in the brain, to invoke a term associated especially with psychologist and philosopher Jerry Fodor.[3] The same is probably true of any complex human behavior; certainly the situation is similar, again, for language. The old-time notion that Broca's and Wernicke's areas account for language processing turns out to be woefully inadequate. However important these cortical regions may be in linguistic capacities, they are neither the whole story nor wholly dedicated to language.

The cognitive processing of music involves, in a first approximation, many neural systems or networks working in tandem. These reach from the ear to the brain and, within the brain, from its most recent parts (evolutionarily speaking) to ancient, deep-brain structures. The networks operate with varying degrees of independence from one another. Most of them seem to be involved also in other functions, some very general (separating sonic events in "auditory scene" analysis, grouping proximate percepts into larger Gestalts, gauging time and periodicity, and so forth) and some more specific to fine auditory perception, musical and nonmusical (for instance our astonishing abilities to analyze and discriminate timbres or tone-colors). All these networks show, in their recruitment in diverse capacities, a *generalization* in the functioning of what cognitivists often call *domain*. Other networks, for example those processing pitch in the special way it occurs in musicking, different even from pitch in tonal languages, are arguably dedicated uniquely to musicking—that is, *domain-specific* for music—though lively debate continues over the existence of *any* musical domain specificity. Altogether a picture takes shape of a multitude of brain functions involved in musicking that coalesce somehow into a manifold-but-unified percept, like the merging of diverse percepts in language or even like consciousness itself.

All these functions stand ready to be activated in any musicking—and can be activated even in ostensibly simple musicking—though individual musical experiences might not engage them all or equally.

On an almost weekly basis, evidence mounts that these capacities for music processing are innate in the human brain—that the brain is, in the vernacular, hard-wired for music. This statement can imply several things, all of them controversial, but here it is enough to take a relatively "soft" stand on "hard" wiring: In a fashion that once again calls to mind language, many basic capacities required for music processing seem to be provided for in neural functioning or architecture either present in the brain at birth or programmed to develop across normal ontogeny. Saying this by no means disallows a huge potential for the individual shaping of the musical brain across individual lives. The position is not a tacit espousal of genetic determinism set against the complexities of ontogenetic development, or a denial of the current focus of much cognitive work, neuroplasticity, the changes a brain undergoes throughout its life. Learning and acculturation play a huge role in any musicking, and they have been central to the preformation and coalescence of musicking across the whole million-year span considered here. As with language, however, the most basic underlying functions that enable music processing come to be present in all normally developing human brains. We know that children need to be exposed to language through a critical learning period in order to develop full capacities for syntax and lexicon, despite the innate brain structures that predispose them to both. Similarly, it seems that all nonhandicapped humans, given the exposure to others making music that is a ubiquitous part of human sociality, become musical. This is part of what it means to assert that humans are musicking creatures.

The recruitment of deep-brain networks in musicking might seem to point to music's great antiquity, but the domain generality of many of these networks belies this indication. That is, though these networks express themselves in capacities that must be very ancient, they tell us little about the final appearance of full-fledged musicking, instead forming a crucial prehistory for it. A vista encompassing some 1,000,000 years, as I have indicated, will afford a fairly comprehensive picture of the ways in which older capacities were shaped, sharpened, and redirected so as to take part finally in the coalescence of modern musicking. Looking back so far takes the measure of these premusical developments, without suggesting that hominins were making music eight hundred millennia before *Homo sapiens*.

The multiple pathways of music processing in the brain imply that we will make little headway constructing our narrative if we view musicking as a monolithic whole. Instead we need to separate carefully the capacities that are most basic to it and gather what traces we can to form hypotheses as to their several emergences. There is little reason to think that these separate functions took shape simultaneously, every reason to think they did not, and the evidence presented here will suggest a broad timespan for their formation. In retrospective vantage, this requires that we piece together an *incremental* narrative of the emergence of music all told.

Such an incremental approach to music's emergence is not entirely new. It has been mooted, for example, over the last decade or so in work led at Cambridge by Ian Cross.[4] From a more cognitive than evolutionary perspective, meanwhile, special issues of the journals *Music Perception* and *Cognition* also have raised the question of this incrementalism.[5] And Stephen Mithen's book of 2005, *The Singing Neanderthals: The Origins of Music, Language, Mind, and Body*, merits special mention. An ambitious attempt to describe a chronology of music's evolutionary emergence from a paleoanthropological perspective—the first such attempt, and pioneering in its way—its narrative is in some measure incremental, though its ability to discern clearly the component capacities of musicking is hampered by Mithen's freely confessed lack of musical expertise.[6]

The incremental stance, moreover, has not been restricted to music. As an approach to the emergence of language, a hotly contested area much intertwined with thought on music (see Chapter 3), it reaches all the way back to Darwin. It has recently been advocated by many linguists, including post-Chomskyan luminaries such as Ray Jackendoff, Derek Bickerton, and Steven Pinker and Paul Bloom. It has also been formulated, from the wider perspective of evolutionary anatomy and biology, by a number of researchers led by Philip Lieberman.[7] This work gestures toward still broader incremental models of the evolution of the whole suite of capacities and behaviors that characterize modern humanity, including research on modern cognition and emotion, human consciousness in general, and modern human kinship systems.[8]

Archaeologists studying the emergence of modern humans have also embraced the incremental model. They have marshaled the kinds of chronologies basic to their endeavor in the effort to understand the formation of capacities not directly legible in the material record they study. As framed by Sally McBrearty and Alison Brooks, this position issues a wholesale challenge to

the notion of a "revolution" in human behavior at the Middle/
Upper Paleolithic border some 40,000–50,000 years ago. They
view this as a Eurocentric idea, an artifact of the development of
Paleolithic archaeology, until recently primarily European. They
gather evidence pointing to a long, gradual, and sporadic piecing
together of modern capacities and behaviors in Africa, a development embracing ancestors of *Homo sapiens* and reaching back
300,000 years or more.[9] By now even the staunchest advocates
for an Upper Paleolithic revolution have taken note of this kind
of evidence and embrace some measure of incrementalism in
describing the advent of human modernity.[10]

A productive incremental approach to the emergence of music
will require both teasing apart the component capacities that
underlie modern musicking and constructing compelling scenarios for their emergence. The first endeavor will rely especially on
cognitive, psychological, and primatological and other ethological
evidence, the second on archaeological and paleoanthropological traces and their interpretation. This tacking back and forth
between modern and ancient evidence will be a repeated gesture
in my account.

It hardly needs saying that an incremental approach cannot
relieve us of the obligation to put together, eventually, the pieces
of the puzzle. At some point the snapshots need to be gathered
together so as to present a moving picture. I will narrate not only
the emergence of the increments—relevant pre- and protomusical capacities, perhaps also some domain-specific musical functions—but also the ultimate coalescence of these into full-fledged
musicking. The evidence indicates that this coalescing of full-
fledged musicking occurred late, well within the species-span of
Homo sapiens, therefore well within the last 200,000 years or so.
Chapters 6 and 7 delve into the chronological specifics.

Perils of Adaptationism

If many individual cognitive capacities underlying music are not
domain-specific to it, their emergences, by the same token, need

31

not have had anything to do with music. A reasonably comprehensive incremental account will need to take in capacities not originally evolved for the emergent behaviors it aims to describe.[11] This points, more broadly still, to two prerequisites for *any* well-formed account of the evolution of a complex, universal human activity (technology, language, religion, numeracy, etc., in addition to music): an inclusiveness reaching to relevant capacities *not* domain-specific to it, and a chronological reach long enough to encompass their various emergences.

Chapters 2–5 are for the most part concerned with hominin behaviors that appeared before musicking itself and that came to be recruited for it only later, in some cases very much later. Obviously, the evolutionary mechanisms that led to the cognitive capacities behind such behaviors cannot have involved musicking. In their later, musical forms, these capacities may represent specific traits selected for one function and later coopted for another one—not adaptations for music but *exaptations*, to use a term associated especially with Stephen Jay Gould and Elisabeth Vrba.[12] Or they may have emerged from more involuted coevolutionary mechanisms of the sort outlined later, in which traits originally selected for nonmusical advantage were reorganized or reshaped into musical traits. But in either case the full range of capacities recruited in modern musicking will not be explained—in principle *cannot* be explained—as music-induced evolutionary developments.

This enters on a question that has preoccupied, in some cases almost mesmerized, researchers over the last decade or two: whether music is adaptation or exaptation. Debate has simmered ever since Steven Pinker made some categorical and (musically speaking) ill-informed judgments on the matter. For him music was a brain-tickling "technology," reliant on the exaptive coopting of capacities selected for far more important functions, especially language, but not adaptive in itself.[13] Others have fought back, either piqued by Pinker's lack of musical expertise or stung by his demotion of music to a level well below the exalted adaptive status he reserved for language.

In arguing for the adaptive status of music, one common strategy has been to adduce putative selective advantages of musicking as a whole, viewing music, in other words, as adaptive in some kind of very big picture. The options among selective pressures are various. Some argue that singing arose as courtship display in the pursuit of mates and thus conferred reproductive advantage, an idea reaching back to Darwin himself. Others seek the beginnings of song in the imitation of emotion-laden animal cries—presumably the better to lure or frighten off these animals. Then there is the argument that song represents a complex vocal learning strategy akin to those of songbirds. Others, more plausibly, suggest that the power of group musicking to establish social coalitions and forge and maintain social order is key. This "social bonding" or "coalition signaling" hypothesis can expand in various directions, from the easing of communal labor and enabling of territorial defense all the way to the facilitating of religious trance; it tends to emphasize dance as well as musicking. Still others look for adaptive advantage in the consoling lullabies and singsong talk (Infant Directed Speech, or "Motherese," it is often called) of mothers tending babies across the uniquely long childrearing period of *Homo sapiens*. Some arguments combine more than one of these options; in Mithen's *Singing Neanderthals* most of them sit uneasily side by side, their interrelation left unspecified.[14]

Alone or together, these hypotheses fail as explanations, and always for the same reason: Each seeks a unilateral explanation for a manifold phenomenon. It makes little sense to specify a single selective environment, however complex, for a behavior that, like musicking, involves many cognitive functions bespeaking long, varied, and piecemeal development. As the emergence of the vertebrate eye needs to be understood as a series of evolutionary events rather than a single adaptation selected for the purpose of seeing, so it is at best implausible that the overwhelming intricacies of musical neural networks could result from one selective episode. Evolutionary biologists deride such globally imprecise and teleological accounts as "just-so stories"—in this case, How the Human Got Its Music.

The incremental approach gets us away from just-so stories. Indeed it shows the question, "Is music an adaptation?" to be in a basic way meaningless. No well-defined adaptive status can be assigned to music as a whole, but only (perhaps) to the increments that appear in the phylogenetic record, and—a *bigger* perhaps, as we will see—to their late coalescence in musicking. Moreover, the question of adaptation vs. exaptation, asked of music in general, has the effect of focusing our sights too narrowly on the question of natural selection alone—and usually a threadbare theorizing of it, at that. It indulges in what Jonathan Kramnick has referred to as "adaptationist fundamentalism."[15] Especially regarding the formation of complex behaviors such as language and musicking, the role of other evolutionary mechanisms and processes extending and complicating natural selection needs also to be weighed. Human modernity built itself not merely from differently shaped blocks, but with a variety of tools as well.

Coevolution, Sociality, and Culture

Hominin evolution has always joined the biological to the sociocultural. This points to another feature required of any narrative of the emergence of complex human capacities: It will be a coevolutionary account merging the social behaviors of hominin species with the evolution of their biological capacities. This carries us beyond natural selection theory into an arena not merely neo-Darwinian but, as we might say, post-neo-Darwinian.[16]

Coevolution is not a new term in natural selection theory, but has long been used to refer to the feedback relations by which the evolutions of separate species might be linked. A classic instance is an "arms race" between predator and prey. Selective pressures in an ecosystem might favor changes in a prey species that enable it better to defend itself against its predators. These in turn might alter the selective pressures operating on the predator genome, favoring mutations that manifest themselves in modes of attack able to overcome the new defenses. In effect each species acts as an aspect of the other's ecological niche, each reacting, across natural selective timescales, to changes in the other. Adaptive success in such a situation is determined not merely by the relation of a species' phenotype to a fixed selective terrain, but rather by a dynamic interaction in which other species as well as the nonliving environment take part.

This notion of coevolution has in recent decades been expanded in several directions. Sophisticated new models of ecosystems as networks of feedback relations in dynamic disequilibrium have overhauled older tendencies to view selective environments as static bulwarks, so to speak, with genetic mutations knocking at the gates for acceptance (or extinction). The role of species themselves in shaping the flexible environment, and thus the selective pressures it mounts, has come to the fore. Dynamic systems theory, or complexity theory, has carried this view farthest, modeling the evolutionary interaction of species and environments as an interplay of genomes and multiple vectors of adaptive advantage, or "attractors," on a multidimensional selective landscape.[17] But even more cautious views have taken on board the roles organisms play in constructing their environments—in "niche construction," to adopt a much-used phrase for the phenomenon—and the impact of this on selective pressures.[18]

The implications of such thinking for selection theory are far-reaching. It carries with it a considerable power, first, to blur the line between the genetic and behavioral histories of species. This blurring was perhaps first noted already in the 1890s, when James Baldwin and other evolutionists proposed what has come to be known as the Baldwin effect, in which learned strategies for coping with selective pressures allow species to survive long enough for inherited characters to appear that answer the same pressures.[19] Moreover, the idea of niche construction and its feedback onto adaptive pressures complicates the historical relation of adaptations and exaptations; the first are not necessarily prior to the second, since behaviors originating as exaptations might alter

35

selective pressures in ways leading to new adaptations.[20] (Think, for example, of the flight of the first airborne dinosaurs, thought to have relied on the *ex*aptation of thermoregulating feathers, and the subsequent *ad*aptations this new behavior helped to set in motion.) The complicating power of niche-construction models increases immensely with the lengthening of the time-span across which behavior and genetic selection operate and interact.

Social species involve themselves in a special kind of coevolution, their sociality itself playing a role in altering the terrain on which they find adaptive niches. This is true in one measure or another for all social species, from ants joined in a colony—a superorganism, as it is often now called[21]—to primates living in bands and troupes. The first stone tools haphazardly fashioned by hominins some 2.5 million years ago, as well as the more perishable tools presumably used by earlier hominids—like the tools chimpanzees in the wild employ today—all might be considered learned-strategy elements of the predator/prey scenario sketched above, hence coevolutionary in the original sense of the term. But when, before 1,000,000 years ago, hominins began *passing along* toolmaking techniques from one generation to the next, in effect constructing imitative traditions, a threshold was passed. Now a social network transmitting information and skill connected itself to the feedback loops of coevolutionary selection. An intensified kind of sociality assumed new roles in niche construction and offered high value for survival.

The analysis of the role of sociality in human evolution has taken many forms in recent decades. For Richard Lewontin, Steven Rose, and Leon J. Kamin, in their polemic against genetic determinism of 1984, *Not in Our Genes*, sociality enters into a "dialectical" relation with biological evolution. It knocks down the firewall between nature and nurture that remains even today a thoughtless stumbling block in vernacular discussions of evolution. With their dialectical coevolution they sharply countered a sociobiology that had emerged during the 1960s and '70s; it tended to view genes as determining human sociality through selective adaptations and did not take much account of the feed-back of social behavior and culture on the fitness of mutations. In its place, Lewontin, Rose, and Kamin offered a picture of an all-out interpenetration of organism and environment. They argued that even interactionist approaches, which distinguish organism from environment or nature from nurture or individual from society in order to discern their interrelations, are insufficient, drawing clear borders where only mutually constituting relations exist.[22]

In the years since *Not in Our Genes*, Peter J. Richerson and Robert Boyd have led the way in theorizing biosocial or biocultural coevolution. For them, the social transmission of learned information across generations, as in those toolmaking traditions a million years back, is tantamount to culture itself. Species that evince such behavior—species with cultures—alter the selective pressures that shape their evolution. "Once cultural traditions create novel environments...that can affect the fitness of alter-native *genetically* transmitted variants," they write, "genes and culture are joined in a coevolutionary dance."[23] Richerson and Boyd's conception of culture is rewardingly broad, relying only on three primary features: information learned within a lifetime, its intergenerational transmission, and the imitation that enables this transmission. They are not alone in emphasizing these. As we will see, information and its mimetic journey across generations must be a touchstone in any narrative account of how musicking came to be.

Richerson and Boyd's social information is conceived dif-ferently by coevolutionists Eva Jablonka and Marion J. Lamb. They discern four types of information in the biosphere, genetic, epigenetic, behavioral, and symbolic, each with its own mecha-nisms of transmission.[24] (Since each type has also its own mecha-nisms of inheritance, they come close at times to launching a neo-Lamarckian assault on any strict neo-Darwinism that would limit heritable variation to the genome.) Their third category, behavioral information, encompasses both the intragenerational

37

learning of social animals and the intergenerational transmission that for Boyd and Richerson defines culture. Behavioral information can alter selective landscapes, entering into coevolutionary interaction with the genome, its epigenetic alteration, and—in humans—symbolic culture. In these interactions hominin evolution can be understood as a coevolution unique in its "four dimensions."[25]

Philosopher Kim Sterelny extends the work of Richerson and Boyd in a different way than Jablonka and Lamb. He argues for a particular, very special kind of socially and culturally determined coevolution, one that ranks high among the factors making hominin evolution unique. Early on in this evolution, hominin imitative and communicative capacities became rich enough to enable not only niche construction, not even merely the passing along of techniques for reshaping niches to the next generation, but something more: the *accumulation* of cultural information. What Sterelny calls the "high-fidelity" transmission of such informational archives from one generation to the next allowed for the likewise cumulative reshaping of the lived environment and for a flexibility of response to changing environments surpassing that of any other lineage. Animal niche construction had always modified the physical and social environment, but now the modifications were compounded, as modes of more and more purposive and conscious imitation and instruction among hominins brought about an "epistemic environment," a niche defined by archived information.[26]

This idea of cultural archives is central to my account of how musicking arose. Such archives qualitatively alter the feedback loops of coevolution, since under many circumstances they can insert into them not merely extragenetic information but *systems* of such information; this systematicity will loom large in the chapters to come. Passed through generations, accumulating cultural systems can give rise to their own internal developmental tendencies and vectors, depending on the cognitive, bodily, and environmental constraints they involve. For hominins such constraints are exemplified in the "technical tendencies" that archaeologist André Leroi-Gourhan long ago discerned in lithic technologies—particular patterns of toolmaking cultures determined by the natures of the materials worked, ergonomic possibilities of hands and fingers, and cognitive capacities of brains. Once formed, these independently organized informational dynamics can exercise their own constraints on the coevolutionary systems they enter, in ways anthropologist Terrence Deacon has described.[27]

For now, we may think of these systems as networks of conditions redirecting in certain ways the basic feedback loops of niche construction. Their dynamics can provide not merely additional strands in those loops but other external circuits outside them, sprouting like Ptolemaic *epicycles* from the cycles of cultural transmission and accumulated archives. These, then, can stand alongside the coevolutionary feedback cycles, feeding *forward* into them and altering their give-and-take. The effect of such epicyclic dynamics is not a neo-Lamarckian one in which learned behavior is assimilated as such into the genome; instead they generate complex, novel interrelations in the coevolution of organism and niche. I will say more about these epicycles below, and more still in Chapters 6 and 7; in between, I will describe the formation of several that have been important in the emergence of musicking.

To assert that informational or cultural archives complicate the niche-constructing feedback networks of biocultural coevolution would be an understatement; devising models to describe this complexity is today an important path forward especially in modeling hominin evolution. Deacon's model is particularly rich and leads him to an account of the emergence of symbolic cognition, a foundational aspect of human modernity, that will be described in Chapter 5. Here it is enough to describe just one general dynamic in the changing selective pressures resulting from niche construction that he has defined and added to the set of coevolutionary mechanisms.

As the niche alteration of coevolution progresses, species' phenotypes come into new relations with the environment.

Behaviors once weakly selected can come under more intense selective pressure while, conversely, other behaviors can be uncoupled from selective shaping as they are accorded a smaller role in reproductive success. The strengthening and redirecting of selective pressures have figured centrally in all coevolutionary accounts, but Deacon pays special attention to the consequences of weakened selection.[28]

When selective pressures on particular behaviors are eased, genotypes governing them are likewise less constrained and can degrade through the accumulation of mutations, in a process for which Deacon borrows from cellular developmental biology the term *dedifferentiation*. In the wake of these genetic changes the behaviors no longer under either strong genetic governance or selective constraint, rather than necessarily disappearing, can be "offloaded," to be passed more and more through social interaction, learning, and intergenerational (cultural) transmission. In the course of this sociocultural transmission, such behaviors can burgeon in variety and in the complexity of their relations to other behaviors, forming a new trajectory in biocultural coevolution as *genetic dedifferentiation leads to sociocultural diversification*.[29] But the cultural diversification itself, then, recruits new neural substrates, new networks in the brains of the animals enacting it, leading to the multiplication and complication of brain controls on the diversifying behaviors.

All this can set in quickly and indeed has arguably been observed in long-domesticated species, where human decisions govern reproduction and so mask selective pressures that would be felt in the wild. One of Deacon's favorite examples involves the Bengalese finch; he and others have argued that its song developed a striking increase in variety over wild strains because two centuries of domestication decoupled it from reproductive pressures and loosed it from innate controls.[30] Our examples, instead, will come from the prehistory and early history of musicking, where the pattern of weakened selection and cultural intensification can be repeatedly discerned.

Even this is not the end of the story, however. Culturally diversified behaviors uncoupled from selective pressures will reenter the biocultural loops of coevolution, giving rise to new epicycles with their distinctive emergent dynamics and to new reshapings of the relations of organism and selective terrain. There is good reason to think—Deacon advances strong arguments in favor of the proposition—that the mechanism starting from weakened selection and cultural offloading has been basic in the evolution of the hominin lineage. Given the uniquely complex cultures, epistemic niche construction, and accumulating informational archives of our heritage, we might expect nothing less.

The Biocultural Coevolution of Hominins

The positions outlined here all teach us that we must come to grips with culture in order to understand hominin coevolution, but this path presents pitfalls and disorienting mazes. A first obstacle is the question of priority between cultural and noncultural forces in coevolution. In broad phylogenetic perspective, all cultural patterns have sprung from earlier, noncultural evolutionary processes; in this sweeping vantage, priority is clear. When we scrutinize the role of culture in more specific evolutionary dynamics, however, this clarity of causal direction disappears. Accepting animal cultures as formative forces in their engagements with their environments—ingredients in their niche construction that help to shape their selective terrains—entails seeing that culture cannot be localized as an outgrowth or aftereffect at the final stages of an evolutionary career. Culture must instead be built into coevolutionary interactions from the moment of its first, rudimentary appearance. For hominins the archaeological evidence of lithic technologies establishes this with ever-greater clarity, as we will see. But the principle must hold also for cultures of other clades, embracing, for example, the teaching of the young that is a defining aspect of songbird cultures. We must think not only of avian biology shaping birdsong, but also of birdsong cultures shaping biology.

All but the most narrowly focused of recent accounts of hominin evolution have attended to culture, but too often they have done so in a one-sided way, tacitly carrying over the priority of noncultural forces in the broad view to fine-grained views where it cannot hold. They have taken as starting points basic evolutionary mechanisms that can operate independent of culture, while treating culture as the patterns, forever dependent, that those mechanisms give rise to and might more or less directly explain. This sums up Kramnik's "adaptationist fundamentalism," mentioned before, in which noncultural selective pressures unidirectionally drive the appearance of cultural phenomena such as storytelling or plot archetypes. At the level of the formation of the mind that creates human culture, this stance has long also been the foundation of evolutionary psychology and human sociobiology. In musical studies, such blunt adaptationism characterizes most of the nonincremental accounts that take music as a whole as their explanandum, seeking monocausal selective pressures to explain it—sexual selection, group solidarity, enhanced child rearing, and the rest. The approach characterizes also positions such as Pinker's that start from a likewise nonincremental, global sense of music in order to *reject* its adaptive status.

The deep history offered here aims to counter such adaptationism in the cases of hominins and of the cultural patterns that would eventually coalesce into musicking. Culture—defined, again, as the transmission to future generations of learning acquired during a lifetime—was an active force among our ancestors at least two million years ago, and no useful narrative of our evolution over that span can start from culture-free evolutionary patterns and point to cultural outcomes. Our narratives must instead attempt to analyze from the start biocultural reciprocities in which deep, multiplex cultural histories shaped noncultural dynamics of evolution at the same time as they were shaped by them.

If this injunction involves propositions somewhat more controversial than the unassailable need to take account of culture in describing hominin evolution, it still does not fully describe the peculiarities of coevolution for complexly cultural animals. The reasoning must be followed a few steps farther.

The assertion that hominins have been, for two million years and more, cultural animals involved in biocultural coevolution does not deny that culture came to play an *increasing* role across this period. Hominin cultural complexity was achieved slowly, sporadically, and in several or many taxa or species. The archaeological record suggests that it had reached a level unprecedented in the earthly animal kingdom already by the time of *Homo ergaster* (in ballpark figures, 1.5 million years ago). A million years later, by the time of *Homo heidelbergensis*, this deep archive was a more consistent and striking feature, one reflected, sometimes stunningly, in traces of technology and sociality. As it deepened, cultural complexity played a burgeoning role in the feedback relations between behavior and environmental affordance that defined the selective terrains for hominin groups. Advantageous cultural patterns led to decisive modifications of selective terrains, hence eventually and inevitably to alterations of the genotype.

Though these alterations were inevitable, they are not easily delimitable or describable in their specific natures or impact. No "hand ax gene" (for example) could result, since both the behavior/affordance interactions of hominin technologies and the networks of biocultural feedback they entered into were too complex to select for genes determining the patterns of behavior involved in making a hand ax. In the same way, at a later stage, no "language gene" or "music gene" could be forthcoming. Instead genetic changes conduced to more general capacities with many phenotypic effects, among them, in the late hominin line, the learning of technological skills and even the forging of technological innovation. Saying this is tantamount to reverse engineering, in coevolutionary terms, Richard Dawkins's "extended phenotype" hypothesis, in which genetic changes are selected by the whole range of an organism's interaction with its environment.[31]

Since this is so, they cannot arise in a one-to-one correspondence to complex, agglomerated patterns cherry-picked from that interaction.

This is one reason why our narratives and descriptions of biocultural coevolution will necessarily remain reductive in the face of the historical realities they model. Another reason is the sheer difficulty of pinpointing reciprocal influences in a situation involving evolutionary timescales, shifting affordances, and the behaviors of complex animals. Yet another is the absence of straight-line causality in the nonlinear system of feedback relations connecting culture and all the other forces in hominin evolution. In these circumstances, definitions of the changing components of our models may seem to evanesce even as we attempt fix them.

Even this level of complication, however, misses an element of hominin coevolution, mentioned above, that will be basic in my account: the presence not merely of cultural feedback cycles, but also of the *systematized epicycles* they spawn. The failure of most accounts to identify this element, even more than the complexities of behaviors, selective terrains, and their reciprocal interactions, has made it difficult to model the emergence of the distinctive capacities of modern humanity, musicking among them.

Scrutinizing the sedimented cultural archives of late hominins, we will see that they gave rise to many repeated patterns or formalisms in behavior and environmental accommodation. According to their various natures, these assumed the character of more or less complex, independent, and self-organized systems. These systems, then, came to stand *within culture but detached from the coevolutionary feedback* from which they arose. Such detachment from the reciprocity and control of feedback is the defining feature of *feed-forward* elements in any network, and, while the measure of the detachment from the feedback loops differed from one instance of cultural systematization to another, in every case it enabled the cultural systems thus formed to persist and to feed forward into coevolutionary patterns. Systematization, detachment, and persistence together characterize the epicycles I will describe and exemplify in the deep history of musicking.

Ultimately, the proposals made in defining this epicyclic mechanism are two: that culture can alter the fundamental feedback pattern basic to coevolutionary processes by generating formal systems; and that these can exert a force characteristic of their systematicity, influencing through feed-forward action the processes as a whole. Figure 1.1 renders the feedback cycle of biocultural coevolution in a simple form, without deep cultural archives or epicycles; Figure 1.2 adds to it the impact of the epicyclic mechanism.

It is worth pondering a bit more the independence of the epicycles, with their feed-forward effects, from the broader action of biocultural feedback. The systematizations or formalisms of these epicycles could not, of course, be truly divorced from the broader feedback networks, since that feedback gave rise to them in the first place. But the natures of their individual formalisms enabled them to establish varying degrees of autonomy from the feedback mechanisms, and with the increase in this autonomy came a multiplication of the effects of their feed-forward impact. There could be no cultural system that was, so to speak, dropped into biocultural coevolution from the outside, a feed-forward ingredient of utter independence from the coevolutionary network; all such systems could only arise from the network itself. But once they began to arise, and once their systematic formations took shape, they had a special power to alter coevolution *as if* dropped into it from outside.

The force that could result from the autonomy of cultural formalisms is ancient, reaching back a million years and more; but it is positively explosive in the history of *Homo sapiens* over the last hundred millennia. I will describe this explosiveness in Chapters 6 and 7, offering a model for the final coalescing of species-wide capacities for musicking, language, and more.

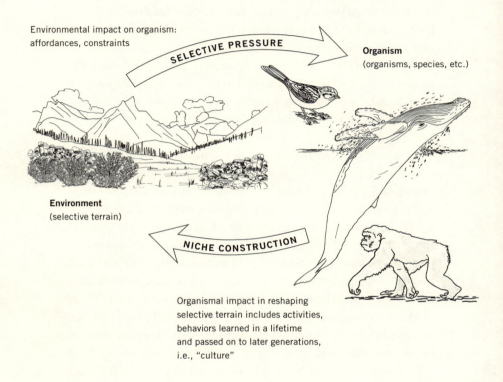

Environmental impact on organism:
affordances, constraints

SELECTIVE PRESSURE

Organism
(organisms, species, etc.)

Environment
(selective terrain)

NICHE CONSTRUCTION

Organismal impact in reshaping
selective terrain includes activities,
behaviors learned in a lifetime
and passed on to later generations,
i.e., "culture"

Figure 1.1 Simple biocultural coevolution
(chart by Virge Kask).

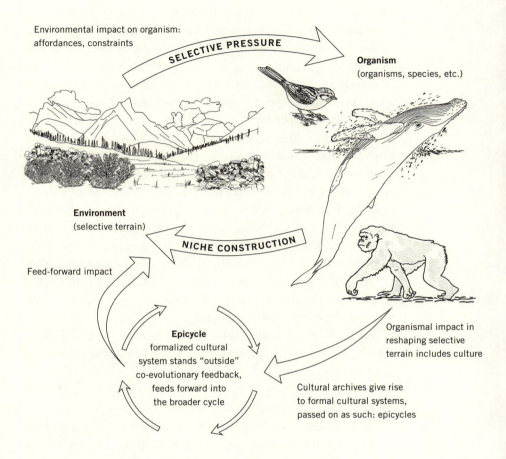

Environmental impact on organism: affordances, constraints

SELECTIVE PRESSURE

Organism
(organisms, species, etc.)

Environment
(selective terrain)

NICHE CONSTRUCTION

Feed-forward impact

Epicycle
formalized cultural system stands "outside" co-evolutionary feedback, feeds forward into the broader cycle

Organismal impact in reshaping selective terrain includes culture

Cultural archives give rise to formal cultural systems, passed on as such: epicycles

Figure 1.2 Epicyclic biocultural coevolution (chart by Virge Kask).

Looking Forward

Musicking and most other characteristic traits of human modernity could not have emerged from their cultural and noncultural antecedents without the action of coevolutionary pathways
such as those outlined earlier. This account of the emergence
of musicking cannot, then, be a story of selection for it as an
advantageous adaptation, or even a story of several incremental
adaptations later pieced together. It will instead involve, from
deep in music's prehistory on down to the coalescence of modern
musicking, the changing social and cultural lifeways of our hominin forebears. These shifting patterns of behavior, through which
hominins encountered and altered the environmental affordances
around them and built their cultures, will be both action, more
or less self-conscious, and necessary reaction to the constraints of
those environments. The environments themselves will comprise
not only the surrounding material world, inorganic and organic,
inanimate and animate, but also shifting social encounters with
others of the same species. All the parts of any coevolutionary
account must be understood to be interacting, moving; none can
take irreversible priority over others.

Here, then, is an abstract of some moving parts that will
appear in the coming chapters, offered so as to signal issues that
must be confronted:

- Musicking was always technological. Its modes of cognition
  were shaped from the first by the extensions of the body that
  were the earliest tools and weapons, in ways that left a deep
  imprint on both sociality and the genome. Musical instruments as such came late, but this broader, crucial instru-
  mentality appeared long before there was music. We need to
  identify and describe this prepoietic poiesis.
- Musicking was always social. If the cognitive capacities basic to
  it emerged from a constant, intimate interplay with available
  materials, their affordances, and their manipulation, all these
  took place, through the whole of the history here described, in

48

the context of copresent interactions between individuals and within groups. The technological and the social were always bound together, and this *technosociality* formed the matrix in which musicking took shape.

• The information comprised in musicking came long before it into hominin cognition and was tightly bound up with experiences of motion and emotion. The deep heritage of musical information lies in a set of mainly emotive communicative acts. The analysis of the acts fills out a history of protomusical semiosis, and the consequences of the heritage remain today as determining factors of musicking.

• The increasing musicalization of such communication could only develop hand in glove with increasing *theory of mind*. This capacity to think of others as endowed with minds like our own emerged in mutual interaction with more and more sophisticated—but still non- or prelinguistic—communicative modes.

• Pre- and protomusical semiosis needs to be distinguished from the appearance of semiotic modes specific to modern language but incidental to musicking. The distance of musicking from symbolic cognition that persists to this day is not a recent aesthetic formation but was an aboriginal and constitutive state for both musicking and language.

• These ancient differences reveal ways in which the history of musicking was tangled with that of language already before either existed. The communicative functions of vocalization that preceded musicking and language helped to determine both deep connections and deep differences between them.

• Hierarchic and combinatorial cognition of several sorts preceded the musicking and language that today embody it. These hierarchies reveal fundamental features of the cognitive flexibility of early humans; they are first legible to us in hominin interactions with the material world.

• Musicking was founded on hominin possibilities for cognitive flexibility. From the first it expressed the diversity such

49

cognition enabled, as it captured in its informational flow responses to varied social and physical environments.

- Musicking is implicated deeply in *thinking-at-a-distance*. It developed alongside a "release from proximity" whereby humans gradually gained the capacity to imagine things not present to the senses. Its coalescing marshaled and helped to shape cognitive byways involved in this release.

- This aspect of musicking made it, finally, a transcendent cultural force. In a cognition increasingly able to think at a distance, musicking pushed toward hierarchic levels beyond sensual stimuli. The bond of music and metaphysics reaches back to the first inklings themselves of other worlds. No happenstance alliance, it is, like the puzzle of musical vs. linguistic semiosis, aboriginal.

- Musicking always elaborated a social structure of hierarchic difference. Social institutions, when they emerged, did not simply foster the use of music or attach themselves to it willy-nilly. It is closer to the truth to say that musicking created institutions.

- The final coalescing of musicking was not an independent development but a coformation involving language and the metaphysical imaginary. All three are characteristic, even definitive gestures of human modernity, and none of them could have taken their modern forms without the simultaneous formation of the others.

Now that I have laid the foundations for my narrative and offered some tokens of its conclusions, it is time to consult the archaeologist's oracle: stones shattered, chipped, and fashioned into implements in the hands of hominins one million years ago.

CHAPTER TWO

1,000,000 Years Ago:

Acheulean Performances

Marteau sans maître

Million-year-old stone tools record for us, in the violent beauty of their crystalline surfaces, both plain truths and mysteries. We start by pondering a foremost mystery.

Think what it would be like to manufacture a sophisticated tool without planning to do so. (Probably you cannot; perhaps the thought experiment is impossible, because your brain is not the same as the brain that could.) Now imagine passing your unthought toolmaking skills to others around you, creating an enduring cultural tradition without awareness, even without consciousness of a human sort; and imagine, further, transmitting this tradition in the absence of anything resembling modern language—no semantic vocalization to speak of, no syntax, no propositional utterances of any kind.

What sort of cognitive capacities could enable such a situation, what kind of social interaction? How does technological complexity emerge without prior planning or even a mental image of the desired end product? What relationships among cognition, sociality, and the opportunities afforded by the material environment might inform this emergence? These are the puzzles that have faced archaeologists as they have analyzed the best-attested, longest-studied Paleolithic tool industry: the Acheulean biface.

The answers that have been supplied to such questions point well beyond toolmaking itself. Hidden among them is evidence for basic developments in early hominin interaction and sociality.

And in these, in turn, we can discern foundational capacities for human musicking. The dawning of protomusical capacities can be read in traces of lithic industry reaching back to an era long before there existed either music or *Homo sapiens* to make it.

Acheulean Industries

Across the last half-century or so, archaeologists working at sites from sub-Saharan to Mediterranean Africa, from England to Sri Lanka, and from Spain to China have reconstructed with pain-staking precision the courses of Oldowan, Acheulean, and more recent Paleolithic technologies. Any census of this work would see that it has been devoted mainly to detailing the tools themselves: their types, the materials from which they were fashioned, the sources of these materials and the means by which they were obtained, and especially the processes involved in fashioning the tools. In recent years, however, the nature of the questions asked of these artifacts has expanded. Topics once thought imponderable or peripheral have assumed greater importance; the analysis of manufacture has focused more and more on the relation of body and mind behind the tool. A serious "archaeology of cognition" has taken shape. These new questions extend from hands and stones in two different directions: inward toward the brains of the toolmakers, and outward toward the sociophysical environments in which the tools were created.[1]

Oldowan tools, named after the Olduvai Gorge in Tanzania, where generations of Leakeys and many others have unearthed some of the most famous paleoanthropological finds, make up the earliest indisputable artifacts. The first choppers and sharp flakes of this industry, found at various African sites, reach back as far as 2.7 million years. Uncertainties surround these tools. First of all, because of the almost absolute lack of hominid fossils associated with them, we are not sure who made them. Most archaeologists speculate that the earliest hominin species, *Homo habilis*, was involved, though this consensus comes in the context of vexed questions as to when, where, and how the *Homo* line itself emerged. Some think that late australopithecines might also have produced Oldowan artifacts.

The tools themselves are basic enough in many cases to raise doubts as to whether they are artifacts at all and not *geofacts*, byproducts of geological, hydrological, and climatological processes. The examples that are indubitable show little standardization, but the manner of their fashioning resulted in a basic dichotomy of artifacts: stone cores with sharp edges and the flakes broken off those cores in fashioning the edges. Even here doubts intrude, as we are not sure whether the cores or the flakes or both were exploited as tools.

In the midst of all this uncertainty, however, one thing is clear: Significant manufacturing skill was required to knap cobbles in these ways. Even at the earliest appearance of the tools this skill could involve a gauging of the materials in hand, the use of a stone hammer, and an ability to join together a short sequence of calibrated blows to the core. Often these blows struck the core adjacent to one another, resulting in characteristic overlapping scars where flakes were removed; Figure 2.1 shows typical cores produced by such actions. Apes today, even with careful coaching and encouragement, seem incapable of managing as much.

Acheulean industries, named after Saint-Acheul, a northern French town where specimens of the technology were unearthed in the nineteenth century, began to displace Oldowan industries about 1.7–1.6 million years ago—a million years or so after their first appearance—though the earlier techniques never disappeared completely. The earliest examples of the new technology appeared in East Africa, and after that it arose in other parts of Africa, in Asia, and in Europe. Once achieved, it settled in as an industry of awesome stability, enduring for over a million years until it was gradually replaced by more complex lithic technologies, especially after 300,000 years ago. We fashioners and fetishizers of incessant technological innovation need to pause at the notion of an industry fundamentally unchanged across a span five times as long as the career of our very species.

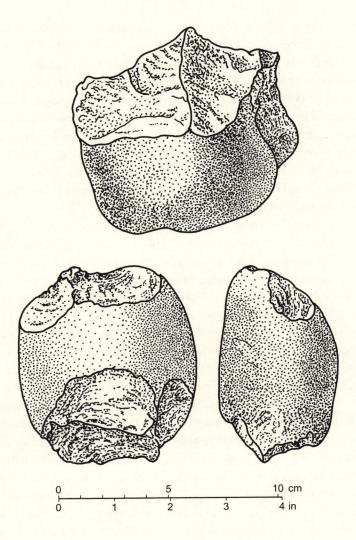

0   5   10 cm

0   1   2   3   4 in

Figure 2.1 The Oldowan industry: 1.8-million-year-old flaked cores from Olduvai Gorge. Redrawn by Virge Kask after M. D. Leakey, *Olduvai Gorge: Excavations in Beds I and II, 1960–63* (Cambridge: Cambridge University Press, 1971).

Archaeologists associate Acheulean assemblages with a number of hominin species, though (as with Oldowan tools) not without debate. The differences of view again reflect both the rarity of finds combining tools with hominin remains and our fragmentary knowledge all told of hominin speciation and dispersion. Early Acheulean tools are connected especially with *Homo ergaster* and *Homo erectus*, two species whose relation to one another and to their successors remains elusive. (The prevailing current view considers *erectus* an Asian variant of *ergaster* that branched off after its dispersion out of Africa almost two million years ago.) Later in its long history the industry was associated with *Homo heidelbergensis*, probable precursor of Neandertals in Europe and perhaps also the African ancestor they shared with *Homo sapiens*; with an earlier, little-known European species, dubbed by some *Homo antecessor*; with likewise shadowy immediate predecessors of *Homo sapiens* in Africa; and with Neandertals themselves—though they ultimately expanded their toolkit well beyond Acheulean techniques.

Acheulean assemblages yield the first seemingly standardized tool types, though there is much disagreement about the extent and implications of this standardization.[2] The tools seem to cluster around three somewhat fuzzy categories: bifacial cleavers, distinguished by long blades or "bits" at one end (see Figure 2.2); relatively rare "discoids," stones flaked into a discus-like shape with a worked edge all around; and—the emblematic Acheulean implement—bifacial hand axes in elongated or ovoid form (Figures 2.3 and 2.4).

What characterizes these tools above all else—what makes them bifaces—is their bilateral symmetry. From the earliest examples (Figures 2.2 and 2.3), they seem to show a tendency, not evident in Oldowan artifacts, toward a mirroring around one or two planes: a plane running lengthwise from tip to tip and bisecting each face of the tool, and a plane coinciding roughly with the cutting edge and separating the two faces. There seems to be a trend across this long-lived industry toward increasing

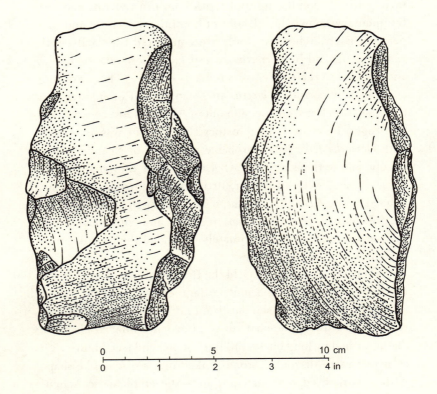

Figure 2.2 Acheulean cleaver from Olduvai
Gorge, 1.4 million years old. Redrawn by
Virge Kask from Thomas Wynn, "Archaeol-
ogy and Cognitive Evolution," *Behavioral and
Brain Sciences* 25 (2002), pp. 389–402; after
Leakey, 1971.

precision in these symmetries, though the dating of Acheulean artifacts is usually anything but secure.[3] The hand ax in Figure 2.3, with its rough but clearly non-Oldowan symmetry, is typical of early Acheulean manufacture; while the finer workmanship of Figure 2.4 characterizes a later period—perhaps from only 600,000–700,000 years ago. (Note, in Figure 2.4, the scars remaining from the removal of small flakes along the cutting edge, a feature little evident in the larger, deeper scarring of Figure 2.3.) No detailed chronology of this increased precision has yet been achieved; some view it as a gradual change, others as a sudden, punctuated event separating two long periods of technological stasis and perhaps associated with the advent of *Homo heidelbergensis*.[4] Chronological precision might elude even further research and more secure dating, given the immense time span involved, the huge geographical dispersion of the industry, and the wide variety of different lithic materials used in it—not to mention the simple, staggering fact that several or even many different species practiced it. The notion of a technology shared among species is another idea that should bring us up short.

Notwithstanding all these difficulties, three features of Acheulean technology, at least, seem manifest: its awesomely long and stable persistence, an unprecedented tendency toward symmetry, and an increase over time in the precision of this symmetry.

Embodied Symmetries

The Acheulean industry shows a clear increase in sophistication over the Oldowan and offers some of the most eloquent evidence we have concerning the capacities of the hominins who created and exploited it. In the large literature by now devoted to these issues, the symmetry that is the Acheulean hallmark has often been understood as a token of the planning that went into the design of the tools; it has been presumed (often tacitly) to mark a self-conscious intention behind the technology. It has some-times even been appreciated in explicitly aesthetic terms—an

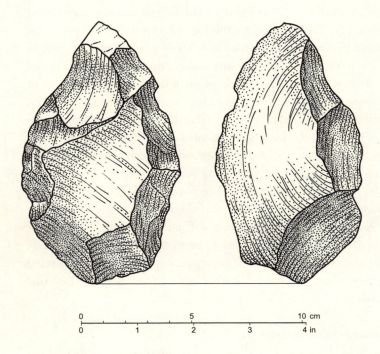

```
0          5              10 cm
0     1     2     3      4 in
```

Figure 2.3 Acheulean bifacial hand ax from
Tanzania, 1.4 million years old. Redrawn by
Virge Kask after Thomas Wynn, "Archaeology
and Cognitive Evolution."

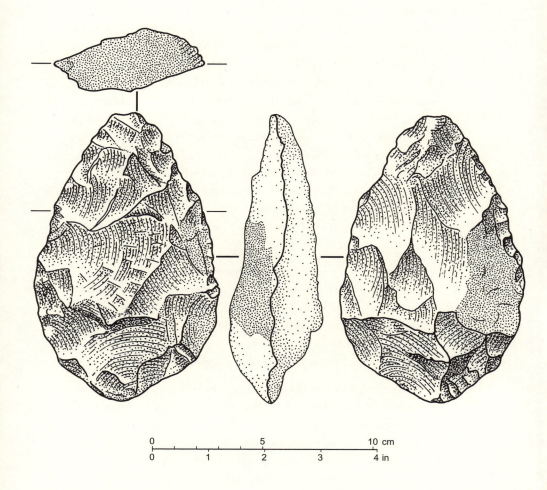

Figure 2.4 Late Acheulean hand ax from
Spain. Redrawn by Virge Kask after José-
Manuel Benito Álvarez.

anachronism understandably hard to resist in the presence of exquisite artifacts such as the one pictured in Figure 2.4. (If you are unmoved, find a flint cobble. Find a hammerstone. Try making such a tool yourself.)

According to such views, with Acheulean hand axes we are in the presence of a standardized, carefully planned and implemented technology. Or are we? In response to appreciations of Acheulean tools, warnings began to surface in the 1990s against the presumption of careful planning in their facture. These gathered force until they destabilized much of what had once seemed unremarkable truths about this industry. By 2004 Thomas Wynn, a leading student of bifaces and chief proponent of the archaeology of cognition, could sum up the new uncertainty in almost nihilistic fashion:

> Currently, two perspectives dominate the interpretation of these tools. The first is that they result from "mental templates" held by the knappers and reflect shared cultural norms. The second is that their shapes were an unintended result of a knapping procedure and the use life of the artifact and have no implications for culture or cognition.... Neither of these stances appears tenable.[5]

To trace the history of this gathering uncertainty among archaeologists is to entertain some of the most provocative conceptions of pre-sapient hominins to emerge over the last twenty years.

Ian Davidson and William Noble were among the first archaeologists to sound the warning against overinterpretation. They argued that the standardization of Acheulean tools had been exaggerated by an unwitting circularity, since archaeologists tended to devote their attention only to the most symmetrical artifacts. Insofar as the symmetry exists, they added, it might have emerged as a byproduct of the manufacturing process and constraints of the materials used. They adduced evidence that the flakes chipped off a core in the making of a hand ax were sometimes more useful tools than the hand axes themselves. And they pointed out that the tools often show signs of being works in progress, refashioned as they were used and changing their nature across their use-life; what remain to us may be not finished implements but only stages of an ongoing process individual tools reached by the time they were discarded, lost, or forgotten. For all these reasons, Davidson and Noble concluded, Acheulean hand axes cannot be presumed to represent end-products conceptualized and envisioned from the beginning by their makers. To make this presumption is to indulge in the "finished artefact fallacy."[6]

In 1999, Clive Gamble extended this reasoning to hominin technologies as recent as 300,000–500,000 years ago. He cautioned against ascribing even to these late Acheulean toolmakers any a priori planning, any execution that started from a mental blueprint or template of the desired end-product and chipped away at a stone core until something like it materialized in the hand. Gamble, Noble and Davidson, and other proponents of this position challenged us to conceive of Acheulean workmanship without the aid of modern foresight or mental representation, without a teleological approach to a preconceived end—without, finally, a recognizably modern human agency at work.[7] They issued this challenge not only because of the nature of Acheulean tools, but because other evidence we can muster for the capacities of *Homo ergaster* and *erectus* shows little sign of an ability to displace thought away from immediate circumstances—the kind of displacement required for a mental template foreseeing the endpoint of a multi-step constructive process. This brain is not yet our brain.

The question of the emergence in hominin evolution of such cognitive displacement, of a mental "release from proximity" or, simply, of *thinking-at-a-distance*, will feature centrally in chapters to come.[8] For now it is enough to define the capacity, roughly, as the ability to think beyond the immediacy of face-to-face encounters with others and with the momentary flux of environmental conditions. Some have described this thinking, in cyberspeak, as offline rather than online. In online thinking a hominin reacts to the saber-toothed cat in front of it; in offline thinking it imagines possible reactions to a cat while sitting safely at a campfire.

In the world today it is clear that offline thinking does not extend very far beyond *Homo sapiens*; in sophisticated versions it seems to be unique to our species. There is likewise little in what we know of the Lower Paleolithic world (or, as it is called in Africa, the Early Stone Age) to suggest any significant capacity for thinking-at-a-distance or future planning. To the best of our knowledge, hominins 1,000,000 years ago did not transport materials across long distances, a likely symptom of planning for future use. They did not create stable campsites to which they might return after scavenging or foraging; indeed social structuring of the landscape was probably minimal even by hominins 500,000 years more recent. There is no evidence for symbolism of any sort or for the sort of social structures symbolism serves, and the kind of language intimately entwined with both of these in modern humans still lay far in the future.

Nevertheless, these creatures created stable and enduring *traditions* of toolmaking. How did they do so in the absence of planning—indeed, in the absence of the capacity to plan? Gamble, considering the late Acheulean period about 500,000 years ago, sought the answer in the idea of a performative sociality, in patterns of actions that gave shape to technology and culture rather than in any abstract plan guiding them.[9] In the world today, clear instances of such performative, unplanned sociality are offered by primate groups from baboons and vervets to chimpanzees and gorillas. Their societies are built from the bottom up, starting from the gestures and interactions of individuals and building complexity according to simple rules, rather than from the top down, as the expression or reflection of a general order or conception of society. Such performative sociality requires little thinking-at-a-distance. It is closely related to conceptions of *embodied cognition* that resist the Cartesian separation of thought from matter and emphasize the situatedness of cognition in material matrices extending out from the body.[10]

Neither bottom-up sociality nor embodied cognition limits the complexity of social behavior as narrowly as we might imagine;

recent primatological studies have shown this clearly.[11] This means that caution in inferring offline thinking beyond humans in the world today does not severely restrict the complexities that are attained in nonhuman societies. The complexity they attain, however, is mostly constructed from successions of simple operations; and this is akin, finally, to the complexity of flocking birds or that built up in a computer from bits of information and simple algorithms governing their relations. Theorizing this kind of process turned Artificial Intelligence study on its head around 1990, when Rodney Brooks and a few other robotics specialists demonstrated its potential to generate complex behaviors. Brooks called it, alluringly, "Cambrian intelligence," and there can be little doubt that it is a sort of interaction with the world and each other that living things have exercised for a very long time indeed.[12]

In the first instance, then, we must not underestimate the potential of prehuman hominins to create complex technologies from cognitive foundations very different from our own: technology from bodies and materials up.

The Chaîne Opératoire and Taskscape

The bottom-up generating of social complexity was coming to be a well-developed theme in discussions of Paleolithic society by the time of Gamble's book of 1999. In order to scrutinize more closely the gestures of such performative sociality, he and others turned to a fundamental insight of one of the most visionary of twentieth-century archaeologists, André Leroi-Gourhan. In his *Gesture and Speech* (*Le geste et la parole*, 1964), Leroi-Gourhan developed the notion of the *chaîne opératoire*, the operational chain or sequence, to describe the succession of gestures involved in technologies like the Acheulean. This gestural chain created a matrix where social behavior and material conditions met; from the meeting a stone tool emerged. Such joining of materiality and sociality in the operational sequence formed the key concept in Leroi-Gourhan's sweeping attempt to understand Paleolithic cultures as embodied cognition. In its material crudescence of

gesture, the operational sequence represented for him a pros-
thetic externalization of cognition, anticipating other exter-
nalizations—those of all later technologies, or that of memory
achieved much later in writing. Leroi-Gourhan's was a prescient
vision of bottom-up performativity, embodiment, and emergent
complexity before such things had names.[13]

Given its radical stance, Leroi-Gourhan's project was slow to
be taken up by Anglo-American archaeologists. *Gesture and Speech*
had to wait almost thirty years, and the arrival of new generations of processual and postprocessual archaeologists, before it was
translated into English.[14] In the meantime, it had never faded from
the minds of archaeologists and anthropologists in France.[15] And
it exerted a telling influence on more general theories of society
and technology there. Bernard Stiegler's extended meditation on
technology and being, *Technics and Time*, accords it a central place.[16]

Much earlier, Leroi-Gourhan's intuition of a feedback relation between human gesture and the material world played a
role in the grammatology of Derrida.[17] Building on French traditions of both phenomenology and material ethnography (Berg-
son, Merleau-Ponty, Mauss), Leroi-Gourhan defined operational
sequences not by rational planning and control of resources but
by the mutual interactions between embodied minds and the
material affordances of the environment. For Derrida this feedback system opened out, in an imaginative excursus not at all
foreign to Leroi-Gourhan's own ranging thought, toward cyber-
netics, toward the informational control systems of all life, and
finally toward the (then recently discovered) genetic code itself.
Derrida saw the inscriptive gestures of hominin hands making
tools as part of a limitless proliferation of the inscribed sign,
the *grammè*, that would undo all narrow, logocentric definitions
of writing and challenge the metaphysics that had backed them
since Plato. From Leroi-Gourhan, in other words, Derrida leapt
directly to his grammatological arche-writing.

Thirty years on, in a similar move, archaeologist Gamble
extended the *chaîne opératoire* toward an encompassing Paleolithic

phenomenology. While many particulars of Leroi-Gourhan's archaeology and paleontology had by then been superseded, Gamble seized upon his conception of the operational sequence as something broader than a procedure for crafting tools. With large bodies of new evidence in hand, he elaborated Paleolithic spaces of interlinked social and material action in (and on) the world. Borrowing a term from anthropologist Tim Ingold, Gamble distinguished these spaces from more neutrally inhabited landscapes by calling them *taskscapes*.[18] For Ingold, another attentive reader of Leroi-Gourhan, the taskscape emerges from the varied actions of a social group, the mobile performance of these actions, their structuring of the lived environment, and indeed the sounds they make. Over against the stable, seen features of the landscape, the taskscape is not external and static but changeable and manufactured; it is not so much seen, in the manner of an unmoving *tableau*, as made and heard. The taskscape creates, from the rhythms of action sequences that form it, its own temporality, one based on moments of mutual attention commanded among its participants by movement and gesture. It describes hominin movement through time connecting the material and the social.[19]

Within this taskscape, Gamble concluded, the Acheulean biface itself was not "the physical representation of an idea shared by all, but instead a social skill negotiated through gestures and inscribed in the bodily movements and rhythms which we call knapping."[20] In early Acheulean industries these gestures were narrowly localized, extended neither through time—by separate stages of manufacture of an implement, for example—nor through space—by transport of raw materials across sizeable distances. The biface was a product of the social negotiation of rhythmic gesture, in feedback relation with environmental affordances, that defined the taskscape. Its production required little in the way of mental templates or thinking-at-a-distance.[21]

A bottom-up, performative account of this sort offers a preliminary answer, at least, to the puzzle of the stability of the Acheulean industry across hundreds of thousands of years. Our expectation of change and progress in this technology is in part an implication of the planning we too easily assume to be behind it. Each new toolmaker, we imagine, sizes up familiar implements, forming a mental template on the basis of their looks, their manufacture, their uses, and their advantages, before setting out to make new tools. Each forms, in other words, a conception of the intentions of those who had made such tools before; and how could this synthetic *theory of mind* (as it is usually called) result in an unchanging process? How could a technology thus conceptualized *not* progress?

Where there is no advance plan, however, no a priori template, but only an enacted operational sequence, the situation looks different. If the tools that result from the sequence are adequate to their uses, there is little reason to expect progression in the technology from one form to another, more complicated one. Habituation of individual toolmakers into a stable gestural chain will be the order of the day—or of the millennium.[22] The advancement of so many technologies familiar to us reflects, in the end, the projection across whole industries of individually conceived intentionality and teleology. These in turn rely upon modes of cognitive displacement and thinking-at-a-distance that seem to have been foreign to Acheulean toolmakers. The Acheulean may confuse us precisely because we are so far in cognitive attainment from what we might call (after Rodney Brooks) a Cambrian industry. Imagining a toolmaking tradition passed along without intent is tantamount to inhabiting mentally our ancestors' sociality, formed without anything like a modern theory of mind.

This kind of performance of gestural sequences may help to account not only for the stasis of the industry but also for the symmetries of Acheulean tools. Wynn has argued for intentionality behind this symmetry, and many others have tacitly presumed as much. However, in the light of other evidence concerning the hominin species involved in the early stages of Acheulean industries, it seems unlikely that their tools resulted from an a priori conceptualization of desired symmetries; Wynn himself, as we have seen, concedes this point. (By contrast, hominin capacities were radically different by the latest stages of Acheulean industries, and different explanations of symmetrical production may be required for them.) What meanings might Wynn's "intentionality" entail if we reject the forming of a mental template leading to the material execution of its facsimile?

A number of answers to the question have been proposed. A simple step-by-step gestural sequence, first, can result not only in complexity of behavior but also in symmetry of design. Patterned movements in the world, human or not, often lead to symmetrical patterns incised on it, even very complex ones—a fact we can savor by recalling Darwin's classic analysis of beehive design in *On the Origin of Species*. As hominin capacities for sequenced knapping moved beyond the rudimentary levels of Oldowan technology, the elaboration of the *chaîne opératoire* toward standardized sequences of gestures might have created incipient symmetries such as those pictured in Figures 2.2 and 2.3. The interlinked rhythms of the taskscape itself might have brought about symmetrical products. In this model of bottom-up generation of behavioral complexity, whatever intentionality lay behind Acheulean symmetries emerged from habituated biomechanical activities.[23]

If this may seem to veer close to an unsatisfactory "It just happened," we can refine the hypothesis with the assistance of ecological psychologists. They push the idea of embodied cognition in the direction of environmental affordances, approaching the mind as an organ symbiotically connected to the materials it encounters. (This position too was anticipated by Leroi-Gourhan and basic to his thought.[24]) Preconceptual action sequences are structured according to these material affordances, the energy required in working them, and the biomechanical limitations of the worker; and all these together can be enough to engender systematic patterns tending to produce material symmetries.[25] From this vantage, thinking of the hominin mind dictating symmetries has it backwards; it is the body-stone interaction from which symmetries (and perhaps even the mind) emerge. The variability of raw materials, more than varied conceptual plans, will lead to variability in tools produced as well as varied embodied thought.

There is a rich and provocative opportunity glimpsed here of reversing our habits in conceiving early hominin experience. It is not that stone tools are proxies of mind but something closer to the reverse: mind as an outgrowth of the body-stone interface. The reversal can be carried out also on more purely theoretical grounds, as art historian Whitney Davis has shown. Starting from the lithic analyses of archaeologist Harold Dibble, he builds a Derridean deconstruction of *any* tendency to read planning and intent into operational sequences. Since the sequence interposes a series of actions between the beginning and end of a manufacturing process, it decenters any putative mental template in favor of a continual, gesture-by-gesture, recursive shifting of aims: "the tool writes the toolmaker as much as the toolmaker writes the tool."[26] Anyone who has tried flint-knapping will recognize the body-mind experience here described.

This reversal, despite its heuristic appeal, might delimit too narrowly the role of the early hominin mind; but the role we can restore need not involve the reassertion of an a priori template. Psychologists have argued that tacit perceptions of mirror symmetries, requiring no conceptualization as such, lie deep in human perception. Tests concerning the confusion of mirror-image facsimiles, especially ones symmetrical along a vertical axis—for example the *d/b* confusion common in dyslexia—suggest that modern humans encode such stimuli in the brain in linked fashion, an image connected to its mirror version. This may have much to do with the bilateral symmetry, along the vertical axis, of the human body itself; and it may be a phylogenetically deep coding. If so, toolmaking gestures, even very ancient ones, might have fallen into sequences leading to rough vertical symmetries as a result of perceptual hard-wiring more than advancing conceptual skills.[27] This model too could describe an early Acheulean operational sequence deployed without mental template or thinking-at-a-distance.

All these approaches extend the kind of thinking behind Leroi-Gourhan's *chaîne opératoire*—his meeting of body and material world in a rhythmicized taskscape (to reintroduce Gamble and Ingold also)—in the direction of the epicyclic, technosocial systems introduced in the coevolutionary outline of Chapter 1. In suggesting how early Acheulean symmetries could have emerged from bottom-up processes, they provide explanations more in keeping with our picture of million-year-old hominins than models involving mental templates, multistep foresight, and top-down planning.

In all this it cannot escape our attention that notions of *chaîne opératoire*, taskscape, and toolmaking, for Leroi-Gourhan, Gamble, and Ingold alike, come to rest in the performed rhythms of sociomaterial interaction. It would be folly to assimilate these rhythms to those of later human musicking. Given all we can reconstruct of hominin sociality 1,000,000 years ago—or even much later—we need to resist visions of our pre-sapient ancestors drumming and dancing around a campfire. (This too Leroi-Gourhan understood: "The distance between musical rhythm, which is wholly a matter of time and measure, and the rhythm of the hammer...which is a matter of immediate or deferred procreation of forms, is considerable."[28]) But it would likewise be folly to dismiss these Leroi-Gourhanian rhythms as mere metaphors in the unfolding of this archaeological strain. One million years ago they were more than this, at last nothing other than repetitive action sequences through which quotidian temporalities of hominin society were created. They reflect the rhythmicization of brains, bodies, and hands inscribing the world and giving dimensions of space and time to daily life.

Mimetic Traditions

If analysis of the *chaîne opératoire* leads us toward a performative, embodied, bottom-up picture of the manufacture of a stone tool, the concept of the taskscape does some additional work. It points outward from the individual maker to the broader interactive matrix, involving other hominins, in which these body-stone meetings occurred. This social emphasis defines the taskscape, distinguishing it from the inhabited landscape. Meanwhile the taskscape grounds our abstract notions of social order in its featuring of action sequences that join the social to the material—creating the social, we might say, through its material correlates. In this, the taskscape helps illuminate the making not merely of Acheulean tools but of Acheulean *traditions*.

Again questions proliferate, involving the nature of the habituation by which hominins came to replicate the action sequences of older members of their bands and the imitative or mimetic capacities that fostered traditions of toolmaking and stabilized them across hundreds of millennia. Must we conceive of such traditions as the product of active pedagogy—a pedagogy unfolding, remember, in the absence of language and much else we presume to be basic to the term—or could their complexity have emerged from another kind of learning? Moving from operational sequence to taskscape and thence to traditions of operational sequences, we spiral out toward an Acheulean sociomaterial epistemology—toward the status of the knowledge involved in the group deployment of the gestural sequences of the technology.

Such an approach recognizes that Acheulean traditions were *cultures* in the sense advanced by Boyd and Richerson (see Chapter 1), transmitting nongenetic information from one generation to the next, and that this information took the form of Sterelny's accumulations or cultural archives. There will be more to say later about this information; here it is enough to characterize generally its Lower Paleolithic nature. It existed independent of any systems of referentiality or symbolic communicative capacities; these appeared much later in the hominin line. This suggests that the information passed from one Acheulean toolmaker to another could not have been much more than the operational sequences themselves. As Derrida appreciated earlier than most,

Leroi-Gourhan's *chaîne opératoire* in its social context was nothing other than a material medium of information.

These gestural sequences should not be thought of as a semantics of toolmaking. This would be to distinguish in anachronistic fashion an action from its conceptualized implications. The operational sequences carried no implications or abstractable concepts and were nothing more than patterns of movement and registers of difference for the hominins that witnessed and performed them. They eventuated in stone tools, but they did not signal or forecast them; they generated cognition more than being generated by it, we might almost say. Their transmission was founded on a kind of agency that emerged not from ideation but from the play of intersecting contexts of action—even coupled contexts of action, as we shall see—that together formed the taskscape.[29] Acheulean traditions comprised embodied information in linkages of unprecedented complexity.

In recent years something of a consensus has formed among archaeologists concerning the kinds of social transactions involved in early Acheulean traditions.[30] Young hominins, inhabitants of an elaborated taskscape, watched their elders fashioning tools, came to be familiar with the patterns involved, and set about duplicating them, thus growing up in a "community of practices" involving ancestors and descendants.[31] Their own expertise resulted from both repeated observation of gestural repertoires and a capacity for mimicry and practice. The skills they honed required no direct, and certainly no verbalized, pedagogy; this was a social transmission in which learning was largely tacit and detached from active teaching. The stability of the Acheulean industry reflects this tacit replication of operational sequences, while the local variability of the tools produced reflects, instead, the absence of any narrowing, precise pedagogy or strong enforcement of cultural norms. From this absence came the freedom of toolmakers to adapt gestural sequences to the raw materials at hand.[32]

One close analysis of several South African Acheulean sites sums up this consensus. Its authors conclude that these industries show "no direct social imposition of standardized values and no strong lines of social learning.... Rather, knappers attempted to reproduce what they had seen around them all their lives." Habituation and mimicry were the standardized channels for the transmission of Acheulean toolmaking. The end products, the implements themselves, were instead the nonstandardized and largely unforeseen consequences of this consistency of social interaction.[33] Technological complexity burgeoned on the Acheulean taskscape not in spite of but *because* of its grounding in habituation, familiarity, and online cognition.

Mimesis was a crucial ingredient of this taskscape. Evolutionary psychologist Merlin Donald recognized this a few years before the new consensus concerning Acheulean industries took shape. In his influential book of 1991, *Origins of the Modern Mind*, he dubbed "mimetic culture" the stage of cognitive capacities reached by Acheulean hominins. For Donald mimesis is a special cognitive attainment, unique to the hominin line and distinguishable from the mimicry of birds and the imitation of monkeys and apes. It is defined by the ability to form a particular kind of mental representation of perceived events. This representation is "self-initiated" and subject to voluntary control; it is primarily visuomotor in orientation, exploiting cognitive connections between visual perception and "self-cued" action; and it does not rely on any linguistic communication. Such representations build on a foundation of more ancient cognitive attainments—distantly the procedural memory of all animals with central nervous systems, proximately the short-term, "episodic" memory of events that higher mammals and especially apes possess in abundance—but they channel these capacities in new directions. Donald saw *Homo erectus* (today the central species would be *Homo ergaster*) manifesting these novelties particularly in two areas: in its toolmaking skill—the Acheulean industries we have dwelled upon—and in an increasing voluntary control of vocalization, to which we return in Chapter 3.[34]

Donald refined and strengthened his ideas on mimesis several years after *Origins of the Modern Mind* in an important foray into debates on the emergence of language.[35] Early linguistic behavior, he argued, was founded on capacities, new in the primate line, for self-directed motor control and the deliberate refinement of actions. They operated through a novel feedback network that initiated the hominin break from the preprogrammed behavior to which most species are limited. This "rehearsal loop" involved four steps: self-initiated performance of an action, observation of the results, remembrance of these, and renewed performance of the action with one or more of its aspects modified. With few exceptions—song learning in some species of birds seems to be one—such practice routines are restricted to humans in the world today, absent almost completely even from nonhuman primates. (A baboon, Donald notes, might pick up a stick and throw it in a fight, but no one has ever seen one target practicing.) We can see how such a rehearsal loop, operating in the manner of the feedback control systems Derrida was attracted to in Leroi-Gourhan, might aid in the learning of the gestural sequences of lithic production.[36]

Donald defines a number of other basic features of this "ability to self-programme motor skills" and the rehearsal that comes with it.[37] As it was elaborated in the hominin line, the ability came also to be generalizable across all cognitive domains controlling those skills. This domain generality, or, as Donald calls it, *supramodal* extension is what enables modern humans to transfer perceived rhythms to any skeletomuscular system in the body: we can tap out a pattern with our foot, wiggle our fingers to it, wag our head, click our tongue, or move our whole body.

Donald also argues that the loop required a mental representation of perceived and executed actions, though the precise nature of this representation, as is common in uses of this slippery word, is unclear in his description. The arguments of cognitive archaeologists against mental-template thinking suggest that we should tread carefully here. "Representation" in this instance may mean little more (but no less!) than the rise to salience of an aspect of a hominin's environment—in this case an enacted sequence of physical gestures imprinting itself in neural networks that fire again when it is repeated. Or, as we shall see, it might mean a set of interconnected neural oscillations. Even with these caveats, however, the self-initiated nature of the rehearsal routine highlighted by Donald remains an important novelty.

Given its fluid progress from observation through memory to performance, Donald's rehearsal loop, deployed in a social context, would inevitably have turned itself outward so as to duplicate actions perceived in the surrounding environment. Indeed, nonhuman primate sociality today suggests that the observational element of the loop among ancient hominins was at first not *self*-observation but rather observation directed toward other individuals in the group. In social animals armed with rudimentary mimetic capacities, in other words, the perception of another's action stimulated emulation, which in turn carried the action into the cogs of the internal rehearsal machine.

We are coming closer to a description of the interlinked loops in the taskscape that connected action to cognition, individual to individual, and living body to external materials. Through emulation and rehearsal the operational sequence of one toolmaker was observed, practiced, and duplicated by another. Relatively complex series of repetitive actions were passed along from one generation of hominins to the next without any need for instruction or abstract planning, and the taskscape came to be elaborated as a place of cultural traditions in the form of motor sequences. Embodied cognition was extended into *embodied social memory*, a group experience of the past that could build on it toward a not dissimilar future.

This shared memory was embodied in that it took shape not in language, with its narratives and abstract propositions, but in the accumulated archives of operational sequences themselves. From the very first, lithic technologies had the potential to act as "artificial memory systems," to use the term of choice of archaeologist Francesco d'Errico, or as an external locale for "information storage," to use that of Donald, or as the medium of an "exteriorization of the brain," to return once more to Leroi-Gourhan—if we can go there without invoking a preconceived idea thus exteriorized.[38] Technologies needed only the consolidation and mimesis of the *chaîne opératoire* to act in this way, and both of these are manifest in Acheulean industries. It is therefore a mistake to imagine, as d'Errico, Donald, and Leroi-Gourhan all do in different ways, that external memory storage needed to await the invention of something like modern graphism or symbolism. Instead it emerged, long before writing as it is conventionally defined, or modern language, or symbolic semantics, or *Homo sapiens* itself. It took shape first as *memory archived* in the form of patterned gesture, transmitted from one body to another.

This counters the many writers who have presumed that sophisticated toolmaking had to be founded upon sophisticated linguistic skills.[39] Donald's mimesis and rehearsal, as he emphasizes, require no propositional language. One million years ago, these mechanisms transmitted information among hominins without the referentiality of words, whatever vocalizations no doubt accompanied them (for these, see Chapter 3). In this, Acheulean mimetic traditions exemplify a distinction that will be important for us between information, on one hand, and modern referentiality, representation, semantics, and symbolism, on the other. While human language today is inconceivable without a referential lexicon, musicking relies instead on the transmission of information not semantically loaded. Modern musicking *comes into* referentiality frequently, but it does so incidentally, so to speak, through its ubiquitous contact with a language and symbolism external to it. An incremental history of music's emergence takes us back to a time before both linguistic referentiality and music, but not before the social transmission of information. It leads us to broach, in this passing of information without reference, a general congruency between modern musicking and the pre-sapient transmission of socio-material skills. To broach and no more, for now; the complex relations of information and signification in the final emergence of human modernity will be left for later chapters.

Meanwhile, the joining of Donald's mimesis to the action sequences and taskscape of Leroi-Gourhanian archaeology grants a vivid sense of hominin sociality on the East African savannah 1,000,000 years ago. We can envision a small band creating its transient social space through a matrix of gestures, marks etched upon the material world; we understand the complexity of the matrix to emerge from the interwoven rhythms of these operations, individually simple. But now, in the wake of our analysis of mimesis, we sense something in this sociomaterial taskscape we had not noticed before. The intersections of these actions are not haphazard; instead the performance of one sometimes summons a related performance. Action sequences evoke more or less voluntary responses in the form of other, similar sequences. *Chaînes opératoires* come to be linked through patterns of likeness. In a word, they come to be *synchronized*.

Entrainment

The synchronizing of action routines in Lower Paleolithic taskscapes must have been of the loosest sort. These hominins did not join their various stone-knapping gestures, like some lithic percussion section, in the coinciding rhythms of modern field-laborers reaping or soldiers marching or rowers rowing to a shared beat. More generally, their synchronies do not indicate that *Homo ergaster* or *Homo erectus*—or even later species involved in Acheulean toolmaking—were musicking creatures, however much their routines reshaped the soundscape they inhabited. Nevertheless, the mimetic coincidings we can discern as the basis for their traditions signal the emergence of a foundational new capacity *to shape voluntarily specific gestures so as to mirror those of the surrounding world.*

The voluntary aspect is crucial. The Acheulean rehearsal loop, building no doubt on older patterns of primate sociality, brought under voluntary control more and more elaborate action

76

sequences. It inserted a new step into the eons-old feedback loop between organism and environment, a step in which, under some circumstances, a hominin not only controlled but also measured out, so to speak, its reaction to environmental stimulus. This shift of neural resources from the involuntary to the voluntary column has to be a major, general theme in any history of hominin evolution. It is basic to the behavioral flexibility that ultimately enabled hominins such as Neandertals and early modern humans to survive demanding, shifting Ice Age environments, to populate a huge range of ecologies, and much more.

In the case of Acheulean technologies, the measuring out of voluntary response was novel in its linkage to perceived regularities in the environment, that is, to those patterned operational sequences, ceaselessly iterated, from which the loosely repeating shapes of tools resulted. Earlier, the Oldowan taskscape had shown little in the way of such repetition, but now the weak synchronies of the Acheulean taskscape took shape from voluntary social interaction among the hominins involved. They formed a kind of self-initiated *social entrainment*.

In musical usage, *entrainment* names our capacity for "beat-based processing" or "beat induction": our ability to perceive the regularity of an even or *isochronous* series of pulses, to predict the continuation of the series, and to coordinate our activities in advance to this continued regularity. (It indicates other musical phenomena as well, as we will see.) The term *entrainment*, however, has a much wider catchment than this musical one. In its most encompassing usage it can refer to the linked synchrony of any repeating cycles. These might occur in nonbiological realms, for example, the synchrony of the tides and the revolutions of the moon, or the famous "odd sympathy" first described by Christiaan Huygens: the tendency of two pendulums mounted on the same beam to fall into linked periods (and opposed motion). In biological uses, recently much elaborated by chronobiologists, ecologists, and ecological psychologists, entrainment can refer to all linkages between the regular life patterns of organisms and regularities of their environments: plants to the seasons, activity/ rest cycles of animals to the cycles of night and day, many other daily or "circadian" cycles (flowers opening at dawn and closing at nightfall, for instance), and so forth. In whatever realm they occur, all instances of entrainment share two basic features: the presence of two or more cyclical phenomena—*oscillators* is the term of art—and their linked interrelationship.[40]

Entrainment thus broadly conceived has proved to be a powerful tool for conceptualizing not only physical, biological, and physiological processes but also the social interactions of species from insects to humans. Its usefulness springs from its dynamism, which allows it to model interactions not as static arrays but as moving patterns unfolding in time, and from its featuring of repeating cycles resembling the periodicity of many social patterns. In the theory of social entrainment proposed by Joseph E. McGrath and Janice E. Kelly, an organism itself is viewed as "a loosely coupled population of oscillators," that is, of interlocked, repeating patterns across a spectrum from the molecular level (metabolic cycles) to the cellular (neurons, pacemaker cells in the heart) to the organismal (reproductive and life cycles). Each member of a social group brings these biological, "endogenous rhythms" to its interactions with others. The linkages among these manifold oscillators burgeon into complex, nonlinear patterns ("dynamic" equilibria), struck up within organisms, among organisms, and between organisms or groups of them and the environment. Those that arise within groups of conspecifics define the realm of social entrainment.[41]

Human sociality is the complex product of both voluntary and innate or uncontrollable rhythms, and of rhythms both cyclic and aperiodic and unpredictable. Human social entrainment arises when cyclical rhythms, endogenous or voluntary, come to be synchronized between one individual and another, and such linked oscillations are widespread in human experiences ranging from the pacing of people walking together or of conversational dialogue to the cycles of international economies. This conception of

entrainment embraces also the loose structuring of human interactions according to broad rhythms of turn taking, where breaks
in the pattern constitute disruptions in expectation with affective
and communicative consequences. This connects humans to a
larger group of species, including present-day monkeys and apes.

Among the most precise forms of human social entrainment
are musical ones, especially entrainment to musical meters.
Starting from this metrical entrainment, Mari Riess Jones,
Edward Large, and an expanding group of collaborators and
other researchers have developed a far-reaching model of our
perception of temporal events.[42] This "dynamic attending theory"
aims to describe the mechanism behind our flexible attention to
changing sequences of events, thereby moving beyond more limited and static theories that rely on encoded memories of rhythms
or rigid internal clocks measuring them.

The proposed mechanism involves multiple neural oscillations, like the endogenous rhythms posited by McGrath and
Kelly, synchronizing themselves to oscillating sequences of external events. The internal, "attending" oscillations are set in motion
by the regularities of external events and show a number of traits:
They are self-sustaining in brain activity; each oscillates at a specific, characteristic frequency; and they are at once resistant to
minor perturbations of regularity in stimuli and also adaptable to
out-of-phase events. The first of these, the self-sustaining quality
of the oscillators, enables the prediction of continued regularity
in the stimulus—"future directed attending," as this aspect of
the entrainment is sometimes called. (Because of this anticipatory capacity, to offer musical examples, we can play together
with one another in ensembles or dance to beats not yet heard
at the instant we program our next move.) Multiple, interlinked
neural networks oscillating at different frequencies, meanwhile,
create multileveled perceptions of complex events (for example
the hierarchies of quicker and slower pulses or cycles entailed in
musical meters). Moreover, Large and Jones's analysis of these
interlinked oscillators suggests that their interaction can exert a

force tending toward synchrony, or restoration of synchrony after perturbations in one cycle or another. Synchrony, in this model, is a flexible attractor, a region (rather than point) of stability toward which the relation of the oscillators tends.[43] (This flexibility allows for much variability of stimuli—*ritardandi*, Chopinesque rubato—without breakdown of the entrainment.)

Is this view of interlinked oscillators and rhythmic cycles more than a model? In psychological experiments measuring perception of and reaction to regularities and perturbations of music-like rhythmic stimuli, Jones, Large, and others have begun to uncover evidence of its functioning in vivo.[44] Recently, moreover, evidence of a different kind has come from electroencephalography (EEG), measuring electrical currents in cortical neural networks, and magnetoencephalography (MEG), measuring the magnetic fields generated by these currents. Both methods indicate that the cortical networks involved oscillate in regular cycles linked at multiple frequencies—hierarchies of oscillators, in other words—and suggest that these cycles are fundamental to cognitive processes such as attention and expectancy. There are strong reasons to think that the oscillators of dynamic attending theory are very real brain functions, that they engage with cyclic phenomena in the environment, and that these linkages are responsible for entrainment. The gaps in our knowledge between conceptual models, observed behaviors, and measured neural processes are narrowing, at least in this area.[45]

Meanwhile, another imaging technique, functional magnetic resonance imaging (fMRI), opens an additional line of evidence. Able to probe deep-brain structures, unlike MEG and EEG, which are limited to the cortex, fMRI suggests that our beat-based processing is not accomplished in the cortex alone. Instead, it reaches to subcortical regions, especially the cerebellum and basal ganglia. The rich range of functions of the first remains in good measure unclear but seems to include the control of skilled motor performance. The basal ganglia also are implicated in motor issues, especially sequential timing and patterned movement.[46] fMRI thus suggests that musical entrainment is closely bound to motor centers in the brain.[47] Together with EEG and MEG, it suggests also that entrainment of this sort recruits a wide network of brain functions, some of them relatively recent in evolutionary terms, others older.

Beat-based musical processing shows every sign of being the tip of a cognitive iceberg. It is a precise, focused instance of the much broader phenomenon of entrainment, a phenomenon that in human experience seems to underlie our general capacity to attend to and correlate sequences of events around us. And it is an expression of motor networks widely dispersed through the brain, both in phylogenetically recent and more ancient structures. Given this participation in broader cognitive capacities for attention and this multiplex recruitment, it is no surprise that the behaviors we can shape in response to beat entrainment are generalizable across domains, as we have seen with Merlin Donald: think again of tapping our feet, snapping our fingers, or moving any voluntary muscles in our bodies to the beat. Altogether, the emerging picture of metric entrainment outlines a relatively modern, specific exploitation of general capacities with a long history in the hominin line. John Bispham has put it all into one rather large mouthful; for him the existence of domain-general oscillators in the brain suggests that "entrainment in music constitutes an evolutionary exaptation of more generally functional mechanisms for future-directed attending to temporally structured events."[48] Beat entrainment represents one channel in modern *Homo sapiens* along which our capacities for voluntary attending and self-initiated motor sequences have developed. In their social dimension these voluntary capacities bring mimesis and entrainment close to one another, as multiple individuals conform their actions to each other or to the same external stimulus.

The Acheulean Increment
All these features of entrainment are dimly visible as we look out across the Acheulean taskscape. *Homo ergaster* or whoever first

was making these tools left behind the earliest solid evidence we have of hominin brains *joining in interlocked cycles of action sequences*. The *chaîne opératoire* of the Acheulean biface acted as an external oscillator, striking up attending oscillations in the brains of those who watched it. Social animals enacted it through a choice to act that was in some degree conscious, if without planning and foresight as to the byproduct that might result. Others in the group, adept at mimesis and armed with the self-controlled motor mechanisms of the rehearsal loop, observed and set in motion their own, similar sequences. The taskscape as a whole was not merely a matrix of action sequences, as I have characterized it above, but something more: a complex system of interlinked oscillators from which emerged social bonding, cultural traditions, and—not least—usable tools.[49]

We do not know what precise ends Acheulean tools served; these were probably many over the long history of the industry, though it is hard to doubt that they included cutting, chopping, and scraping. Whatever uses the tools were put to, the endurance of the industry as a whole suggests that hominins able to master it gained advantages by doing so. It suggests also that they passed on to their offspring the capacities that enabled them to learn the tradition. The tools were the crudescence in the material world of the cognitive patterns that stood behind them. That is the unremarkable way to describe them, but we shouldn't forget the inverse, even if it seems more uncanny: The actions involved in their making shaped cognition as much as they strengthened or changed the hand.

And the tools functioned as material extensions of the body that altered the selective landscape and its pressures. As the toolmakers were advantageously selected, so were the capacities that enabled their industries: self-initiated motor sequences, mimesis of others, rehearsal loops. No doubt many looser forms of social bonding marked the primate line long before hominins emerged, and in the broad view outlined above these also must be considered loose examples of social entrainment. But now entrainment entered the hominin line in a new, powerful, and more focused form. Now it was defined by oscillating replications of elaborate action sequences that bore relations more determinate than before to the affordances of the material environment. And now, also more than before, it served accumulated stores of information passed from one generation to another; it was *cultural* entrainment.

These novel swerves in ancient forms of correlation might shed a somewhat brighter light on the puzzling persistence and stability of Acheulean industries. Pausing over the puzzle in their ruminations on biocultural coevolution, Richerson and Boyd "entertain the hypothesis that Acheulean bifaces were innately constrained rather than wholly cultural and that their temporal stability stemmed from some component of genetically transmitted psychology"—this even while the tools called for "the same sorts of manual skills that we transmit culturally."[50] The apparent conflict of a cultural stability genetically maintained suggests to Richerson and Boyd a compelling strangeness about the cognitive makeup of *Homo ergaster* or *erectus*, and a more circuitous route from that cognition to our own than we tend to assume.

The model of increasingly focused entrainment of action sequences assuages the strangeness, but does not aim to dispel it entirely. It posits a long-lasting stage in the development of mimesis and joint action that sprang from several sources. These included an embodied knowledge that resulted in cultural *transmission* but little or no cultural *transformation* of the kind we know so well, and capacities for shared attention and the attributing to others of intentions like our own. The foundation on which this social matrix was built remained an entrainment, ancient but newly attuned through voluntary mimesis, of oscillating gestures and cycles of gestures. But the causal line did not flow only from embodied knowledge to culture. Instead the patterns of cultural accumulation redrew, through social mimesis, horizons of embodied knowledge and organismal relation to material affordance, and through this redrawing led to alterations in selection and selective terrains.

At any rate, some kind of continuity of cognitive evolution in the hominin line reaching from coordinated motor patterns of Acheulean toolmakers all the way to those of modern humans seems inescapable. The limitation of Donald's rehearsal loop and mimesis to the hominin line, all but absolute within the primate clade, indicates as much. With this continuity comes another: the continuity connecting those ancient entrained operational sequences to modern modes of embodied social entrainment, including musical ones. In those million-year-old movements and the mimesis that linked them we can discern outlines of capacities that would eventually underlie musical rhythmic cognition. I have taken up this crucial increment of modern musicking first because the evidence suggests that it was the earliest to form, its roots reaching all the way down to the social entrainment that enabled Acheulean industries to proliferate and persist. At this distant historical moment there was not music but a *techno-sociality* incising the material world through loosely conjoined rhythmic action. One of the outgrowths of this advent, far down a divagating path we will follow in chapters to come, was musical entrainment.

Whatever we do not know of this advent, we already know enough to reconceive the transmission of Lower Paleolithic toolmaking skills as emergent, embodied, and entrained cognition. This suggests a final return to Acheulean hand axes.

Poiesis

The return requires a detour through the disclosure, revealing, or unconcealing (*aletheia*) that Heidegger names as the forgotten essence of technology in his famous essay on the subject.[51] This unconcealing is a process of bringing into presence something not present. It therefore places technology under the aegis of *poiesis*, the broader name the Greeks gave to such bringing forth or "presencing." Technological unconcealing touches at the heart of *Dasein*, insofar as this names for Heidegger our openness to the presencing (or disclosure) that arises from our intersubjective

and material connections to the world. Technological unconcealing, moreover, has a history, divided in the West into two
epochs. These are distinguished especially by the increased distance, in the modern age, between technological effects and
unconcealing—a distance that hides the essence of technology
while capturing the energy of resources in standing reserves at
human command.

From the beginning, however, technology names a particular
kind of poiesis, not a bringing forth of something in or through
itself, as for instance a blossom blooming, but instead a presencing guided from without by the craftsman or artist. This ability
to reveal what does not reveal itself is, already for the Greeks,
a defining feature of *techne*. For Heidegger, it arises from the
craftsman's prior mental conception: "Whoever builds a house or
a ship or forges a sacrificial chalice reveals what is to be brought
forth.... This revealing gathers together in advance the aspect
and the matter of ship or house, with a view to the finished thing
envisioned as completed, and from this gathering determines the
manner of its construction."[52] Throughout its long history, in
the Heideggerian account, technology is action springing from
mental-template thinking.

So it remains in Bernard Stiegler's 1994 study *Technics and
Time*. Stiegler takes Heidegger as his starting point, and his whole
project is a furthering of Heidegger's thoughts on the relations
of technology to the temporality of Being or *Dasein*. But in his
first volume it is archaeologist Leroi-Gourhan who earns pride
of place.[53] In analyzing Leroi-Gourhan's project in both *Gesture and Speech* and earlier writings, Stiegler perceives much
that is germane to the Acheulean technosociality I have dwelled
upon. He sees with his predecessor the fundamental importance
of Paleolithic technology in defining the natures of the species that mastered it.[54] He accepts, if with qualification, Leroi-
Gourhan's "universal technical tendency" that couples from earliest times hominins to matter; and, conflating categories that
Leroi-Gourhan also sought to join, he describes the coevolution

of technological development (*technogenesis*) and biological and social developments (*anthropogenesis*).[55] If this does not lead him to break down as fully as he might the dichotomy of nature and nurture, it nevertheless provokes a memorable characterization of the "epigenetic sedimentation," standing outside and counteracting biological determinism, involved in the transmission of technologies.[56]

Finally, Stiegler considers the exteriorization of memory Leroi-Gourhan had perceived in artifacts and their traditions. Following Derrida, he connects this movement to all writing systems, to the *grammè*, and ultimately to *différance*, "which is nothing else than the history of life." The movement, he avers, quoting Derrida, "goes far beyond the possibilities of 'intentional consciousness.' It is an emergence that makes the *grammè* appear as such (that is to say according to a new structure of nonpresence)."[57] This Derridean response to Leroi-Gourhan, in naming an emergence of the sign—and the tool—innocent of agency and intent as we normally think of them, recalls the question with which I began this chapter: How can we imagine the manufacture of a sophisticated tool without planning, foresight, or mental image of the product-to-come?

Stiegler, however, retreats from the question and, in the same motion, from an understanding of the Acheulean toolmaker. His interest remains not so much Derrida's nonpresence as the presencing and unconcealing of Heidegger's *Dasein*. He turns from Derridean possibilities beyond "intentional consciousness," possibilities akin to the Acheulean ones I have described, back to a Heideggerian model in which technology as *poiesis* is founded in an anticipation or foresight arising with the temporality of *Dasein*. "It is the process of anticipation itself that becomes refined and complicated with technics," he writes; without it, "humans could not make tools." At the end of his long analysis of Leroi-Gourhan, Stiegler, having defined the human by means of technology, conceives technology according to a too-familiar human:

Either the Zinjanthropian is nothing but a prehominid who cannot anticipate, that is, who is not in time and who in no case accomplishes its future since it has none...or else the human is human from the Zinjanthropian onward, in which case there is a technico-intellectual intelligence as such in a single stroke. The latter means that there is anticipation in the full sense of the term, just as there is idiomatic [i.e., epigenetic] differentiation...and no longer simply species-specific [i.e., biologically determined] differentiation.[58]

Here we meet Stiegler's early hominin, and it is us, possessing a full armature of mental representations from which to plan and execute its immersion in the material world, experiencing temporality in the fashion unique to Heidegger's human *Dasein*, distant from those nonhuman primates who cannot anticipate, cannot be "in time," cannot bring about the future. We see no sign of the self-organizing complexity that might have led to Acheulean symmetries, and that has been used by Manuel de Landa, much more broadly, to define a whole Deleuzian "machinic phylum";[59] no sign of the entrained couplings, beneath conscious intentionality, that linked Acheulean operational sequences; and no sign of a *poiesis* building the products and sociality of a taskscape in the absence of a modern, recognizably human interiority.

If instead we resist Stiegler's perspective on Lower Paleolithic industries, steeped in the Heideggerian magic of the tool, we are confronted once more, but in new terms, with the nearly imponderable: a technological tradition that knows little self-possession and no gathering-together-in-advance, that results in products but does not thereby realize a future. Or let us resist in Heidegger's own terms. That an Acheulean revelation occurred, an unconcealing from the stone core of a shape replicated in countless instances, we cannot doubt. But this earliest poiesis relied on no mode of abstraction, no cognitive distance, no knowing craftsman; it was poiesis from the bottom up, to recall Rodney Brooks. There is, ironically, a precisely Heideggerian trajectory in this: hominins opening out through the rhythms of their *techne* toward the presencing offered by their material surroundings and their encounters with others. But there is no template-magic: no mental blueprint, not even the possibility of one. So Acheulean technology stands categorically apart from Heidegger's two later technological eras, far outside the Western metaphysics of being—indeed outside any human metaphysics at all—necessitating a third era in his poietic history: pre-sapient, primordial, nonhuman *Dasein*. Cambrian *aletheia*.

Into this social *techne*, another, different revelation insinuated itself: rhythmic synchrony. The taskscape formed as a sharpening of more general modes of mammalian and primate entrainment, more general capacities, even, for attention in social interaction. This sharpening, like the tools themselves, was an accidental poiesis, the achievement of creatures unfathomably distant from us in their cognitive capacities, rather than the mark of our birth. But its ramifications—musical also—are with us still. These, finally, are the lessons taught by Leroi-Gourhan's Acheulean *chaîne opératoire*.

CHAPTER THREE

500,000 Years Ago:

Lower Paleolithic Voices

The Vocalized Taskscape

The Acheulean taskscape 1,000,000 years ago was more than a soundscape, reverberating with the varied noises of hominin activity and industry. It was also a *voice*scape, in which lungs, larynx, and vocal tract helped to negotiate environmental affordances and social entrainments both general and specific. Its synchronies, indeed all its social interactions, must have resounded with calls, cries, growls, purrs, whimpers, grunts, hoots, and more. The many varieties of vocalization in primate societies in the world today indicate this much.

The mimesis, rehearsal, and cultural transmission of early Acheulean industries suggest something more: that this early hominin voice was not merely an innate one, elicited by external stimuli in preprogrammed ways and involving little voluntary control, like a wolf's howl or a cat's hiss. Instead, it had already begun to shift along the biosocial spectrum toward modest voluntary control and social complexity. It was a construction molded, in even greater degree than in those primate societies today, by encounters with others amid the materials, dangers, and rewards of the environment.

Whatever the complexities of this construction, however, it is safe to say that it little resembled modern language. No evidence suggests that Acheulean hominins possessed even a rudimentary lexicon or syntactic manipulation of it. Semantic referentiality and the combinatorial and hierarchic processing of syntax, had they existed, would have relied on too many distinctive cognitive capacities and fostered too many new elements of sociality not to leave traces in the archaeological record—in technology, in the transport and exchange of materials, in patterns of movement, settlement, and affiliation, in predation, and so forth. Such physical evidence exists for our much more recent ancestors, the sign that language had arrived. Semantics and syntax also would likely have upset the long-lived stability of the Acheulean industry—the stability that is our significant gauge for the embodied cognition of its makers. This was an era of social vocalization and communication before language, an era of what paleolinguists often call *protolanguage.*

Debates about the nature and development of this protolanguage have simmered and occasionally boiled over across the last thirty years or so, a time in which the venerable question of the origin of language has been reinvigorated by new evidence, subtle inference, and rich speculation. The debates have drawn attention to basic questions in hominin evolution: the emergences of cooperative sociality, of social "mindreading" or *theory of mind*, and of the cognitive foundations of modern language. The questions raised have ranged beyond vocalization to consider communicative gesture—an issue that cannot be unimportant in the material mimesis of the taskscape even 1,000,000 years ago, and another area where today's nonhuman primates have much to tell us.

At the same time, questions of the nature of protolanguage have too often been limited by a unilateral teleology. They have tended to look back from the single vantage of modern language—often not even modern language in all its varied attributes, but instead language viewed through the narrowing lens of lexicon and syntax. In this they have reflected the emphases of post-Chomskyan linguistics and the disciplinary allegiances of those who have stepped into the protolanguage arena, mostly linguists or language cognitivists.

A musicologist sees protolanguage from a different place. The basic features of human song and, more generally, musicking differ in some respects from those of language, in other ways overlap with them; in still other ways they seem to exploit similar or identical cognitive capacities to different expressive and informational ends. Song offers itself, in this complex relation to language, as a second modern behavior that protolinguistic analyses need to account for. This too can lead to fruitless teleology: As far back as Vico and Rousseau, the putative origin of human communication in song lured speculators down a path hiding many pitfalls; Darwin himself stumbled into them, as we will see. Cautiously tracked, however, the special attributes of song and music can widen the question of protolanguage from language narrowly conceived. The opportunities along this direction need to be gauged against what we can reconstruct of the capacities of Lower Paleolithic hominins and the conditions of their lives—against, that is, the experience of the Acheulean taskscape.

Copresence

The taskscape 1,000,000 years ago was structured in part from action sequences under some measure of voluntary control, passed mimetically from one hominin to the next through the mechanisms of the rehearsal loop. The stone tools that resulted from this kind of sociality were something more than its happenstance byproduct, and something less than a preplanned product. Whatever advantages they afforded groups equipped with them led probably to some selective pressure for the perpetuation of the capacities behind them. At the heart of this taskscape was a social entrainment more focused and more intense than ever before in the hominin line. The attunement of oscillatory neural processes in this entrainment laid the basis for the far more pronounced and precise rhythmic synchronies that would emerge much later.

On this taskscape interactions were close, in the moment, and online. Mimesis of another's action sequence started from habituation and familiarity—from the actions that knappers and neophytes saw around them everyday—then internalized these, repeating and rehearsing them. In the absence of anything like propositional language, there was no offline learning of the sequences, no abstracted instruction, statement of principles, or discussion and reflection about the tool made earlier that day. At most there may have existed some deictic "instruction" closely bound to immediate contexts: a huff of acknowledgment for a particularly effective blow struck.[1] Society was performed from the bottom up, as a sequence of face-to-face encounters, rather than as the expression of any general, governing conception of social organization. Acheulean cultures were, in short, cultures of *copresence*.

The taskscape was characterized down to its foundation by this inability to interpose distance between sociomaterial inter-actions and cultural knowledge transmitted across generations. We open such distance continually, we are virtuosos at using language and other means to do so, and we take it so much for granted that the elements of our culture otherwise transmit-ted almost disappear from view. Early hominins could not. The constitutive proximity of their sociality and its eventual transfor-mation—the "release from proximity" introduced in Chapter 2— will form recurring themes here and in future chapters; they are critical to thinking about how musicking arose. They are central also in Clive Gamble's analysis of European Paleolithic societies from *Homo heidelbergensis* (the species widely accepted as the earliest hominin in western Europe) through *Homo nean-derthalensis* to *Homo sapiens*. The story he pieces together from a wealth of archaeological and paleontological evidence narrates the increasing capacity of hominins across this period to extend interactions away from the immediacy of face-to-face encounters toward greater distance and wider social networks.

The move beyond copresence involved a gradual growth in social flexibility, voluntary control of action, and complication of *discourse*. It reflected also an increasing nuance in the exploration of the affordances of the material environment, moving beyond shallower responses holding close to the immediate dimensions of those affordances: imagine the difference between using a stick as an implement (which a chimpanzee in the wild can manage) and whittling a point on the end of it (which the chimp cannot). The introduction of distance into social networks rested on new modes of sustained attention shared among individuals, and ultimately, at the end of a long development, on symbolic exploitation of materials. From this general perspective, symbolism can be understood as one outcome of the surmounting of immediacy that emerged in the hominin line.

All these developments unfolded slowly across the last million years. As recently as 500,000 years ago, our picture of the earliest European societies of *Homo heidelbergensis* shows simple outlines.[2] It reveals modest signs of the extension of social interaction beyond copresence and a sociality that, if it has tightened somewhat the loose entrainments we discerned for *Homo ergaster* or *erectus*, should nevertheless give pause to those who would too readily extend sapient capacities far back in the hominin lineage.

Gamble's evidence comes especially from lithic technologies and from a small number of well-studied sites: Boxgrove, in southern England; Bilzingsleben, in eastern Germany; Notarchirico, in southern Italy; and a few more. In the stone artifacts at these sites, the emphasis remains on an opportunistic *chaîne opératoire* closely bound to its situational context rather than on a finished expression of a mental template. Tools were fashioned quickly from raw materials close to hand, near to the scavenged or hunted carcasses they were used to butcher. Operational sequences were short, limited to the rhythms determined by these material proximities and short-lived joint activities. After their use, tools were sometimes carried away from the scene, as study of the flakes left behind from their manufacture reveals. But transport of materials across long distances, which might imply advance planning for tool making, was rare. Often tools were simply discarded at the site of their manufacture, and the repeated visits of hominins to the same scavenging or hunting locales, perhaps across many years, might explain the occurrence at some sites of

accumulations of hundreds of discarded bifaces. The social network revealed in these lithic arrays was intense but local, reaching little farther than the shared attentions of individuals focused
on tasks before their eyes. No convincing evidence has been found
for the distancing of materials from their primary affordances
toward what archaeologists think of as symbolic use—shells perforated for stringing on a necklace, for example, or geometrical
patterns incised in bones.

Gamble's picture of Lower Paleolithic sociality is more
cautious than that offered by some others. He takes issue, for
instance, with the interpretations of the Bilzingsleben researchers, led by Dietrich Mania, who discern traces of built structures
there. For Gamble, instead, the site reveals a looser, more ephemeral cluster of gatherings in its scattering of bones, tools, and
stone and bone anvils—an episodic rather than consistent occupation of the landscape. Bilzingsleben confirms his sense that in
this period, "The focus of social life was not the organized social
occasion, centered on hearth or hut, but rather the opportunity,
intercepted, encountered and available for subsequent negotiation." Gatherings took the form of "performances that involved
the rhythms of manufacture as bones and stones were smashed
and fashioned." These may have solidified social bonds, especially
in the locales that offered repeated scavenging or hunting opportunities and were often revisited. But the emphasis was firmly
on sociality at the moment of face-to-face collaboration, and the
gatherings created "no lasting effect once co-presence was broken."[3] To speak of something like modern memory or calculation
here would be pointless.

Such caution is wise especially in the face of dramatic speculations sometimes advanced concerning Lower Paleolithic attainments. A famous recent instance is the assertion of researchers
led by Juan Luis Arsuaga at Atapuerca, in northern Spain, of
ritual funerary behavior at least 400,000 years ago. The excava-
tion there in the Sima de los Huesos ("pit of bones") of remains
of twenty-eight individuals, assigned by the excavators to *Homo*

heidelbergensis, is stunning and most likely reflects extraordinary events; we lack a convincing explanation of how this concentration of hominin remains came about. But in itself—or even in combination with the single biface found among the bones and supposed by some to be an "offering" accompanying the "burials"—it is not enough to support convincingly the widespread presence of capacities resembling those of modern humans for which there is no corroborating evidence at this period, and little for another several hundred thousand years after it.[4] As with design features of modern language, if such capacities were part of the general makeup of *heidelbergensis* (or whatever we call this hominin) we should expect them to be reflected in numerous other features of their sociality, in the process leaving physical traces.

This does not exclude the possibility that the Sima de los Huesos represents a microburst, a sporadic outbreak of behaviors not generally present at this period—if not offerings to the afterlife, at least some conscious recognition of an extraordinary (and perhaps extraordinarily traumatic) event.[5] We will see in Chapter 4 a likely instance of such local and episodic cultural attainment in wooden spears from the same era, and this idea of microbursts of innovation will figure importantly in considering still more recent archaeological evidence—and will be a necessary backdrop for my account of the emergence of musicking. Moreover, evidence from sites other than Atapuerca has been analyzed along less cautious lines than Gamble's without leading to credulous claims. Chris Stringer and others, for example, have discerned at Boxgrove evidence of something more than early human scavenging—evidence, in fact, that these hominins were capable of hunting the megafauna whose butchered remains have been unearthed there. Accepting such analysis substantially alters our view of the hominins, since stalking and killing Middle Pleistocene hippopotamuses would have required both a technology and social collaboration more complex than those Gamble describes.[6]

Even Gamble's cautious approach, however, need not lead us to underestimate the elaborateness of the half-million-year-old social networks he describes.[7] If they reached little beyond copresence and immediate affordance, they packed considerable variety into their narrow taskscapes. Gatherings to butcher carcasses may have been fleeting, quickened by the threat of other animals lured to the kill, but they were nevertheless a far cry from those nonhuman scavengings. The few well-studied sites reflect concentrated matrices of collaboration that depended on joint attention and, if we had to guess, emotional interactions of considerable power if short range. Nearby stones had to be collected in order to be fashioned quickly into bifaces or flakes; larger stones or large bones might be pressed into service as anvils or chopping blocks. The butchering itself had to be accomplished—no easy task, especially in the case of big carcasses.

This variety and the urgency of the situation probably resulted in spontaneous, transitory divisions of labor, as some individuals searched for stones, some quickly fashioned tools, some sliced hide and sinew and hammered bones, and some, perhaps, stood watch and drove off four-legged scavengers. Or perhaps each individual undertook several of these tasks, with the meeting at the carcass supplying the matrix for intense, face-to-face negotiation. Much of the nutritional sustenance to be had—marrow from crushed bones, certainly, and perhaps flesh—was consumed on the spot, and the rest soon after the butchering. This probably entailed gestures of sharing as well as hoarding, cooperation and dispute, with many of the emotions still attendant upon human neighborhoods in the here and now.

And, finally, there is the evidence—especially those accumulations of discarded hand axes—of repeated gatherings at particular sites. The site at Boxgrove was on the shore of a waterhole, where carrion or prey might have been especially plentiful. Such repeating patterns, at one level, might differ little from the cyclical, seasonal life-rhythms of countless mammals, with predators and prey drawn to resources shifting across changing ecosystems. The cultural learning of Acheulean hominins, however, unique in its intensity on these Middle Pleistocene landscapes, suggests that their repeated gatherings could be something more, an aspect of the conversion of the landscape into a taskscape of inter-linked cultural rhythms. We can draw no sheer divide between four-legged predators or scavengers gathering in cyclic fashion where opportunities abound and two-legged ones, armed with sharp stones, doing the same. Nevertheless, hominin gatherings involved a complexity above and beyond those animal gatherings, in which, at the least, nearby lithic resources were exploited and learned technologies brought to bear. Their remains reveal to us new kinds of social networks.

Mindreading and Shared Attention

The current picture of late Lower Paleolithic sociality, if it is one of broad outline, does not for that lack intricacy. It reveals in these hominin societies collaborations more complex than those evident among great apes in the world today. Chimpanzee group hunting is often adduced as an example in apes of coopera-tion toward a shared goal, and it might seem close to Acheulean sociality. But the analysis of Michael Tomasello and his fellow researchers suggests that this puts too human—or hominin—a face on it. Though chimpanzees might appear in hunting to work toward a common goal, in fact they seem to be otherwise moti-vated. Each aims only to achieve its own ends, situating itself at every moment so as to maximize its chances of making the kill and gaining the best of the spoils. The organization of the hunt as a whole emerges, from the bottom up, as a dynamic inter-section of individual interests: It is flocking raised to a higher power. Apes do understand the intentions of other apes, but they seem to react to these competitively rather than cooperatively, unable to enter into an intentionality shared and sustained among the group.[8]

In a hominin group butchering a carcass at Boxgrove 500,000 years ago, instead, the variety alone of activities involved—even merely the toolmaking and the butchering, the two activities directly reflected in the archaeological record—suggests an endeavor different from chimpanzee hunting. It suggests col-laboration governed to a modest degree by individuals' abilities to see a broader picture in which immediate cooperation with those around them, along with division of labor among members of the group, will bring them to their (individual) goals more surely than competition alone. A distinction appears between individual goals and the joint means that will best attain them, and both are accommodated in collaborative activity.

The difference between today's nonhuman primates and the Boxgrove hominins can be illuminated also from other directions. For Shirley Strum and Bruno Latour, baboons' sociality involves their ability to perceive simultaneously a variety of stimuli and react to these through bodily gesture, momentarily stabilizing social spaces. It is a question of moment-to-moment embodied performance. Human societies, instead, merge such performance with larger schemes created through the deployment of material resources (and ultimately symbolic ones). These umbrella con-ceptions for ordering society exert a top-down organization that leads to a reduction in the complexity of baboon-like, bottom-up performance.[9]

Gamble posits a resemblance between Strum and Latour's baboon societies and his Lower Paleolithic ones, with their "min-imal extension of copresence beyond the gathering,"[10] but here his retreat from incautious claims about this era may carry him too far. The social performances of Acheulean hominins involved something more than baboon sociality, a something revealed especially, again, in the cultural archive of information about material resources—in other words, the mimetic traditions of toolmaking. Such an elaborated drawing of materials into the social matrix has no counterpart in baboon interactions, and it indicates that Lower Paleolithic hominins had already begun to move in the direction Strum and Latour see as indicative of human sociality. The society evident at Boxgrove remained limited in range and variety, with passing collaborations and restricted to face-to-face communication; but in the midst of this overwhelming copresence its lithic technology, opportunistically exploited, adumbrated a different kind of social order.

The new order rose above cognitive foundations developed modestly beyond the earlier Acheulean entrainment described in Chapter 2, and this difference between hominin sociality 1,000,000 and 500,000 years ago will be basic to the attempt here to describe Lower Paleolithic vocalization. Ecological psychologists Günther Knoblich and Natalie Sebanz have plotted a line of evolving social interactions that can help sharpen the distinction.[11] For them the simplest kind of sociality stems from the response of an organism to the affordances of its environment. Two organisms reacting similarly to the same material possibilities might enter into a rudimentary "ecological" entrainment or, in a more complex scenario, one organism might simulate the actions of another, within limits determined by their basic action repertories. The second scenario proposes a set of neural networks in the observer enabling various basic actions; when one of these actions is perceived, the corresponding network is activated, setting off a more or less involuntary simulation.

This "ideomotor theory" received a boost in the 1990s with the discovery in monkeys of "mirror neurons." These are neurons involved in particular actions that fire also when the same actions are not performed but *witnessed* being performed by others. Here we seem to be close to the synchronized neural oscillations basic to the entrainment models of Mari Riess Jones and Edward Large. The interactions of *Homo ergaster* in performing the Acheulean taskscape might have relied on not much more than this second scenario of Knoblich and Sebanz.[12]

What is missing still from this stage, and was probably missing also from early Acheulean entrainment, is a well-developed capacity for sustained, shared attention directed toward the environment and taskscape. From this capacity might come the kind of elaborated cooperation involved at the butchering sites of Boxgrove, Notarchirico, and Bilzingsleben. It appears in Knoblich and Sebanz's third scenario, and it brings with it several corollaries.

Shared attention presupposes the ability to separate another's perceptions from our own so as to gauge them and perhaps voluntarily to join in them, and it entails the ability to understand the directedness of another's attentions—what they point to, so to speak. There is then a deictic aspect to it, even in the absence of language, that draws near to an important borderline between reading others' *at*tentions and understanding their *in*tentions. This suggests a more than rudimentary *theory of mind*—an ability to understand that other minds are like our own and occupied with similar kinds of thoughts and motivations.

The collaborative, joint intention missing in chimpanzee group hunting but likely present in Lower Paleolithic gatherings indicates the nascence of this full-fledged, characteristically human, shared intentionality. Along with it there begins to take shape what Tomasello calls "recursive mindreading," the ability not merely to understand other's intentions but to understand that they understand ours. In its mutual recognition of similar minds around us, recursive mindreading is a basic ingredient of our theory of mind. Modern humans can carry its back-and-forth mutuality a turn or two farther, understanding that others understand that we understand their intentions and so forth.[13]

In Tomasello's view recursive mindreading transformed hominin sociality, enriching the perceiving of another's intention with the dawning of shared intentionality. It turned merely joint activities into cooperative ones, since its recursion enabled individuals to conceive and expect mutual and reciprocal help and sharing, an expectation all but absent from chimpanzees or gorillas. In cooperative circumstances, intersecting foci of attention became the common ground for more and more sustained shared attention. The expectation of mutual cooperation that mindreading fostered began to build top-down structures that could in some degree govern sociality and strengthen its bonds, thus pushing sociality beyond Strum and Latour's baboon interactions toward human ones. All this begins to suggest how recursive mindreading could come to be the bottom line of Tomasello's account of the emergence of human communication, its elementary particle.[14]

Already in the half-million-year-old gatherings at Boxgrove or Notarchirico, the archaeological evidence suggests, developments such as these had begun to recast copresent societies of mimesis and semivoluntary entrainments into societies incorporating sporadic but vital collaboration. To pursue the implications of this nascent mindreading for Lower Paleolithic vocalization requires a detour into paleolinguistics.

Protolanguage

Informed speculation on the nature of protolanguage can be traced at least back to Darwin, and today it comprises an intricate tangle of intersecting and opposing positions. It came of age, and moved to the center of approaches to the origins of language, about 1990. In that year, cognitive psychologists Steven Pinker and Paul Bloom offered a compelling case for the emergence of language from neo-Darwinian processes of natural selection, contesting some powerful voices, in particular Noam Chomsky and Stephen Jay Gould, who maintained that only other, nonselective forces could explain language's complexities. At a moment when biological bases for language construction were ever more widely accepted, Pinker and Bloom argued that universal design features of modern languages, especially grammatical ones, were lingering symptoms of adaptive responses to selective pressures. They put the idea of an incremental, selected evolution of language on a new footing, more secure than before in both its linguistics and its biology. Though they did not take up explicitly the question of protolanguage, they made it inevitable.[15]

At the same moment linguist Derek Bickerton was tackling the question head-on, offering a detailed analysis of the differences between protolanguage and full language. He could hope for this to be something more than pure speculation because, he argued, protolanguage was not merely an extinct stage of communication in hominin history; instead, it has left its traces in certain language uses of modern humans. These "fossils of language" arise in circumstances where normal language is absent, impracticable, or half-developed: in the notorious case of Genie, a California girl imprisoned, isolated, and deprived of exposure to language from infancy until the age of thirteen; in certain colonial situations where native speakers of several languages are cast together and improvise a pidgin to communicate effectively; and in the multiword utterances of infants near the beginning of language acquisition.[16]

The protolanguage that takes hold in these circumstances is in effect a lexicon without grammar. It deploys words in simple series to form messages but does not link them to one another through more than a rudimentary syntax. It is not, then, a fully *compositional* or *analytic* language, and it mostly lacks an array of features syntacticians have discerned that seem to be pervasive in modern languages. Chief among these are significant, expressive word order; grammatical inflections; recursive possibilities for the expansion of utterances through the "nesting" of a construction in another one of the same sort; "null elements" not expressed with a word but reliably inferred from grammatical structure; and multiple categories of "arguments" entailed by verbs (subject, direct and indirect objects).

Something like this present-day protolanguage, this lexicon without syntax, Bickerton surmised, must have been the historical form assumed by the antecedents of modern language. He worked with evidence available in 1990 to associate this ancient protolanguage with *Homo erectus* about 1,000,000 years ago. He pictured it to be limited by a narrow range of sounds as well as by its lack of syntax, for the vocal tract of *erectus* had not yet taken a shape that would enable all the timbral and articulatory variety of the modern human tract. Modern phonology as well as modern syntax, in this hypothesis, emerged only after wordlike sonic symbols had come into use—when, that is, a protolinguistic set of vocalized signifiers fell under the sway of grammatical rules for ordering and syntactic relation.

Since 1990, Bickerton has continued to elaborate this lexicon-first model. In recent writings he has emphasized reciprocal altruism—like Tomasello's reciprocal help and sharing—as a "social calculus" that had to appear in the hominin line before even a lexical protolanguage could take hold. He has speculated how vocalized signs or protowords, initially iconic pantomimes or onomatopoeic imitations of sounds in the world, might have been "displaced" from a reference restricted to immediate context so as to enable them to refer to things absent in space or time. This displacement emerged, in general, as a product of coevolutionary niche-production, and Bickerton has confidently proposed a single situation that pushed for referential displacement among our distant, meat-seeking ancestors: their need to recruit group members to band together and scavenge the distant carcasses of megafauna.[17]

Bickerton's view has been an influential one, standing behind many incremental approaches to the emergence of language. Linguist Ray Jackendoff's model, for example, starts like Bickerton's from vocalized symbols and considers mainly the stages through which full compositionality, lexical and syntactic, might have emerged. He reserves the term protolanguage not for the initial stages in this development but for a later point already showing considerable communicative complexity: rudiments of expressive word order and a "protophonology," that is, a combinatorial building of vocalized symbols out of something akin to *phonemes*—the elementary sonic bits that make up modern words. (Because these bits are discrete and contrast from one another, linguists sometimes refer to this aspect of modern language as *contrastive phonology*.) Jackendoff sets aside entirely the earlier development from which these protowords first emerged and came to be displaced, though he acknowledges it as a "major evolutionary step."[18]

Meanwhile, the general emphasis on syntactic compositionality in models of protolanguage such as Bickerton's and Jackendoff's has been challenged by an alternative approach. Linguist

Alison Wray has tackled the problem of the emergence of a lexicon of vocalized signs by positing "holistic" utterances, indivisible vocal gestures conveying complete messages. These arose, she speculated, from earlier calls akin to those of nonhuman primates today. They were effective especially in manipulating the emotions of others in intimate social circumstances—ideally suited in this to societies limited to face-to-face encounters. In such copresent interchanges they could take on deictic meanings gleaned from context: "go away," "give this to her," "bring me the meat," and the like.[19]

Wray's hypothetical utterances differed in one crucial respect from even the most eloquent ape vocalizations: They were made up of something like modern, discrete phonemes. Starting from this contrastive protophonology enabled her to construct a simple set of steps through which words emerged: Individual phonemes often recurred as parts of different holistic utterances; sometimes they recurred in different utterances that happened to overlap in meaning; from these initially haphazard moments of overlap, individual meanings were gradually linked to specific phonemes, converting them to *morphemes*, meaning-bearing linguistic bits. Phonemes were conventionalized, in other words, in a process like that of infants learning to divide up the continuous stream of vocal sounds that comes to them from adults through the frequent repetition of certain bits. Then the holistic utterances could be segmented into words, and this segmentation eventually opened the way to modern compositionality.[20]

Wray's holism has the advantage of highlighting a deictic, gestural aspect of protolinguistic communication. Among its advocates is archaeologist Steven Mithen, who proposes that the gestural aspect of her holistic vocalizations took the form especially of intonational patterns—that is, of shifting and sliding contours deployed in utterance. He agrees with Wray that such vocal gestures must have been effective especially in copresent emotional manipulation. All three of these features—emotive immediacy and gestural and intonational distinctiveness—seem to Mithen to relate holistic protolanguage to modern music. His elaboration of Wray's views thus militates for a musical protolanguage—a theme to which I will return.[21]

Whatever its attractions, Wray's holistic protolanguage, like Bickerton's compositional one, raises questions it does not answer. She has a tendency, bordering on silliness, to offer made-up phrases like *tebima* or *maputi* as the starting point for her evolutionary scheme; but these embody a combinatorial phonology very far indeed from the nonphonemic primate calls that she envisions as their precursors, and she offers little explanation as to how the one emerged from the other.[22] We can see this difficulty lodged in Mithen's rehearsing of Wray's ideas, since his emphasis of gesture and intonation does not merge comfortably with clusters of phonemes or protophonemes. All this poses a more general question: What might it mean to call an utterance like *maputi* holistic when it comprises contrasting smaller units?[23]

In the simplest of summaries, holistic and compositional models of protolanguage differ in this: The one takes phonemic clusters and conventionalizes and segments them, then subjecting them to syntactic connection; the other starts from vocalized symbols or protowords, already segmented, conventionalizes them, and gradually comes to bind them syntactically. The two positions work at cross purposes, or at least focus on different stages of protolinguistic development. It is significant that, after dismantling Wray's holistic arguments at length in a recent writing, Bickerton can come around to a distinctly Wray-ish generalization: "the earliest protolanguage words...would have been indivisible chunks of sound." Wray, for her part, has sketched a compromise scenario that grafts Bickerton's analytic protolanguage onto an earlier, holistic communication.[24] This brings her close to an important, multitiered view of human language and its origins elaborated by anthropologist and linguist Robbins Burling, taken up later.

Wray's and Bickerton's positions, along with Jackendoff's and other outgrowths of them, can be seen to be linked also in their emphases of linguistic combinatoriality (whether of phonemes into words or words into sentences) and compositionality. This orientation manifests a kind of post-Chomskyan, generative-grammar linguocentrism, even a *syntactocentrism* (to coin a term) that perhaps comes along with the disciplinary turf of modern linguistics. It has remained at the center of discussion of the emergence of language, and there is no doubt that it spotlights important issues.[25]

Syntactocentrism can, however, carry us only so far in speculating about Lower Paleolithic communication. This is because, as will gradually become clear across the following chapters, the evidence we can muster suggests that *combinatoriality and compositionality are relatively recent innovations*—at least as recent as the Middle Paleolithic. Setting one or another of these modes of linguistic complexity as the explanandum directs our attention away from the efficacies vocalization must have displayed long before grammar or combinatoriality gleamed in hominin eyes. In obscuring these earlier communicative powers, moreover, syntactocentric approaches open a gap between primate communication systems and the beginnings of modern language. They lead to *discontinuity* theories, and all their advocates can (and often do) enlarge on the categorical differences between human language (learned, symbolic, combinatorial, conventionalized, generative, etc.) and the vocalizations of chimpanzees or gorillas (innate, emotive, nonsymbolic, nongenerative, etc.). However real these differences may be, their emphasis runs the risk of ignoring the considerable complexity of ape communication and neglecting what it might tell us about hominin developments.

We need, in short, to explore a broader approach to early hominin vocalization.

Protodiscourse and Gesture-Calls

Collaboration on the late Acheulean taskscape, we have seen, arose not only from coinciding intentions but also from a nascent capacity for recursive mindreading (or theory of mind) exceeding that of present-day apes. Tomasello's arguments along these lines start from the gestures apes employ to express intentions and gain attention—gestures rather than vocalizations, for the latter are mostly inflexible and innate in apes, while the former admit of some learning and negotiation, if not much imitation or cultural transmission. From these beginnings, Tomasello traces a continuous path to modern language. Shared intentionality founded on mindreading skills, he proposes, expressed itself in cooperative gestures, which in turn generated three fundamental kinds of communicative interactions: requesting help, informing (offering helpful information), and displaying emotions. At first these involved pointing gestures and rudimentary iconic pantomimes of actions requested or situations needing joint attention, which came to be basic communicative modes as cooperative interaction took hold.[26]

These gestures underwent displacement or, as Tomasello calls it, a "drift to the arbitrary" as they were repeated, distanced from specific contexts, and passed on to young learners who might infer their meanings from elders (through deictic, contextual clues) even without catching their iconicity. In this fashion conventionalized, situation-free reference originated in "action-based gestures within collaborative interactions structured by joint attention"—all arising from growing theory of mind. Hominin mimetic skills such as those of Acheulean taskscapes must have entered into this process; there is little evidence of such mimesis in modern-day apes. The imitation and conventionalization of action gestures and iconic pantomimes resulted in meaningful utterances. These, finally, deployed in sequences of gestures (vocal or not), pushed toward the most basic rudiments of grammar: simple predication, agent-first word order, and so on.[27]

Tomasello's model, like Bickerton's, accounts for the displacement of communicative signals through the conventionalization of signals initially resembling their meanings by virtue of similarity, either iconic (pantomimic) or onomatopoeic. Like Wray's model, it emphasizes the gestural or deictic aspect of the signals and ties them to nonlinguistic primate communication. But unlike either, it provides a set of stages or developments plausibly linking simple sequences of communicative gestures along the lines of those witnessed in monkeys and apes in the wild—sequences that show no evidence of syntactic ordering[28]—to something like rudimentary human language. It bridges the chasm opened in discontinuity theories, founding its stages on growing capacities for shared attention, cooperative intention, and recursive mindreading.

This approach broadens the focus of paleolinguistic studies well beyond issues of compositionality and generativity, and it describes something close to what linguist Jill Bowie has called *protodiscourse*. Discourse, for her, refers to the moment-to-moment social enactment of communication, linguistic or otherwise. It is "sequenced communicative behavior" in whatever mode, a performative interplay of vocalized and other gestures shaping face-to-face transmission of emotions, intentions, and meanings. These discursive sequences build on deep foundations similar to Tomasello's: structured interaction, usually in the form of alternation or turn taking, the sustaining of shared attention across a number of turns, and, ultimately, recursive mindreading.[29]

Discourse thus defined has wide and deep phylogenetic roots. It is broad enough to take in the ancient sociality of Lower Paleolithic taskscapes, before sentences, combinatoriality, compositionality, or words. The kinds of gestures involved in such discourse are varied and not only vocal; ultimately they include all the communicative stuff of copresence. In this, Bowie's shift from protolanguage to protodiscourse blurs the borderline between vocalizations and nonvocal gestures, since all face-to-face gestures contribute to its efficacy. Facial expressions, body language and posture, quickness of response and the pace of turn taking, regular or uneven alternation, interruption, pointing gestures, action pantomimes and more are part of the communicative exchange. In vocalization itself, nonlexical and nonsyntactic gestural attributes left aside by the post-Chomskyan mainstream come to the fore, especially momentary expressive emphasis and intonational patterns and shapes. Though Bowie does not mention them, other attributes of voice also play a role: the rhythmic pacing of an utterance and its quickness of onset and decay (contrast a bark with a growl, for example), its volume and general pitch range, and its timbre and timbral variety.

The concept of protodiscourse casts a wide net in defining communicative gesture. The preceding list features several kinds of signals that admit of nothing like the contrastive phonology and syntax that have preoccupied debates on protolanguage; yet they are fundamental to the communication of both humans and nonhuman primates in the world today, and they must have been so also in Lower Paleolithic encounters. Anthropologist Robbins Burling reserves the term *gesture-calls* for these kinds of signals.[30] In fact, Burling describes a whole gesture-call system that humans deploy in a parallel communicative channel alongside compositional language, an array of bodily and vocal signals especially effective in conveying emotional states and general intentions. Human gesture-calls include laughs, sighs, groans, sobs, gasps and so forth, on the vocal side, and also bodily gestures such as frowns, smiles, and shrugs.

Gesture-calls differ from full-blown language in a number of basic ways. They are largely innate and comprehensible across societal, cultural, and linguistic borders. Smiles, frowns, sobs, and laughs may convey nuances that are not transparent when encountered in unfamiliar settings, but there is almost never any question that they are (respectively) smiles, frowns, sobs, and laughs. Gesture-calls, moreover, are closely tied to the emotions they express. Like those emotions they are not subject to as full a voluntary control as language, often emerging automatically in interactive contexts, and emotions are revealed but not easily concealed by them. Gesture-calls are far less versatile than words in signaling things beyond these internal states, such as meanings or propositions about the outside world. Their semantic possibilities are narrowly limited, as in the famous predator warnings of vervet monkeys, which number three or four more-or-less dis-crete calls.[31] Except in conjunction with human language, they show no conventionalization or displacement.

These referential limitations reflect the fact that gesture-calls are not combinatorial. A laugh or sigh cannot be broken down into smaller, discrete parts that might be recomposed into other signals, and there is nothing in either that resembles a contras-tive phonology. Instead they fall along scales of graded continu-ities—from a giggle to a laugh to a guffaw to a snort to a cry, for example, or from a slight to an exaggerated shrug. This sliding continuity and the absence of discrete components led Burling to describe them as "analog" in nature, in opposition to the "digi-tal" systems of phonemes and words basic to human language. Systems of discrete, digital elements, where minimal differences can count as much as or more than larger ones, allow the huge proliferation of distinct signals characteristic of language. (*Gnat* and *mat* are phonologically closer but semantically much more distant than *mat* and *rug*.) Gesture-calls, because of their analog nature, cannot proliferate in this way. They achieve distinctions through distance from one another along their graded scales, and—an important point to which we shall return—proximity of calls leads to indistinctness of the messages carried.

The analog/digital divide between gesture-calls on one hand and words and phonemes on the other is fundamental to Burl-ing's model of language evolution. Because he sees it as absolute it allies him with the discontinuity camp, at least in regard to com-municative signaling itself. His model is dichotomized across a deep phylogenetic history, with compositional language, recently achieved, overlaid on an ancient, persistent gesture-call system. Continuities of communicative evolution need to be sought not along a bridge from gesture-calls to words but elsewhere, in a gradual expansion of cognitive capacities.

At the same time, Burling's dichotomy oversimplifies human communication, as he is quick to see, and he describes several intermediate communicative categories that fill in the divide.

These include gestures closely associated with language—"para-linguistic" gestures, as he calls them: the gesticulation with hands and arms that we tend to join to speech, and the intonational patterns of speech itself. They include also emblematic gestures and vocalizations that convey culturally specific, learned meanings but do not participate in syntactic compositionality: forefinger and middle finger extended in a V for victory, for example, or thumb and forefinger closed in a circle to mean "OK." There are also vocalized emblems of this sort. These are particularly intriguing because they form a class of utterances in all languages that do not fully exploit contrastive phonemes, cannot be incorporated into syntax (except as a quotation), and are largely reliant on intonational pattern: in English, *uh-oh, un-uh, mmm, mm-hmm, ahh, ah-ha*, and the like. All these different modes, together with compositional language (whether voiced or signed) and gesture-calls, make up the panoply of human communication.

The gesture-calls, however, stand apart, forming the most ancient, least language-like element. In all their features they resemble communicative gestures of our closest relatives in the world today, monkeys and apes. More than this, gesture-call systems extend far beyond primates and can be witnessed in all mammals—in the baring of teeth or barking or whining of a dog as well as the warning call of a vervet, the pant-hoot of a chimp, and the sigh of a human. There is reason to believe that these similarities reflect the homology of these signaling systems, that is, their evolutionary derivation from shared ancestral gestures.

The wide dispersion of the mammalian gesture-call system makes it implausible—indeed, incredible—to exclude our hominin forebears from it, but we can marshal arguments other than this negative inference for their participation. For in fact *the foremost traits of gesture-calls are closely congruent with the features of late Acheulean sociality.* Gesture-calls are a communicative mode of copresence and immediacy, eloquent and emotive in the kind of face-to-face expressions and responses that dominated interactions on Lower Paleolithic taskscapes. Their semantic restrictions and lack of displacement would not have hampered their deictic directing of attention and their forging of shared intentions regarding things and circumstances at hand. What we know about these hominins does not warrant any thoughts of compositional language, symbolic representation, or anything more than a rudimentary, pointing referentiality; but it fits perfectly with a well-developed gesture-call system.

In fact, the collaborative complexities of late Acheulean sociality resulting from even a cautious interpretation of a site like Boxgrove suggest that these hominins carried the gesture-call system to an unprecedented level of communicative power. They indicate that the gesture-calls formed ingredients in moments of shared attention sustained longer than earlier hominins could manage. This suggests that the calls were coming under increasing voluntary control that allowed more governable discursive interactions, including predictable turn taking.

And the social complexity brings with it other likely consequences: As the situations in which the calls were deployed grew more intricate, fostering a more richly contextualized deictic deployment of them, their emotional and intentional messages must have gained precision and carried new informational payloads. In effect, the gestures and calls came to occupy finer gradations along their analog spectra. This in turn would have allowed them to multiply and diversify—all before the cognitive foundations for modern language had evolved, all without combinatoriality or contrastive phonology and with little displacement. The late Acheulean taskscape probably resounded with vocalizations of unprecedented variety and emotive potency—and perhaps of newly sharpened deictic meanings as well.[32]

Myths about Musical Protolanguage

In their gestural and intonational aspects especially, the gesture-calls of protodiscourse veer close to Wray's holistic utterances, and these, as we have seen in Mithen's conception of them, can seem tantamount to a protomusic. Similar thinking has suggested to many others that the key to understanding protolanguage is to be found in the hypothesis of a musical origin for language all told.

The idea that language arose from song has ancient roots, and it was developed with a vengeance in modern times by a whole line of eighteenth-century thinkers, including Vico, Condillac, Rousseau, Herder, and many others.[33] In evolutionary thought it has also played a role, one presided over by Darwin, who related it to selection—specifically, sexual selection. He imagined ancestors of modern humans endowed with cognitive powers already advanced beyond those of modern apes, powers supporting rich imitative abilities. (The mimetic Acheulean taskscapes described in Chapter 2 suggest the prescience of this first step.) These ancestors used their imitative powers to vocalize natural sounds and the calls of other animals. Through an unspecified process of conventionalization, the vocalizations came to have more general meanings, developing into early, onomatopoeic words. Our progenitors also applied their imitative powers to their own emotive cries—to gesture-calls, in effect—and these imitations likewise gained conventionalized meanings, near to the native emotional significance of the cries from which they derived. "I cannot doubt," Darwin concluded in the first part of *The Descent of Man*, "that language owes its origin to the imitation and modification, aided by signs and gestures, of various natural sounds, the voices of other animals, and man's own instinctive cries."[34]

So far these ideas anticipate many later formulations of protolanguage, including Bickerton's and Tomasello's, with their gestural and vocal pantomimes and onomatopoeias. But Darwin quickly steered his protolanguage in a provocative musical direction: "When we treat of sexual selection we shall see that primeval man, or rather some early progenitor of man, probably used his voice largely, as does one of the gibbon-apes of the present day, in producing true musical cadences, that is, in singing.... The imitation by articulate sounds of musical cries might have given rise to words expressive of various complex emotions" (I, 56). Here a congeries of dubious, unspoken categories and presumptions crowds in. Darwin's allusion to singing gibbons invokes the interspecies comparison exploited at countless points in his treatise, but in this instance its results are unimpressive. His discovery of gibbons' "true musical cadences" effaces in one motion yawning differences between nonhuman vocalization and human singing, at the same time indulging in an imprecision of musical terminology he would hardly suffer in other areas. His notion of "musical cries" compounds the confusion, falling back on the Romantic ideology according to which music is a nonspecific, primal language of emotion.

Darwin returned to these matters in the second part of *The Descent of Man*, on sexual selection, in order to make "a strong case ... that the vocal organs were primarily used and perfected in relation to the propagation of the species" (II, 330)—the grandfather, in effect, of the many modern proposals explaining human musicking as an adaptation for sexual display and mate attraction. Here Darwin expands the earlier assignment of human musicality to gibbons, quoting a contemporary observer of their musical capacities: "It appeared to me that in ascending and descending the scale, the intervals were always exactly half-tones; and I am sure that the highest note was the exact octave to the lowest.... I do not doubt that a good violinist would be able to give a correct idea of the gibbon's composition." From true musical cadences gibbons have advanced to chromatic scales, and with a "very musical" "quality of the notes," at that; Darwin's observer, we learn, even transcribed their song in musical notation (II, 332). Monkeys too seem to have discrete "tones," expressing anger and impatience with low ones, fear and pain with high (II, 336).

These precocious musical abilities, once discovered in monkeys and apes, could hardly be denied to human forebears. "Musical tones and rhythms," Darwin continues, "were used by the half-human progenitors of man, during the season of courtship, when animals of all kinds are excited by the strongest passions" (II, 336–37). Despite the advanced precision of these musical formulations—these tones, half-tones, octaves, rhythms, cadences—they all somehow took shape before language, enabling ancestral humans to "charm" each other "before they had acquired the power of expressing their mutual love in articulate language" (II, 337). And their power to charm tapped the deep, innate, primeval emotional expression of music: "...when vivid emotions are felt and expressed by the orator or even in common speech, musical cadences and rhythm are instinctively used.... The sensations and ideas excited in us by music, or by the cadences of impassioned oratory, appear from their vagueness, yet depth, like mental reversions to the emotions and thoughts of a long-past age" (II, 336).

This ostensibly primal emotional expression is double-edged, absolutely modern as well as ancient, and thereby caught up in supplementary dilemmas of the sort Derrida diagnosed in Rousseau; and in fact Darwin's prehistoric music looks back to Rousseauian eighteenth-century noble savagery as much as to the lives of apes. It has even more in common with the high-flying expressive mysteries sensed in music by Romantic writers and composers, and Darwin borrows, from Herbert Spencer, Jean Paul Richter's *bon mot* of post-Kantian musical transcendentalism: "Music...tells us of things we have not seen and shall not see" (II, 336).

In Darwin's account, in short, music becomes not only a repository of ancient expressive mysteries but at the same time a capacity of articulateness before articulation, assigning modern features to deep prehistory. Today most of the accounts of musical protolanguage descended from him still fall into this trap. Often they use an ill-defined "music" to evade the begged questions of the protolanguage debate, replacing one unconvincing assignment of advanced cognition to early hominins with another. Modern accounts that recycle his view of music as an adaptive response to sexual selection are special offenders in this regard. They tend to eschew the careful discrimination of music's various cognitive dimensions in favor of an adolescent, hip-thrusting music redolent of a rock guitarist's fantasies.[35]

A related kind of imprecision is evident throughout *The Singing Neanderthals* of archaeologist Mithen, noted above as an advocate of musical protolanguage. He is frank in disclaiming musical expertise, and it is tempting to give his foibles a pass—except that their effect on his book is pervasive. Since he does not distinguish very clearly the component capacities of modern musicking, he is left in each new chapter to try on, so to speak, another adaptive explanation for musical behavior as a whole—social bonding here, infant rearing there, sexual competition elsewhere. In their bluntness these hypotheses do not coalesce easily into the incremental historical account Mithen is after, and they have only a loose attachment to the archaeological evidence he (expertly) adduces. They are too general to join with that evidence in separating distinct musical capacities or suggesting their accumulation or formation. Because of this musical, not archaeological shortsightedness, Mithen can imagine scenes such as the hominins at Boxgrove, 500,000 years ago, singing and dancing around a carcass—evincing, that is, cognitive resources far in advance of those posited even by capacious interpretations of the archaeological evidence.[36]

Other proposals of musical protolanguage avoid Darwin's musical vagueness but instead repeat his mistake of assigning modern aspects of musicking to our aboriginal forebears. Steven Brown's "musilanguage" hypothesis, for example, aims to locate a common source for both music and language in a stage of "lexical tones," discrete pitches matched to meanings and combined into referential, "melodorhythmic" phrases. Brown does not stop to consider the immense cognitive complexity or the course of emergence of either the discrete perception of the tones or the combinatoriality of the phrases—not to mention the referentiality of both.[37] A deep historical approach to music or language cannot begin by assuming the very capacities and design features it aims to historicize. Moreover, taking precise, complex musical capacities as first principles can only widen the distance between emergent human and broader mammalian communication,

multiplying the mysteries of the phylogeny of acoustic information transmission. As we imagine such cognitive feats as Brown's
musilanguage—or the singing and perfect pitch Mithen assigns
to Neandertals, to cite another instance[38]—we move ever farther
from the kinds of capacities discernible behind the archaeological
record for the hominins in question. In this way many proposals
of musical protolanguage offer discontinuity theories like those
of the linguists rather than protodiscursive continuity models.

Some proponents of musical protolanguage are aware of this
gap and look to close it with a comparativism extrapolated from
Darwin. They usually reassert his anthropomorphic presumption
that the acoustic signals of animals—not only "dueting" gibbons
but warbling birds, squealing, chuttering whales, and many other
species—are all analogous to human singing. "Birdsong" and
"whale songs" are fascinating communicative systems, and their
relations to human musicking have inspired inquiry that will not
soon end, it is safe to say; but a connection cannot be presumed
prima facie. And in any case these nonhuman activities must be
less relevant to a historical account of the emergence of human
musical capacities than the communicative capacities and activities of human ancestors themselves. The first step in comparing
nonhuman "song" to human singing needs to be not categorical
judgment about signals innate or learned, not complex questions
of cultural transmission of such signals, and certainly not a feel-
good anthropomorphism by which human capacities are extended
willy-nilly beyond humans. It needs to be a careful dismantling
and scrutiny of the differing notions of "song" that pertain. In the
absence of this, many recent accounts are not as far removed as
we might hope from the preposterousness of Darwin's transcriber
of gibbon songs.

The most nuanced and productive recent advocacy of the
comparative approach, by W. Tecumseh Fitch, takes such care. He
cites complex, learned, combinatorial vocalization in a number
of nonprimate lineages—birds, whales, and several others—as
instances of convergent evolution, selective pressures in separate

species and niches leading to generally similar outcomes. Such vocalization, these instances show, has evolved repeatedly, and it has done so without mapping specific meanings onto the sonic bits learned and combined—in the absence, that is, of anything like the semanticity of human language. This appearance of great complexity without complex meaning is one of the most fascinating puzzles of many phenomena that travel under the rubric of animal song. It encourages Fitch to advance his own version of musical protolanguage among our ancestors, which takes its start from a contrastive, generative phonology not attached to specific meanings—a "bare" phonology, as he calls it. Our ancestors, in other words, sang in the manner of songbirds or humpback whales, or of Darwin's gibbons; indeed Fitch offers his approach in general as a revival of Darwin's. Their songs had only the most general of messages, and their combinatorial patterns only the most rudimentary of syntactic governance (Fitch calls it "phonotactic"). Only after ancestral humans achieved this complex sonic combinatoriality did further developments crucial to modern language follow: first a holistic linkage of complete utterances to meanings (cf. Wray), and later a segmenting of these now-meaningful vocalizations and a blossoming of full syntax (Bickerton).[39]

It is clear that Fitch aims to overleap the syntactocentrists into the deep past of communication, and his proposal of hominins vocalizing discrete, generative songs raises in a different way than they the important question of the emergence of combinatorial cognition in the hominin line, to which I will return in Chapter 4. But even in advance of a closer look at this question his proposal seems implausible, or at least ineffective in resolving the syntactocentrists' dilemma. As his broad comparative purview takes him far from the primate lineage, it also carries him away from our closest relatives' communicative vocalizations, the gesture-calls of monkeys and apes, which, in the world today, show no trace of the combinatorial structuring evident in some birdsong. If (as I have argued) these calls can serve as a guide to early Acheulean vocalization, Fitch's move to other lineages carries him far from this deep history as well.

We can place the problem in an even wider frame: Looking back several million years beyond the hominin lineage to the ancestors we share with chimpanzees, we must come to a point at which gesture-call-like vocalizations were the full measure of hominid capacity. Fitch does not suggest a route from such calls to combinatoriality, so his comparative method sets up a large hurdle in our own ancestry. Ironically, his convergent continuities across distant lineages lead back to *dis*continuities across proximate ones.

Prosody and Melodic Contour

A protodiscourse of gesture-calls instead starts from the precombinatorial, pregenerative, analog side of this divide. As we have seen, this communicative mode conforms well to our picture of hominin sociality on the late-Acheulean taskscape 500,000 years ago, and specifically to the sharpening interplay there of joint intentions, complicated collaborations, voluntary and varied vocalization, and emergent deictic semantics.

The acoustic elements that helped to determine the efficacy of this Lower Paleolithic communication include intonation or pitch, rhythm (both general pacing and the rapidity of onset or decay), volume, and timbre. Their roles in ancient protodiscourse are indicated by their pervasive importance across the spectrum of present-day primate communication, from monkey calls to the gesture-call aspects of human language. In nonhuman primate calls today, these elements help to express stances of dominance or submission and supplication, acts of assertion or requesting, experiences of pain, attitudes of anger, fear, and welcome and more. In general, the calls convey emotional messages linked in deictic fashion to contexts of copresent interaction.[40]

In the study of human speech, the acoustic elements just named are grouped under the more general category of *prosody*. Most linguists discern two major types of prosody. The first, "linguistic" prosody, involves the elements of pitch, rhythm, and so forth as they relate to the grammatical structuring of meaning in utterances. This prosody is tied in complex ways to word morphology and to syntax—to *phonology*, in other words, the systematic encoding of meaning in the sounds of language. Much effort over the last half century has been devoted to modeling and theorizing the complex, fluid relations of prosodic elements to phonological ones, and, in line with generative theories of grammar, contrastive and generative conceptions of the elements of linguistic prosody, especially its localized pitch accent, have proliferated.

We are concerned here, instead, with the second and arguably more basic type of prosody. This is "affective" or "emotional" prosody, the general shaping of pitch, rhythm, and volume for pragmatic purposes in discourse, especially to communicate emotive attitudes or stances. This is the kind of prosody in modern speech that bears a strong kinship to the ancient heritage of gesture-calls and protodiscourse. Like linguistic prosody, emotional prosody can involve all the acoustic aspects named above—pitch, rhythm, and so forth. But unlike linguistic prosody it seems not to work in close connection with phonology, and there is little evidence that it is ordered in a generative, systematic fashion. For this reason it is also sometimes called "paralinguistic" prosody.[41]

The affective intonational contours of phrases and sentences—their "tunes," as linguists sometimes call them—seem in particular to stand apart from the structures of morphology and syntax. The pitch contours of affective tunes show something like an analog coding that seems to help them clearly to mark emotional expression; in this they are like those monkey calls. Their length varies, at the upper end reaching the span of a complete utterance, though in long utterances they can fall into subphrases. Their shapes, if limited within the borders of individual utterances, seem intriguingly to be determined in part through the place of those utterances in broader, back-and-forth exchanges. There is, thus, a discursive element built into them. Sensitivity to the affective tunes of speech appears very early in human infant development, well before language itself is acquired. The tunes are essential in communicating with and socializing infants, and across many (perhaps all) cultures caregivers exaggerate the melodic contours of their utterances to infants in order to enhance their communicative power.[42]

The perception of the intonational tunes of language has a close counterpart in musicking: our ability to perceive general intonational contours of melodies as a kind of acoustic *Gestalt*. The musical capacity, like the linguistic one, emerges early in ontogeny, independent of any special training, and the two seem to be generally related in the brain areas they recruit.[43] As in language, individual musical contours vary in length, and there is a fuzzy upper boundary beyond which we subdivide them into separate shapes. We easily and intuitively recognize melodic shapes, or indeed similarities of generally congruent shapes: melodies that go down first, then up, or up first, then down, or begin high and end low, or the reverse, or are flat and monotonal. Such recognition is not vitiated by small differences in the melodies involved; it depends on broad pattern-processing rather than on individual pitches or intervals. Like language tunes, musical contours seem to be gauged in Burling's analog fashion. All these features mark them as another remnant of gesture-calls.[44]

Such processing of melodic contour is distinct from a second manner in which we perceive musical intonation: discrete pitch.[45] We perceive melodies, that is, not only as general contours but also as arrays of successive pitches (or intervals between them), wholes built from the joining of discrete smaller units. This discretized perception is a primary manifestation of combinatorial structuring and cognition in music, and we will dwell on its phylogeny in later chapters. Here it is enough to note an important implication of its divergence from the more holistic processing of contour that musicking shares with language: The processing of language—even of tonal languages—offers no equivalent to the discrete pitch processing of music. To locate features in language displaying a combinatoriality similar to that of discrete pitch in music, we need to look elsewhere than intonation, specifically, to contrastive phonology, word morphology, and compositional syntax. The tunes of language may seem to be its most "musical" element, and they may even share common contour-processing networks in the brain, but at best this parallel is partial.

Further differences between language and music processing emerge from consideration of the timbral diversity basic to gesture-calls and modern human communication alike (to digress for a moment from pitch alone). Human sensitivity to timbral differences is astonishingly refined and complex, comprising a set of percepts constructed on several different aspects of acoustic stimuli. Especially important in the case of musical tones are the balance of overtones comprised in a pitch and the natures of onset and decay of its sounding.[46] In gesture-calls and modern musicking alike, timbral percepts tend to array themselves along a continuum, one timbre grading indistinguishably into the next; in both, in other words, timbre is an analog signal. For this reason, we can be fooled as to what instrument is producing a given pitch, or unsettled by a not-quite-right facsimile of a particular instrument's timbre (for example, those available on most electronic keyboards). In modern language, on the other hand, while many timbral elements are analog and gesture-call-like—these are the timbral elements of prosody—others play a different role. Among these the timbres that distinguish vowel sounds are paramount, forming an essential part of contrastive phonology. These are rendered discrete in our perceptions; that is, although a vowel in a given language will encompass a family of timbres, there is no continuous spectrum of timbres in any given language filling in the space between the vocalic sounds it employs.

Vocalic timbre might therefore be thought of as similar to musical pitch in this way: A given language comprises a selection of discrete timbres and deploys them in combinatorial fashion, just as a given music comprises an array of categorical pitches deployed combinatorially. The timbral relation of modern language and musicking to gesture-calls at least in part reverses the pitch relation. In schematic and oversimplified form: Pitch is discrete in musicking but not in language; timbre is partly discrete in language but not in musicking; and neither one is discrete in gesture-calls.[47]

These dichotomies in intonational and timbral processing spotlight the distance between the gesture-calls of deep hominin history and modern musicking and language alike. The calls cannot provide, on the language side, a proximate ancestor for a contrastive phonology or its vocalic timbre; and on the musical side they show no counterpart to discrete pitch. These several borderlines between graded (analog) and discrete (digital) processing reveal that an advanced gesture-call system does not amount either to a musical protolanguage or to a protomusic. In the vocalizations of gibbons, finally, there is nothing like Darwin's "true musical cadences," and we will need to move carefully in tracing the route from gesture-calls to the combinatorial pitch of melody. Most importantly, these borderlines show that assigning such gesture-calls to late Lower Paleolithic hominins is not tantamount to equipping these creatures with combinatorial syntax, lexical semantics, contrastive phonology, or discrete musical pitch. *A protodiscourse of gesture-calls marks all these as developments yet to come.* It instead was a communicative system essentially prelinguistic and premusical in its lack of combinatorial organization in any of its aspects.

The Negotiated Voicescape

Only with these distinctions in mind can we begin to trace the path from the intonational aspects of the gesture-calls to those of modern language and musicking. The complexities of the Acheulean taskscape indicate that it pushed to new levels of efficacy an analog signaling that would persist in both language and music. Meanwhile, our production and perception of speech prosody and melodic contour today are far more varied and flexible than those evident in the gesture-call systems of our closest relatives.

123

A coevolutionary mechanism involving weakened selective pressures might explain how this variety began to emerge.

Ape societies today show many nonvocal alternatives to fulfill the emotive, manipulative functions served also by their innate calls, including grooming, gestural assertions of status, and more.[48] We may presume that similar nonvocal behaviors formed a part of the communicative means of ancient hominins. As the intricacies of their sociality increased, they generated a growing repertory of such signals, a repertory expanding along with the fashioning of the taskscape itself. The gestures arose in tandem with the lines of mimesis and the material pedagogies discussed in Chapter 2 and the fleeting complexities of cooperation, division of labor, and mindreading that more and more characterized hominin modes of copresence.

In the context of these nonvocal alternatives, selective pressures maintaining innate vocalizations weakened, initiating a cascade of coevolutionary consequences: partial offloading of the calls to cultural transmission, recruitment of new brain areas in their production, increasing voluntary control over them, and diversification of their prosodic, emotive shapes. The communicative advantages offered by more numerous and varied calls fed back into a social ecology selecting for flexibility of interaction and the shared attention and theory of mind it entailed. Brains and auditory and vocal channels capable of producing and distinguishing versatile prosodic expression—sophisticated deictic signs vocalized in increasing variety—became the target of selection *because of* the earlier offloading of vocalization to culture.

What is described here amounts to a *cultural epicycle of vocalized deixis*. The vocalizations emerging from it remained prelinguistic, differentiated into numerous prosodic shapes but without any conventionalized lexicon or syntactic, combinatorial possibilities. And so affective prosody (unlike linguistic prosody) remains to this day, not subject to the combinatorial structuring marked elsewhere in both language and music. But whereas in the prehistory of musicking and language analog shapes formed context-bound signs of emotional appeal and response, today they are additionally mapped onto three different combinatorial systems: word morphology and syntax in language and the pitch structures of music. Such mapping lay beyond the capacities of Lower Paleolithic hominins; in subsequent chapters (and later epochs) we will seek its archaeological traces.

Have we, then, widened the chasm between Acheulean gesture-calls and modern, combinatorial communication? No; instead the borders drawn here allow us to see routes across them, along which novel structuring possibilities might have emerged from the graded calls. In speculating on the emergence of the contrastive phonology of modern language, Ray Jackendoff has offered a model for thinking across this divide. Modern phonemes differ from one another in a number of acoustical factors, including not only discrete vowels but also the many manners of consonant production; traversing the distance between gesture-calls and contrastive phonemes therefore requires acoustical shifts across several vectors. Jackendoff suggests that these shifts involved an intermediate stage of "protosyllables," which took the form of holistic oral gestures using articulatory motions of tongue and lips to cycle from closed mouth to open and back to closed. Jackendoff's protosyllabary is rooted in the kind of vocalized "motor scripts" the gesture-calls must have involved.[49] From our Acheulean vantage, his suggestion is appealing in highlighting the gestural essence of syllable formation and in connecting it to the broader range of habituated gesture that defined the taskscape.

The suggestion is appealing also in that it envisages an early phonological winnowing, so to speak: a focusing of acoustic nodes, comprising timbres and articulatory gestures, as the protosyllables divided up the continuous sonic spectrum of the gesture-calls. We can apply just such reasoning to the intonational contours or "tunes" of the calls. As these multiplied with increasing signaling demands on the taskscape, a focusing of each on a specific pitch-shape must have been more and more necessary to distinguish it from other, acoustically proximate signals. Diversification of the calls, in other words, would have militated for increased precision as well; this is true of multiplication of signals along any graded (analog) spectrum, if confusion among them is to be avoided.

The systematicity of the cultural epicycle of vocalized deixis was rudimentary but nonetheless effective. It amounted to the collision of cultural diversification with the inherent constraints of differential information plotted along a spectrum of continuous change; from the collision emerged more and more precise signals. At some point this increasing precision could approach the verge of a phase transition to discreteness, a shift in the nature of information transmission from analog to digital.

Protodiscourse, Bowie's "sequenced communicative behavior," took the form of a matrix of gestures, multimodal but in large part vocal, that defined and structured a space of social interaction. This is as much as saying that it functioned on the Lower Paleolithic taskscape as a set of largely *vocal operational sequences*, in which the interactional patterns, turn taking, and grounding in shared attention all reflected advancing social entrainment. We can restate the epicycle described above from the vantage not of cultural diversification of vocalization but instead of its location on a selective terrain emphasizing shared attention:

- as the cognitive capacity for shared attention grew, the coordinated, turn-taking structure of protodiscourse began to coalesce;
- as this structure took shape, the efficacy of gesture-calls was more and more linked to their participation in it;
- this solidified linkage altered the taskscape so that the adaptive advantages of vocalized collaboration grew;
- intensified collaboration and discursive intricacy militated for greater control and more variety in vocalization, along the lines of the acoustical specification of Jackendoff's vocal motor scripts;

• this in turn demanded, for both production and perception of the calls, a deepening of shared attention, thus feeding back into the beginning of the cycle.

The rhythms of bodily operational sequences, haphazard on pre-Acheulean taskscapes, had long since begun to manifest the mimetic coordination revealed by Acheulean technologies. Now this entrainment was transferred in larger part than before to the voices of its enactors—or, viewed differently, the ancient emotive and manipulative vocalizations came under the organizing sway of elaborated modes of social coordination. The calls gained new powers to structure the taskscape, facilitating sustained periods of conjoined emotions and actions and of deictic meaningfulness. Protodiscourse, in this view, is *what happened to primate gesture-calls when mimetic entrainment and shared attention grew strong.*

This was as yet a set of coevolutionary mechanisms operating on hominin *communication* all told, and to distinguish in it between language and music betrays a specious evolutionary teleology. Such thinking is often implicit, sometimes explicit in writers interested in the origins of language, who seem to assume that prelinguistic selective pressures for more efficacious communication are the same as pressures for language. If this were the case we would need to wonder why, in a world filled with communicative, social species, only one ended up with combinatorial, fully semantic language. To wonder thus is not without effect; it raises intriguing questions of general constraints on the transmission of information—abstract-machinic constraints, as we might say—and of the utility of the communicative specificity that humans deploy in unrivaled measure.

Half a million years ago there was no language or musicking—not even a hint of either in any recognizably modern form—and no propositional syntax or symbolic exploitation of the material world. There was only a set of action sequences, partly vocal, under greater control and of greater communicative utility than before. To understand it we need to look backward from it, not forward. In this the protodiscourse model helps because it is retrospective, connecting to the entrainment, ecological affordance, embodied cognition, gesture-calls, and performed taskscape of an earlier period.

Protodiscourse was like hominin technology in its entrained operational sequences shaping copresent interactions. Indeed, as I have suggested, it probably recruited and extended the capacities that underpinned toolmaking. It is fashionable these days to differentiate technologies in hominin evolution from adaptations—the former cultural behaviors learned, deployed in the world, and transmitted; the latter genotypic and phenotypic traits driven by selective pressures. Those who argue in favor of the adaptive nature of language frequently follow this strategy, and some of them have tried to distinguish on these grounds between language and musicking. In this view music is a nonadaptive technology to tickle and delight the hearing—"auditory cheesecake," in Steven Pinker's notorious phrase, tantamount to dessert making, if catering to a different part of the sensorium.[50]

Even apple pie has a deep history, however, one tied to fruit consumption in our arboreal ancestors, to the need for sugars in hominin diets, and to the advantages of cooking in predigesting certain foods, already exploited by our ancestors almost a million years ago. Protodiscourse underscores the lesson taught in Chapter 1: that in any human history of sufficient depth a sharp dichotomy of technology and adaptation will always fade, effaced by the feedback, basic to biocultural coevolution, of niche-altering technologies onto selective pressures. The Acheulean taskscape-as-voicescape described here offers a primer on this coevolution, its outlines simple but telling. Ancient vocal messages entered into the cultural feedback loops of technology; feedback effects moved along new channels and recast the niche in new ways; constraints on innate vocalization were weakened; adaptive advantages of communicative flexibility were redoubled; and acoustical and cognitive features of vocalization came under pressure to create more effective communication.

Social Intelligence, Baboon Minds, and Connectionist Cognition

One of the strongest arguments advanced in recent years for continuity between the communication of nonhuman primates and human language comes from biologist Dorothy Cheney and psychologist Robert Seyfarth. They have spent three decades observing monkeys in the wild. First they detailed the social lives of South African vervets, and also their distinct predator warning calls, differentially signaling the proximity of specific threats. Then, for more than a decade, they studied a troop of baboons in Botswana.[1]

Cheney and Seyfarth did not merely observe these monkeys. Instead, they pioneered ingenious ways of conducting experiments on them without much disruption of their natural lives. Central to these was audio playback, from hidden speakers, of various sounds—especially vocalizations by the monkeys themselves—and painstaking, prolonged observation of the monkeys' reactions. With the vervets, such experiments yielded an analysis of the probabilities that they would respond to a particular call in a manner appropriate to escape the predator it signaled (snake, leopard, or eagle). Among other results, this detailed the growing precision with which juveniles both deployed and reacted to the warnings—evidence of their partially learned nature.

The audio playback experiments on the baboons, for their part, aimed to illuminate the social knowledge in the troop. They relied especially on the "violation of expectation" model used in psychological testing on human infants, in which unexpected situations command stronger reactions and more sustained attention than commonplace ones (pp. 93–95). From playbacks that variously affirmed or contradicted the social rankings they had observed in the troop, Cheney and Seyfarth pieced together as vivid a picture of baboon sociality and the psychology behind it as has yet been achieved. From these experiments, also, they homed in on the nature of baboon communication, leading them to a striking conclusion: that baboon sociality reveals a kind of cognition that might once have formed a precursor to human language.

Is there a non sequitur here? What can general baboon social interaction, rather than baboon vocalization in particular, tell us of antecedents to human language? The logic is one we encountered in Chapter 3 and exploited in adapting models of the origins of human communication advanced by Michael Tomasello, Jill Bowie, Robbins Burling, and others. All these positions ground the emergence of modern human communication in the advantages or pressures of complex sociality; they are versions of a position that has come to be known as the "social intelligence hypothesis." According to this hypothesis, advanced theory of mind, recognition of shared intentions, cooperative interaction, and other features of complex sociality all emerged as consequences of the advantages of group living and the complicated interactions required for its success. These capacities in turn formed the foundations of modern human communication.[2]

The social intelligence hypothesis is best viewed as several related hypotheses, depending upon the feature of primate or hominin societies taken to be the driving force in cognitive evolution. For Kim Sterelny, for instance, this force is the complexity of social interaction, especially as manifested in the burgeoning need for sustained cooperation and trust. He has speculated more subtly than most on the quandaries and ambivalences built into this cooperation.[3] For Leslie Aiello and Robin Dunbar, instead, the focus is group size, from which they construct a much-discussed argument on the emergence of human language. Starting from the evidence that relative neocortex size increases among living primates in direct relation to group size, Aiello and Dunbar hypothesize that encephalization in hominin evolution was driven by the adaptive advantages of larger groups and the social complexities entailed in maintaining them. This leads them through the following steps toward an argument for the emergence of language from earlier primate communication systems: (1) physical grooming is crucial but time-consuming as a means of maintaining complex sociality; (2) among modern nonhuman primates, the amount of time needed for such grooming increases with group size toward a limit of expenditure; (3) the expansion of group size among fossil hominids, estimated from gross cranial capacity, suggests a leap beyond this limit sometime after the emergence of genus *Homo*; (4) this development may have put pressure on these hominins to substitute time-saving vocalizations for physical grooming; (5) and this in turn militated for the increasing complexity of these vocalizations.[4]

Taking their lead from this "vocal grooming hypothesis," many recent versions of the social intelligence hypothesis are especially concerned to understand the origins of language. Cheney and Seyfarth's particular approach pushes this connection as hard as any.[5] Baboon vocalizations, they concede, are distant indeed from human language, very limited in their number and acoustic variety; but baboon social intelligence, on the other hand, narrows the gap. Baboons provide a present-day analogue to ancient developments because, Cheney and Seyfarth write, "The internal representations of language meaning in the human brain initially built upon our prelinguistic ancestors' knowledge of social relations" (p. 269). Long before language itself emerged, language-like capacities arose from social interactions and were selected for them.

Within baboon troops, fundamental design features of language emerge from contextualized social perception (pp. 266–70). Baboons listening to a sequence of calls "associate each call with a particular individual, and each individual with a particular behavior and motivation." In doing so, the "listeners recognize a causal relation between the calls.... Once we accept the notion of causality, it becomes clear that these simple sequences are similar in at least one respect to the words of a sentence: they are compositional."[6] Moreover, on hearing their conspecifics' calls, baboons form meaning-laden mental representations of those uttering them and those to whom they are directed. These representations are "propositional" in that they convey to the hearers motives of the individuals involved in the exchange. They manifest "discrete values" in their differentiating of distinct individuals, thus rendering the calls themselves discrete in perception, despite their graded, "holistic" production. The calls are processed in a hierarchic fashion, in that they reflect knowledge of dominance rankings within the troop that apply both to individuals and to whole matrilinear groups. Perception of the calls within such dominance hierarchies means that they are "rule-governed"—following the directionality of individuals' rankings—but also "open-ended," since new individuals can be freely added to the perception, resulting in numerous combinatorial possibilities. The involvement of our ancestors in situations of similar social complexity, Cheney and Seyfarth conclude, "created selective pressures favoring structured, hierarchical, rule-governed intelligence."

The many strong claims here add up, for Cheney and Seyfarth, to a "syntax of social knowledge," in that the ordering of baboons' mental representations shows features akin to linguistic semantics, proposition, predication, and compositionality. They attribute to baboons, in other words, an advanced "language of thought" of the sort Jerry Fodor and his many followers have seen as basic to human cognition ("mentalese," Fodorians sometimes call it).[7] In this way they hitch their view of baboon social intelligence, and the phylogeny of hominin sociality and language they link it to, to the most prominent model of a representational and computational psychology (pp. 249–51).

At the same time, Cheney and Seyfarth understand that their monkey mentalese is not the whole story. They describe baboons' mental processes also through an alternative model of cognition, likening them to the multimodal "distributed neural representation[s]" by which humans encode and connect the accumulated perceptions that define an object in cognition (p. 241). This is the language not so much of Fodorian computationalism as of *connectionism*: the view that cognition comes about in the interaction of dispersed neural networks formed as a perceiving organism moves through myriad environmental stimuli more and less salient and frequent. For several decades now connectionism has been opposed in cognitive modeling to computationalism. In recent years the divide between the two has narrowed, as research has shown more and more clearly the capacity of connectionist neural networks (and networks of networks) to model even high-level, compositional, and symbolic human thought processes.[8]

It is easy to underestimate the levels of behavioral complexity that can result from such neural connections, sliding then toward the limitations of a narrow behaviorism and the temptation to use familiar human terms in approaching intricate nonhuman sociality—"language," for example. In the face of this temptation, nevertheless, connectionist models have gathered momentum with the growth of complexity theory, which has begun to take the measure of the intricacy of formal design that can emerge spontaneously from dynamic systems. This has suggested the modeling of systems akin to baboon sociality as emergent phenomena of interacting brains: phenomena that can appear abruptly and (to the human observer) unexpectedly, without obvious scalar relation to prior stimuli; that seem to evince general principles in their structuring ("rules," if you like); and that rely on no mental semantics or grammar.[9]

Connectionism in this way holds out the possibility of discerning foundational cognitive capacities, shared across many species, on which behaviors of varying complexity—even hugely varying complexity—are built. The possibility is especially promising for research into human origins, since, if a historical model of continuous development of cognitive modes is to be envisaged, it stands to reason that it will need to start from the bottom up: from basic capacities building complexity rather than from an extrapolation of human modes into the prehuman world.

So let us pursue a bit farther the implications of the computational/connectionist divide in Cheney and Seyfarth's work. The problem with their granting computational minds to baboons or *Homo ergaster* is that it assigns to them a developed language of thought, thereby presuming human capacities (syntax, propositionality, combinatoriality, etc.) in creatures evidently remote from our cognition in many ways. The presumption works from the top down, seeking advanced human cognitive modes in other species. There is in it even an element of circularity, since the model chosen, by invoking the workings of language, forecloses the very distance between baboon and human minds it aims to describe.

What is proposed in Cheney and Seyfarth's assertion that a watchful baboon "understands that *Sylvia threat-grunts and Hannah screams* carries a different meaning from *Hannah threat-grunts and Sylvia screams*" (p. 268)? For them it reveals baboon mentalese in action, processing a syntax of social relations, comprehending identity, rank, and causality extending between ranks, and even generalizing this comprehension to any pair of individuals in the group. It means something near to what a Fodorian would mean in asserting the same of a human observer of the baboons.

But it may mean none of this. From a less representational, more connectionist vantage, a baboon's understanding might reflect no more (and no less) than the neural networks shaped by innate capacities, including advanced perceptual abilities, in flexible interaction with repeated environmental stimuli—some social, some not, some salient, some less so, all related to others by proximity and context. The understanding could be an expression of perceived repetition and similarity among stimuli, which activate anew, and develop in incremental new ways, established, distributed, and pluridetermined neural patterns.

This connectionist approach turns away from imagistic, semantic, and language-like conceptions of monkeys' mental representations. It is described by psychologist Lawrence Barsalou in an analysis of recent neuroimaging work on macaque monkeys, quoted by Cheney and Seyfarth and worth repeating here. When a macaque hears another macaque's bark or coo, Barsalou writes, there occurs a multimodal activation of different cognitive networks that have proved relevant to similar stimuli in previous situations:

> The auditory system processes the call, the visual system processes the faces and bodies of conspecifics, along with their expressions and actions, and the affective system processes emotional responses. Association areas capture these activations as they occur repeatedly, storing them for later representational use. When subsequent calls are encoded, they reactivate the auditory component of the resultant situational knowledge, which in turn activates the remaining components in other modalities. Thus the distributed property circuit that processed the original situation later represents it conceptually.[10]

There is much that remains vague here, as in most connectionist models: the various systems, areas, modalities, and so forth (such vagueness in regard to neural substrates is certainly a part also of computational conceptions and notions of mentalese). But Barsalou's connectionist approach offers this important advantage: the key concept representation, though it remains front and center, is no longer semantic or imagistic. Instead it is *a quite literal re-presenting, a solidifying, affirming, salience-forming set of neural tautologies*. There is no reliance on abstracted social identities such as those humans conceive, on a mysterious language of the mind that does the representing, or on baboon comprehension of causality, proposition, and predication. In their place are the accretion and connection of complex intrabrain and interbrain networks and the responses they enable in the face of situations both familiar and less so. Networks are, within sheer biological constraints, products of environmental affordances, forged through the repeated patterns of an organism's interaction with its sociomaterial surroundings. They are reactivated, re-presenting and reinforcing themselves, in the face of familiar patterns, situations, and stimuli. All the intricacy Cheney and Seyfarth find in baboon sociality may well be explained by just such networks and the forces shaping them, without recourse to anything like mentalese.

Cheney and Seyfarth are not the only researchers to suggest that compositional or combinatorial processing reaches far back in phylogenetic history. Giacomo Rizzolatti and Michael A. Arbib, two foremost researchers on mirror neurons, have done so as well.[11] Mirror neurons, first detected in monkeys, are neurons that fire not only when a monkey performs an action, but also when the monkey witnesses another monkey or a person performing the same action. Such mirror systems, as I noted in Chapter 3, might yield insight into the mimetic entrainment of pre-sapient hominins, if their operation in humans could be illuminated more than it has been to date.

Rizzolatti and Arbib leap far beyond this modest potential, however, arguing that the action recognition and duplication connected to mirror systems underlies human language all told. They view the activity of mirror neurons as a representation of actions either undertaken or observed. This representational capacity gives the mirror system a kind of semantic content, forming a lexicon-like set of distinct motor patterns. From these Rizzolatti and Arbib extrapolate a "pre-linguistic 'grammar' of action," evinced in the hand and arm gestures of ancient hominins, that showed "inherent" combinatorial properties similar to basic sentence structures (pp. 192–93). In their historical scenario, vocalized gestures gradually took on the referential possibilities and combinatoriality of the brachiomanual gestures; in doing so, vocalizations came to supersede the limitations of older, emotive cries. A quick glance at endocasts of fossil crania leads Rizzolatti and Arbib, finally, to the sweeping suggestion that combinatorial gesturing might even have marked the emergence of the genus *Homo* more than two million years ago.

Rizzolatti and Arbib's case for early combinatoriality is even less well founded than Cheney and Seyfarth's combinatoriality among baboons. Their presumption of an inherent combinatoriality in ancient gestures is imprecise and unsupported. Their idea, also, of a semantic motor vocabulary represented in mirror-neuron networks has been effectively countered in recent critiques of such overreaching speculation on mirror neurons.[12] Here again we sense inchoate notions of semantic representation intruding where they might not belong. Like Cheney and Seyfarth, Rizzolatti and Arbib attribute combinatorial structure and language-like protocols to situations of communicative production or perception where the bottom-up complexity of action sequences, deployed in association-rich social situations, might suffice. At the very least, the burden of evidence for such attributions needs to be set high.

We have circled around to familiar territory. Chapters 2 and 3 described, according to bottom-up processes involving action sequences, both Acheulean mimetic traditions and a later, accumulating social complexity. The entrained transmission from generation to generation of Acheulean toolmaking culture and the intense, intimate interactions of collaborative butcherings at Boxgrove or Notarchirico show every sign of arising from cognition like that described by Barsalou. Each could have formed its patterns from multimodal, associated neural networks of relatively modest complexity, and neither seems to call for a mental syntax or a lexicon of mental images. These Lower Paleolithic taskscapes can be conceived as products of a positive feedback between hominin brains and the contexts they created of proximity, mimesis, and growing mindreading skills. More succinctly, the taskscapes reflect the neural consequences of *action sequences in social alliance*. We have

137

already extended these consequences from the *chaînes opératoires* of lithic technologies to a protodiscourse involving enhanced vocalization and other deictic, protosemantic gestures.

In general, the alternative computational and connectionist models of human or humanlike cognition are not neutral in the face of deep history. A computational approach encourages reverse engineering, retrospectively projecting human capacities onto earlier hominins or onto nonhuman species understood as proxies for our ancestors. This is evident in Cheney and Seyfarth's baboons and might be witnessed also in accounts like Tecumseh Fitch's, which assimilates the learning and combinatoriality of birdsong to those of human language. The assignment to distant species of full-fledged, humanlike capacities gives them an ex nihilo feel and fosters a catastrophist history discerning revolutions more easily than continuities in the phylogeny of cognition. A connectionist model, instead, might hope to plot a route in this phylogeny from simple to more complex cognition. It might be more amenable to an incremental history without inexplicable, revolutionary disjunctions.

The erroneous retrospective assignment of human capacities to our distant forebears does not invalidate the social intelligence hypothesis; it only confounds its timeline. It introduces cognitive workings fundamental to language or musicking—especially semantic reference, hierarchic structuring, discrete combinatoriality, and syntax—into ancient modes of sociality and communication that did not require them. How can we plot more reliably the chronology of the emergence of the newer capacities? The reconstructed operational sequences and taskscapes of extinct hominins are certainly our surest guide, but, if we are to read traces of novel modes in the sociomaterial lives of Middle Paleolithic hominins, we will need also a clear understanding of the communicative structures these might reflect. As we take up protomusical issues and ultimately musical ones in the coming chapters, we will continue to shift our attention between basic cognitive functions involved in musicking and these ancient taskscapes.

CHAPTER FOUR

250,000 Years Ago:

Neandertal Digitalization

Protodiscourse as Protomusical Structure

Gesture-calls in nonhuman primates can be eloquent, and we must suppose them to have become even more so at some point in the descent of our hominin ancestors. Their concatenation on the Lower Paleolithic taskscape, described in Chapter 3, resulted in the sequenced communicative behavior that we called protodiscourse. This was at first an additive, bottom-up communication in which the individual calls advanced the broader exchanges gesture by gesture, but did *not* create larger communicative wholes kicking meaning onto a higher level. I have already introduced some words linguists use to describe this kick, the formation of high-level meanings from upstructuring of atomic and molecular bits of language: generativity, compositionality, and combinatoriality. To assign this kind of structure to Acheulean protodiscourse would be to assert that its signal-sequences were built and perceived as a hierarchy in which higher levels evinced emergent, categorical novelties of communicative function and coherence. There is little evidence, we have seen, to support this.

But in the absence of such structuring, what was conveyed in communications of *Homo heidelbergensis* or even late *ergaster* or *erectus*? Not meaning referentially displaced in the manner of language. Instead, there was an expressive, manipulative, deictic connecting of gesture-call to context-bound, copresent referent. Late Lower Paleolithic societies of copresence created signals of emotions and intentions more precise than ever before, which nevertheless evinced only general semantic content and no combinatorial hierarchy. From moment to moment the exchanges of these signals presumably constructed communicative situations involving simple choices: Do I approach him (or flee)? Do I take the meat from her (or leave it)? Do I groom him (or not)? Do I give her this stone (or not)? Perhaps even: Do I share (or not)? Such exchanges would have rendered patterns of *expectation and its fulfillment or denial*, want and its match or mismatch with the social environment, a hallmark of communication and sociality in general on the taskscape.

With the words "expectation" and "fulfillment," we can begin to glimpse music as a distant analogue to this protodiscourse. Growing out of the enhanced shared attention, mindreading, and emotive deixis of Acheulean hominins, there are energies and exchanges structured in a very general way *like music*. This taskscape is congruent with the kind of informational structure music would much later become, in two regards: in the complex organizing of information with little or no referential displacement, and in the formal patterning of stimulus and response according to bifurcating options. We need to approach these features one at a time.

Information, first, must not be confused with reference and meaning. Reference requires a connection struck up in perception between two things: an object and the word called to mind to name it, for example, or a social status and the ornament worn to signify it—or, to stretch the point to Lower Paleolithic taskscapes, a deictic gesture and the copresent emotional stance it indicates.[1] Meaning, for its part, is itself referential in any definition that is not too broad to be useful, connecting a concept, word, gesture, action or collection of any of these to what it is about, be it object, another action or concept, and so forth.

Information is more basic than either of these. It requires no human or humanlike consciousness, not even any perception as such, but only a receiver responding to its surroundings in a way that consistently reflects changes in them. It amounts to a regular registering in one system of differences in another, correlations that Jerry Fodor has called "reliable causal covariance." Fodor is right to see that such correlation is pervasive—much broader than reference, meaning, perception or cognition—and that information is therefore ubiquitous.[2] Across the biosphere and beyond, information is spread wide and thin on the ground.

Musicking in its modern guises structures acoustical information in complex ways without necessary reference beyond itself; it is arguably the most intricate self-conscious human organizing of information of any sort with such pervasive, immanent nonreferentiality. To illuminate this point imagine, looking far ahead for a moment, a band of sapient humans, somewhere in Europe 35,000 years ago, or perhaps Southwest Asia 55,000 years ago or east Africa 70,000 years ago, dancing around a fire to the sounds of a blown pipe and a beaten log drum. A familiar scene of musicking, at least from more recent periods; so familiar, indeed, that we can hardly picture it without wondering also about the significance the gathering might have had—a danced imitation of a hunt, for example, or an offering to ancestors. Such putative meanings bring to the scene a characteristic human specificity and displacement of reference, which deepens if we imagine further these people singing words or speaking to one another in something like modern language.

But in the music/dance itself there is little evidence of referential specificity. It is a highly elaborated mode of entrained sociality, and in this must convey (in a mimetic species with advanced mindreading) deictic, copresent messages of the sort we know from the Acheulean taskscape. But such embodied cognitive modes integrating gesture, movement, and emotion to drummed pattern or piped melodic phrases do not entail a referential leap from an acoustic phenomenon to something else and other. Moreover, the complex as a whole shows no sign of any conventionalized lexicon like that basic to language. Meanings—that hunt, say, or those ancestors—burgeon only in the overlaying of other communicative and semiotic modes onto the embodied production of and reactions to music. In the absence of these, ideas of the music's "meaning" or its "signified" must hover close to motion and emotion if they are not to be a misnomer.

If it is easy to imagine that the music and the dance have no specific and displaced *referent*, it is, on the contrary, impossible to conceive of them conveying no *information*. They organize immensely complex registers of acoustical and bodily differences in the auditory and visual channels, brains, and bodies of both those who enact and those who perceive them. This embodied cognition is separable from whatever referential and symbolic leaps might accrue to the scene. (Or might not; but can we imagine a scene such as this occurring in a taskscape *not* elsewhere replete with referential and symbolic distance? This question will occupy us in subsequent chapters.) In the cognition and actions of musicking and dancing, what is engendered is not some leap from sound and movement to ideas, but a deepening and complicating of ancient modes of entrainment and an elaborating of the deictic significance these could convey. An elaboration, in other words, of reliable covariance toward an embodied, copresent signification.

In a general way, music theorists, psychologists, and cognitivists alike have devoted themselves to tracking this play of covariance. In doing so they have often described how ancient, binary responses stand behind music's significance, and this brings us to the second aspect of the Acheulean anticipation of musicking, its posing of situations of formal bifurcation. Early moves toward this understanding of music emerged in the 1920s from a joining of certain protocognitivist aesthetic philosophies with behavioral psychology. A first landmark was Susanne Langer's *Philosophy in a New Key* of 1942, which added into the mix Cassirer's philosophy of symbolic forms and an earlier musical formalism, reaching back to Eduard Hanslick in the mid-nineteenth century. For Langer, musical significance was "connotative," unlike the "denotative" significance of language, in that it built complex patterns that signify without reference to things beyond themselves. To explain the meaningfulness of this connotation she proposed, following German Gestalt psychologists, especially Wolfgang Köhler, fundamental similarities between these patterns and the "forms of mental life." (Köhler himself had seen so basic a link that he pressed musical vocabulary into service to describe such patterns.) These formal congruencies often took binary shapes, "*tensions and resolutions*" fundamental not only to music but to emotional response; they could embrace a wide range of emotional experience and capture the dynamism of the psyche: "There are certain aspects of the so-called 'inner life'—physical or mental—which have formal properties similar to those of music—patterns of motion and rest, of tension and release, of agreement and disagreement, preparation, fulfillment, excitation, sudden change, etc."[3]

For music theorist Leonard Meyer, developing Langer's intuitions in his classic *Emotion and Meaning in Music* of 1956, binary bifurcations were especially important in explaining emotional response to music, and in his account Langer's nondenotative musical meanings drifted closer to modern information theory.[4] Meyer followed the Cambridge psychologist J. T. MacCurdy in understanding emotion as the psychological outcome when a tendency to respond to a stimulus is inhibited or thwarted. The tendency itself is a patterned reaction to a stimulus, more or less automatic in operation and the product either of learning or of innate structures. Once such a tendency is set in motion, whether it is brought to consciousness or not, it creates an expectation of a particular outcome. The patterns of music, Meyer argued, tap fundamental Gestalt forms of perception, such as grouping, continuation, closure, and so forth; he was much more specific than Langer in demonstrating how they do so. These patterns are second to no other expressive gestures in setting off MacCurdy's tendencies. At every moment and on different temporal levels they elicit expectations and then, fulfilling or denying them, arouse emotions.

Thus Meyer, joining Gestalt psychology to an analysis of musical gestures from several, mainly Western traditions, built a general theory of emotional engagement with music. He raised the possibility of accounting for a complex musical edifice on the basis of overlapping systems of binary expectations met or unmet, and we will see later that such accounts followed fairly quickly. Meanwhile, the theory of emotion as a bifurcated response to a tendency, fulfilled or thwarted, has evolved since MacCurdy and still provides fertile ground for music psychologists. Niko Frijda's influential view, for example, treats basic emotions as gauges of the matching or mismatch of responses to environmental stimuli and has recently been used to extend Meyer's listener-response theory.[5]

More generally still, other analysts have linked these psychological theories of musical affect to the ecological psychology associated especially with James J. Gibson. Such views, even when they do not emphasize Meyer's psychological bifurcations, advance a conception of musical engagement as a complex of innate and learned responses to the *affordances* of an acoustical environment (to employ a coinage I have used before that was a contribution of Gibson).[6] Musical response in these views becomes a part of the intertwined histories of organism and environment basic to biocultural coevolution. In effect, we traverse musical terrains much as we have always managed taskscapes, marking informational structures and deploying responses, often binary in nature, in ceaseless psychic negotiation with our surroundings. Among the consequences of the deployment are expectation, fulfillment or its absence, and affective arousal.

It should go without saying that none of these views pose limits to the complexity modern musicking can muster in structuring the acoustical environment. Indeed the congruencies of communicative patterns posited here between musicking and the Acheulean taskscape are agnostic in regard to such structures. The patterns indicate only deep foundations of our musical responses, and they are too general to model the complexities musicking today inevitably erects above them. Perhaps, on the other hand, it should *not* go without saying that the cognitive modes involved in these modern intricacies were nowhere to be

seen in hominins half a million years ago. Our Acheulean ancestors were not musicking creatures. There can be little doubt,
however, that those cognitive modes were solidly in place by
the Upper Paleolithic in Europe, from about 40,000 years ago,
and accumulating evidence suggests that they were older still in
Africa. What were the basic capacities governing these developments, and when did they appear?

Middle Paleolithic Heuristics

The answer takes shape again in the lithic record, which reveals
that the long, relatively static era of Acheulean technologies,
described in Chapter 2, was broken sometime after 500,000 years
ago. This was neither an abrupt change nor a single event. Instead
the archaeological record in Africa, Europe, and southwest Asia
shows the gradual introduction of novel techniques and operational sequences in the making of tools. New loops formed in the
feedback relations between hominins and material affordances.
The changes took hold in more than one species, and by 250,000–
300,000 years ago they are visible among both Neandertals in
Europe and pre-sapient hominins in Africa.

The period reaching from about 400,000 to 100,000 years ago
witnessed the coexistence of several hominin species, of which
we can name with confidence at least three. *Homo erectus* made its
long last stand in Asia and perhaps elsewhere—and, if astonishing recent finds of Indonesian "Hobbits" are borne out, lingered
in isolated island communities there as recently as 18,000 years
ago. *Homo neanderthalensis* emerged and spread through Europe
and central and western Asia. *Homo sapiens* assumed its modern
anatomical form toward the end of the period in Africa. As
for precursors to the latter two, *Homo heidelbergensis*, the probable ancestor of Neandertals in Europe and the species usually
connected to Lower Paleolithic sites such as Boxgrove in England, survived into the early part of this period; some see it also
as a precursor to *Homo sapiens* in Africa and perhaps, looking
back farther, the ancestor we share with Neandertals at about

600,000 years ago. *Homo helmei*, instead, is the name others assign to our immediate ancestors in Africa, though still others would collapse this taxon, interpreting the specimens of *helmei* as archaic *sapiens*.[7]

The best-founded early association of the new technologies with a single species connects them to the Neandertals, and it is from this Eurasian, Middle Paleolithic connection that most of my analysis will stem. Lying along this path is the interpretive pitfall of European parochialism, the tendency to track the later stages of hominin evolution primarily as a European development. This is of course not a deep-historical fact at all but an outgrowth of the history of archaeological research, which for most of the last century was mainly carried out on European soil, thus biasing our sample of evidence.[8] In an influential study of 2000, Sally McBrearty and Alison Brooks surveyed the African archaeological evidence for novel behaviors, and they made the case for a gradual buildup of innovations there beginning at least 280,000 years ago—innovations generally similar and more or less contemporary with the new behaviors appearing in Europe. In the most liberal estimates this development extends some of the novelties back to a period well before the emergence of *Homo sapiens* (now placed about 200,000 years ago), all the way to the boundary between African lithic eras usually termed the Earlier and Middle Stone Ages.[9] The behaviors exemplified by Neandertals and analyzed below were no doubt not identical to those of contemporary hominins in Africa; but their direction can serve as a useful proxy for the general directions gradually coming to light in our own immediate ancestors.

The *gradualism* described by McBrearty and Brooks, meanwhile, is not the same as *progressivism*. A second interpretive hazard is to impose on the fragmentary and often puzzling archaeological record a scenario of smooth advance. Instead this record, even at its clearest, conveys something other than continuity and accumulating progress. It shows, first, that species other than our direct antecedents were involved in new behaviors during the late Lower and Middle Paleolithic periods (or Earlier and Middle Stone Ages, in the African terminology); this is especially clear in the Neandertal example.

It also shows that the appearances of these behaviors even within a single species may form uneven patterns difficult to decipher. Striking divergences in behavior may result from local forces, regional environments and the specific demands and opportunities they present, rather than from significant or persistent cognitive differences.[10] Taskscapes can, in other words, take very different forms for reasons other than fundamental differences in hominin capacities. It has been suggested, for example, that the puzzling absence of Acheulean stone bifaces among East Asian *Homo erectus* may reflect nothing more than the abundance there of a much more tractable but perishable material from which to make blades—bamboo.[11] The course of Middle and Upper Paleolithic cultural change seems to have been one of fits and starts, extending over several species and falling into different rhythms in different regions. We will witness below, in a recent discovery of early spears, the kinds of surprises this uneven course can bring; and in Chapters 6–7 we will take the general measure of such localism across the last 100,000 years.

If ideas of smooth progressivism are problematic, so are their converse, theories of revolutionary change. Joined to European parochialism, these form one more interpretive trap: the venerable, still resilient notion of a European invention of behavioral modernity coinciding with the advent there of sapient humans some 40,000 years ago.[12] This putative revolution defines the conventional borderline between the European Middle and Upper Paleolithic eras. To be sure, it is reasonable to assume that early *Homo sapiens* in Europe introduced behavioral innovations, perhaps even striking ones. Despite our ever-increasing sense of Neandertal behavioral versatility, we have nothing associated with them that approximates some of the artifacts left by modern humans in this period: cave paintings at Chauvet, carved animals from Vogelherd, and bone and ivory flutes from there and neighboring sites. To say this is not, however, to advocate for a definitive European revolution that ushered in human modernity, at least if we are careful not to assume that the novelties of early European *sapiens* were new to the species when they appeared there.

In fact, the new African evidence marshaled by McBrearty and Brooks and others suggests the opposite: that European innovations had distinct precursors among African humans. Moreover, given the findings of the last twenty years or so, there is reason to expect that future digs will fill out this picture of out-of-Africa modernity. In the face of this new evidence, some once-staunch advocates of the European Upper Paleolithic revolution, for example Paul Mellars and Richard Klein, have more recently revised their ideas to embrace African precedents. Indeed Mellars's descriptions of the advent of human modernity now run the risk of transposing whole-cloth the revolutionary model to Africa. He envisages a dispersion of novel cultural patterns from east Africa, through southwest Asia, and north and westward across Europe, following the spread of *Homo sapiens* after 60,000 years ago. The imported behaviors, he argues, were reshaped by new pressures of new environments, perhaps even with some reciprocal cultural interactions with Neandertals.[13]

This suggests another avenue along which the revolutionary thesis has been countered, now in the local European context: by discerning substantial signs of modernity among Neandertals themselves. The contention over this question grew especially shrill in the 1990s, before clear evidence emerged separating Neandertals and *sapiens* as distinct subspecies or species. Some went so far as to level not-so-veiled charges of racism and cultural imperialism against those who limited modern behavior to non-Neandertals in Europe. The atmosphere is calmer now, but the fundamental question remains: If Neandertals were not painting cave walls and fashioning musical instruments, what *were* they up to? Can we make out a collective place for them in the fits and starts of Middle Paleolithic history?

At present there remain wide differences of view on Neandertal behavior and capacities, differences stimulated by the puzzling aspect the species' history presents across the long *durée*. Neandertals managed to survive in a Europe and western Asia—they spread as far to the east as southern Siberia—of extremely challenging and variable environments through the late Middle and Upper Pleistocene, with sharp climatic shifts, sometimes stunningly quick, and repeated ice ages.[14] More dramatically still, in the Levant at about 70,000 years ago they seem to have replaced an early migration of modern humans out of Africa, probably as a result of climatic and accompanying ecological changes as a new glaciation began.[15] They were toolmakers of unprecedented skill, as we shall see, who successfully hunted a variety of game, including some of the largest and fastest animals they encountered.[16] And more and more compelling evidence suggests that they engaged, at least sporadically, in behaviors usually considered to be markers of the modernity of *Homo sapiens*: interment of their dead, body decoration with pigments, and even the making of ornamental artifacts and marking of cave walls.

In the midst of this evident adaptability and versatility and these extraordinary capacities, however, the Neandertal career, over some 250,000–300,000 years, shows little of the burgeoning cultural change of Upper Paleolithic *sapiens*. This combination of slow, limited cultural change on one hand and flexible resourcefulness and survival in the face of steep odds on the other poses the enigma of Neandertal capacities.

To solve the puzzle, many refinements have been proposed in recent years of the older, blunt views of sheer differences between Neandertals and early European *sapiens*. Steven Mithen, for example, has offered a general cognitive hypothesis. He imagines Neandertals as having a modular mind in which the individual components—dedicated to social intelligence, technical intelligence, and so forth—were effectively walled off from one another, with little general integration. Without connections among these neural networks, individual areas of Neandertal behavior might show

149

considerable development, but the essential cultural innovations of modern humans, dependent on cognitive integration, were out of reach.[17] David Lewis-Williams, in a speculative analysis of early sapient wall painting and related behavior, proposes something similar: that Neandertal brains were not hard-wired in ways that could open to them the altered states of consciousness expressed and fostered in such cultural work.[18] Their artifacts could be complex, but their cultures were foreshortened and flat.

Thomas Wynn and Frederick Coolidge approach the enigma also along cognitive lines, through an analysis of Neandertal memory. Close reading of the lithic evidence suggests to them that Neandertals were strong on long-term working memory, a "procedural" memory that enabled them to rehearse and master repeated actions of unprecedented complexity. Less developed was their short-term working memory, the source in modern humans of attentional and behavioral control across many cognitive domains and in the face of disruptive stimuli. This balance, subtly distinct from modern human capacities, might explain the combining of highly developed expertise with a pervasive dearth of innovation.[19] Clive Gamble instead views Neandertals from the perspective of the taskscapes they created, seeing in them humans whose social rhythms were largely habitual and stable—intensified over those of earlier hominins, enabling a limited cultural variety from one group to the next and furthering the evolution and use of protolanguage, but finally not breaking dramatically with an earlier sociality of copresence.[20] All these positions on Neandertal cognitive modes intersect and are in varying degrees reconcilable with one another as hypotheses.

Other researchers solve the puzzle by minimizing it—that is, by emphasizing the traces of Neandertal cultural change over time. In a recent survey of archaeological evidence, Michelle C. Langley, Christopher Clarkson, and Sean Ulm delineate for Neandertals, much as McBrearty and Brooks had done for our African precursors, a slow but steadily accelerating growth in behavioral complexity over a very long period. Markers of this complexity include new kinds of tools we will examine below, among them composite tools involving hafting. The growing complexity involves also the use of pigments, perhaps for body painting, new sorts of modification of raw materials, including bones with regular patterns incised in them, and some burial of the dead. The incidence of each of these seems to grow incrementally from 160,000 down to 40,000 years ago, suggesting a gradual Neandertal move toward complex behaviors often considered unique to modern humans.[21]

For minimalists of this bent, one archaeological assemblage looms large: a novel industry, called Châtelperronian, associated with Neandertals at the very end of their career, sometime between 40,000 and 28,000 years ago. Along with its distinctive lithic artifacts this industry may offer—analysis of the evidence from a crucial site remains controversial—bones and teeth carefully worked as implements and ornaments. Some of the most strenuous recent debate concerns whether this industry was an independent Neandertal achievement or the result of "acculturation" and technological borrowing in the wake of contact with the earliest European *Homo sapiens*. In the latter view the Châtelperronian represents a Neandertal adoption of the first sapient industry in Europe, the Aurignacian. Settling the case either way would have obvious implications for the nature of late Neandertal capacities and achievements.[22]

More generally, one implication of this enlargement of the spectrum of Neandertal capacities has been the narrowing of the perceived gap between them and *Homo sapiens*. This has, for some, renewed an old debate about the very distinguishing of the two into separate species. João Zilhão, taking a minority position, has recently argued that the two lineages did not develop separately long enough for full speciation before they met in the Levant or Europe. Whatever anatomical differences they showed, in his view, would not have made successful interbreeding impossible.[23] His position concerning interbreeding, at least, if not regarding speciation, has found statistical support in the mapping of the

Neandertal genome, with its implications that enough interbreeding occurred to leave markers in the genomes of many present-day humans of non-African descent.[24]

The narrowing of distance between Neandertals and us, argued along genetic and archaeological lines, is not without drama and is driving for many a wholesale reconsideration of the Neandertal achievement. But, if Neandertals were much like the *Homo sapiens* they encountered over the last 40,000–90,000 years, why, once again, are we faced with what must seem by comparison a lethargic cultural accumulation across most of their history? And, more pointedly, why did they disappear? To answer these questions, Zilhão, April Nowell, Stephen Shennan, and others have turned in a promising new direction. They advance a complex interplay of population demographics, climate changes, and the effects of both on cultural transmission and viability to begin to frame a new kind of explanation.[25] These forces point, I think, to a nonlinearity that characterizes the advent of cultural innovations not only among Neandertals but among *Homo sapiens* as well—and probably, across an even longer *durée*, among all hominin lineages. They can reveal much about the emergence of cultural modernity in *Homo sapiens* over the last hundred millennia, and I leave further consideration of them for Chapter 6.

Neandertal Lithics

In the midst of all these debates and quandaries, the innovations in toolmaking associated with Neandertals are as solidly established as anything in Paleolithic research. The pre-Châtelperronian Neandertal toolkit is often referred to as Mousterian, after the type-site of Le Moustier in the Dordogne, a terminology that admits of qualifications and confusions for several reasons: Mousterian assemblages show several different regional "styles"; they include Acheulean bifaces as well as newer kinds of tools; they are dispersed through Europe, west Asia, the Levant, and northern Africa; and they were produced by *Homo sapiens* as well as Neandertals. Nevertheless, "Mousterian" has come to be accepted

shorthand for the industries most closely associated with Neandertals across most of their existence, and so it will be used here.

The innovations of the Mousterian toolkit can be characterized, in first approximation, as an expansion of the taskscape
involved in their manufacture and use. This was among other
things a geographical phenomenon, as raw materials and tools
were transported over longer distances than before. Among
Neandertals in the Dordogne, according to archaeologist Jean-
Michel Geneste, the distances involved seem to increase across
time, with a spike upward during the last long warm period (or
interglacial) of the Middle Paleolithic, about 120,000 years ago.
The distances attained in these transfers could reach (if rarely)
as much as two hundred miles.[26] In still more recent times there
might be some suggestion of something different than transporta-
tion of materials: long-range exchange of materials from group
to group.[27]

Such mobility suggests a more general advance, compared to
earlier hominins, in the capacity to imagine changing and future
contingencies. Hominin cognition, it signals, was beginning to
take in the possibility of relatively distant future needs, also a
vista of material resources beyond the seen landscape, and perhaps even the prospect of interacting on the far side of the hill, so
to speak, with others at once similar and different. Neandertals,
in short, show a noteworthy and probably unprecedented capacity
for thinking-at-a-distance.

Caution is called for in the face of the far-reaching claims
this might inspire.[28] There is only modest and equivocal artifact
evidence among Neandertals for what archaeologists term, often
imprecisely, "symbolic" behavior.[29] Neither is there any secure
evidence for Neandertal musicking; the famous "Neandertal
flute," much discussed in the 1990s, turned out to be no artifact
at all, but a byproduct of cave bear predation.[30] While such behaviors are of course not an infallible predictor of language in its
modern form, their absence at least suggests its absence also. At
present, after more than a century of research on Neandertals, we

can picture their taskscapes to be extended well beyond earlier societies of copresence, but not so far that they could not have been achieved through the elaboration and intensification of the protodiscourse described in Chapter 3. This intensification probably involved a slow expansion of referential possibilities in the form of a limited conventionalization of vocalized and gestural signals, and it may have entailed, as we will see, an incipient hierarchization of the course of communicative exchange. But it evidently did not amount to fully modern behavior and most likely did not entail modern language.

Even with such due caution, however, the increased mobility of Neandertals' raw and fashioned materials brings suggestive implications for the operational sequences of their toolmaking. Mousterian technology, in the analysis of archaeologists Mark White and Paul Pettitt, shifted away from the immediate, "situational" patterns of earlier toolmaking and use, for example the tools at Boxgrove, fashioned for a particular task and mostly discarded when it was accomplished. Neandertals instead regularly "curated" their tools over a longer period and wider space than in earlier industries. This required greater flexibility than before, as the use-life of transported materials was played out across a wider range of environmental conditions and stimuli.[31] This, too, represents a move beyond copresence, as new forms of distance and variability were interposed between the primary affordances of materials and their technological applications. There is ample evidence for the conclusion that Neandertals "regularly carried tools as a hedge against unforeseen, generalized needs."[32]

This degree of extension of the operational sequence interposes a distance between tool and primary material affordances that is rare in the pre-Neandertal archaeological record. One stunning exception, and dramatic testimony to the fits and starts of Middle Paleolithic history described above, is a set of eight wooden spears unearthed in Schöningen, Germany, in the 1990s. These are sophisticated implements, their wood taken from felled spruce trees rather than from scavenged branches and their points carved from the hardest wood at the base of the tree. They are aerodynamically balanced, in the manner of modern javelins. Such manufacture involves a *chaîne opératoire* of striking length and procedural intricacy. All the more astonishing, then, that the spears reach back as far as 400,000 years and may have been the creation of late *Homo heidelbergensis*, not early Neandertals. And this may not exhaust their surprises. Two of the Schöningen spears bear marks that have been interpreted as notches in which to haft a separate point. This interpretation would make them by far the oldest composite or multipartite tools yet discovered—and would seem implausible at this period but for the otherwise extraordinarily elaborate facture of the spears.[33]

Ranging far from immediate material affordances would become much more prevalent in later, Mousterian industries. Even without confirmation of the Schöningen hafting, recent researches have pushed ever earlier the horizon for the first appearance of composite tools. Stone points once hafted onto wooden handles have been unearthed at late Mousterian levels of Levantine sites, associated with Neandertals. In one dramatic instance, dating back some 50,000 years, the broken tip of a spear was found in the fossilized vertebra of an ass, the remains of an ancient kill. In another, traces of bitumen that had been heated to high temperature, presumably to make a hafting adhesive, were recovered from several stone implements dating back 60,000 years; in still another, hand-worked birch-bark pitch from a German site, probably another hafting adhesive and some 48,000 years old, bears the uncanny trace of a fingerprint.[34]

The distance here between raw material affordances and technical use is substantial. In the adhesive technology, for example, we need to imagine the tools used to recover raw bitumen and the container or perhaps flat stone in or on which it was heated. If fiber or hide straps were used in addition to the adhesive, as seems likely, we also have to picture a multistep process in which these were cut with their eventual function in mind. A new kind of *hierarchization* of the *chaîne opératoire* appears, in which more and more complex tools are fashioned for the purpose of making other tools.

More significant still, hafting technologies produced composite designs involving the assembly of several components, with the resulting implement engineered so as to fulfill its function as a whole. Composite tools are not merely additive forms of technological complexity but *emergent tools* that join together discrete elements so as to reveal new properties: A thrusting spear or javelin with a stone tip can fell a horse, or dispatch a wounded ass, in ways that a stone point alone cannot. The part-whole relationships involved in such compound implements form *compositional* hierarchies in which elements join together to compose larger systems. Middle Paleolithic composite tools in this way represent compositionality in material form.

Francesco d'Errico and a group of coauthors have suggested one inference that might be drawn from these developments. "The evolution of toolmaking from simple to composite, and the further development of using tools to make tools," they write, "might even be seen as the archaeological reflection of the transition from a proto-language to a language with a more complex structure."[35] There is a large step built into this hypothesis, and we certainly lack the evidence to take it with confidence. Indeed I have suggested already that the case for fully modern language among Neandertals is dubious, given the near-static nature of their cultures and the paucity of evidence for other symbolic behavior; if we accept the weak short-term memory Wynn and Coolidge read in the lithic record, this might pose another impediment to full-fledged language.

Nevertheless, the general point of d'Errico and his coauthors is a powerful and important one and can be pressed further. These Middle Paleolithic technological innovations create in material form *combinatorial patterns* of composition. These are different from the compositional forms of language, in that neither the parts of composite tools nor the finished product carry semantic meaning; in language, such meaning in the parts of an utterance is raised to a new power in their syntactic binding to one another. In composite tools, instead, the relation is one of *function*, in which the use-potential of the individual parts is altered in the functioning of the whole. Composite tools and other, broader developments I will take up next provide the clearest glimpses we have of Neandertal minds. What they show are cognitive patterns that seem to be at least loosely related to those on which modern language is founded, and we will see shortly that these hierarchic and combinatorial patterns underlie modern musicking also.[36]

The evidence for composite implements, hafting, adhesive technology, and so forth remains sporadic and, across the long course of Neandertal evolution, mostly late. Probably such technologies appeared and disappeared more than once across many groups and the life of the species. But even in the absence of these special technologies, Mousterian stone artifacts embody in their own ways both the Middle Paleolithic lengthening of *chaînes opératoires* and a pervasive hierarchization of technology. To appreciate this we must step back for a moment and gain a wider vantage.

In Paleolithic analysis, an important advance toward processual, operational-sequence thinking was the distinguishing of two general and opposed approaches to the making of stone tools. Because the dichotomy first came into use among French archaeologists in the generation of Leroi-Gourhan, especially François Bordes, researchers tend to retain the French terms for the approaches: *façonnage* and *débitage*.[37] *Façonnage* names the process by which a raw nodule or cobble is reduced to a finished tool. It involves removal of material from the cobble; the tool is the core material that remains, as in the making of an Acheulean biface. In *débitage*, instead, the operational sequence leads to tools being chipped off the core, and what is left over is either waste material or a smaller core from which further tools might be struck. *Façonnage* and *débitage* are not mutually exclusive and do not pose a chronological succession of toolmaking strategies, the one superseding the other. In fact, both processes are present from the earliest Oldowan technologies, if we can presume there a dichotomy of two types of tools, with both the choppers (*façon-nage*) and the sharp-edged flakes removed from them (*débitage*) put to use.

Nevertheless, the expansion of toolmaking techniques in the Middle and Upper Paleolithic ushered in a wealth of new, sophisticated sequences giving a new prominence to *débitage*. The most important of these in the Middle Paleolithic was Levallois technique, named after a town near Paris where flint tools were unearthed in the late nineteenth century. Levallois refers, in current thinking, not to a specific technique but to a set of related operational sequences.[38] They began to appear at least 250,000–300,000 years ago and perhaps as much as 100,000 years earlier; but in any case by about 250,000–200,000 years ago Levallois assemblages in Europe are well attested, widespread, varied in specific approach, and closely associated with Neandertals.[39]

European Levallois is a technology unified in several basic aspects, though these can be applied in many distinct ways. It is known as a *prepared-core* technology because it requires a set of preliminary steps to shape the core from which a point or flake is to be struck. First the edges are struck off a cobble, roughly yielding a desired size and shape (Figure 4.1, steps 1–2). Then, using the edges created by this first flaking as multiple striking platforms, flakes are chipped off the top of the cobble, forming there a convex surface (steps 3–4). Next, one end of the cobble is taken as a striking platform for the production of the desired point or flake (step 5); perhaps this platform is itself prepared by lopping a large flake off this end. Finally, a single strike at the proper place on the platform will flake off an implement either finished or requiring minimal retouching (step 6).

Levallois operational sequences admit of many variations and degrees of sophistication and precision. In their classic form, they depend on a number of standardized procedures that have been conceptualized by Eric Boëda.[40] The first is the distinguishing

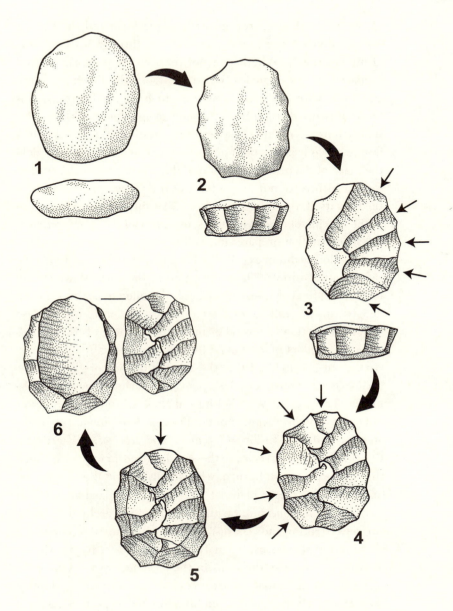

Figure 4.1 A simple Levallois sequence.
Redrawn by Virge Kask after François Bordes,
"Mousterian Cultures in France," *Science* 134
(1961), pp. 803–10.

of two parts of the core, the striking platform and the flaking surface, divided by a secant plane cutting through it (the "plane of intersection"). Whether or not the striking platform is itself prepared, it is categorically distinct from the flaking surface and forms with it a "hinge" behind which the final percussion is made. It is also distinct from the multiple platforms of the earlier stage (steps 3–4). These enable the preparation of the flaking surface, with convexities both on its sides and at its tip, so as to yield the shape of the resulting point or flake. We can see that Levallois sequences involve not only a *functional differentiation* of parts of the core itself, reminiscent of the similar differentiation involved in the making of composite tools, but a *temporal hierarchization* of the sequence that prepares it and finally strikes a tool from it.

Levallois techniques gave the knapper a novel control over the resulting flake tools. The preparation of the core allowed these to be much finer than earlier flakes had tended to be, cutting less deeply into the volume of the core and often enabling its reuse in the production of several or many tools. The tools themselves were the product of *débitage* at the moment of the final hammer-strike, but it is evident that the shaping of the core before this final strike was related to the *façonnage* of earlier Acheulean techniques. This has led Mark White and Nick Ashton to see in it not only a gradual development out of those earlier sequences but also an unprecedented fusion of *façonnage* and *débitage*. What underlies this fusion, for them, is the standardized practice by which the core is prepared. In turn, what stands behind this are, on the one hand, the secant plane of intersection realized at the final moment of *débitage* and, on the other, the hierarchy of distinct surfaces (striking and flaking) created by the initial *façonnage*.[41]

Levallois sequences, like hafting technologies, are not simply additive, in the way the steps in the *façonnage* of an Acheulean biface had been. In that facture, material was successively chipped away from the core in a set of undifferentiated (or, at most, weakly differentiated) gestures, to leave finally a more or less symmetrical tool with a cutting edge around it. In Levallois sequences, instead, the steps took the form of operations, or groups of operations, that differed qualitatively: the steps required to shape the core (even here perhaps of two different sorts), the step required to create the striking platform, and the step required to produce the point—not to mention the fine work involved then in retouching it. The new kind of emphasis on *débitage* in Levallois technologies formed the endpoint of a hierarchy not only of material surfaces but also of separate conceptual categories of processes shaping them.

All these niceties of lithic analysis represent no less than a reorganization of Middle Paleolithic information transmission. If composite tools reflect a passage of technological information structured in compositional, combinatorial patterns, Levallois sequences, widespread at an even earlier date in the archaeological record, materialize more general informational hierarchies. They form "nested" hierarchies—*containment* hierarchies—in which gestures are grouped at more than one level and each group overarches and contains groups at the next level down. Such hierarchies are more basic than the compositional hierarchies represented in composite tools, in that the elements at one level do not form systematic wholes at higher levels (compositional hierarchy, that is, is a special kind of containment hierarchy). Containment hierarchies can be represented by large brackets over smaller brackets, over still smaller brackets, indicating however many levels of nesting the hierarchy entails, and in them the impact of the organization can accumulate from the interrelations of several levels. Modern perception of such hierarchies takes in simultaneously these levels, without necessarily hiding the contribution of any of them, and in this way they retain the imprint of their stratification. They also can show strikingly different properties or functions at different levels—emergent properties, by which one level is categorically distinguished from the next level down.

A Levallois flake is the cumulative product of a containment hierarchy temporally distributed across a set of gestures, meshing together interdependent, nested processes working at different levels of functional generality. Behind the technology stood minds organizing procedures at multiple levels, with functional differences between them and with the potential for new properties to emerge, like phase transitions, across the border from one level to the next. The transmission of the technology across generations signals the entry into culture of these new, hierarchic structures.

The new sequences must have relied at least on a well-developed long-term procedural memory and the rehearsal and learning of complex action sequences it facilitated, and indeed Levallois techniques are the chief evidence Wynn and Coolidge use in assigning just such capacities to Neandertals. In their scenario, the Neandertal "expert mind" and the new technologies emerged hand in hand across the Middle Paleolithic era, as increasingly complex operational sequences came to be devised, practiced, and passed on in mimetic traditions. In other words: Cognition and culture shifted in coevolutionary coordination, and new hierarchic possibilities took shape in each as the loose entrainments of Acheulean performance were replaced by more intricate bonds of structured procedural training.

As ever, changing communicative modes could not have stood entirely apart from this taskscape. The transmitted patterns of technological mimesis must have grown more precise in tandem with the increasing power and communicative specificity of protodiscourse. The relations of communication and procedure, moreover, could not have been unidirectional. Feedback loops would have fostered greater specificity of expression in the gesture-calls even as they brought about new intricacies of technological procedure. But these changes interacted now with procedural patterns involving novel structures and reflecting novel cognitive patterns. Categorical differentiations of function, hierarchy of gesture and conception, and discrete combinatoriality must have begun simultaneously to reshape protodiscourse and technology.

These shifting patterns were linked to the new variety and

depth of interaction with environmental affordances apparent in the lengthened operational sequences of the Middle Paleolithic archaeological record. Hominin cognition once again extended the sequences of steps between raw materials and usable technologies, but now the sequences themselves underwent new forms of arrangement and organization. Material affordances, operational sequences, protodiscourse: the claims of the taskscape sharpened as never before into directed activities, a technosociality exploiting new abilities to distance thought and new flexibilities of engagement and response.

All this grants Neandertals considerable cultural sophistication and powers. The cognitive intricacies beneath Mousterian industries are symptoms of the novel mobilities, physical and ideational, that allowed them to survive in their challenging environments. These intricacies organized embodied gesture into hierarchies and elaborated these toward combinatorial generativity, the first creating products determined by categorically distinct nestings of gestures, the second emergent tools affording uses not possible with their separate parts. Each seems to represent something new in the transmission of the archives of hominin culture.

Further Protomusical Structure

The nascent hierarchization and combinatoriality of Neandertal cognition are not evident in Acheulean protodiscourse, and they correlate with the kind of mind required for modern speaking and musicking. This is not to assign modern language or music to Neandertals; what we can reconstruct of their lifeways, it is worth repeating, suggests that their cultural archives accumulated at a rate too slow and sponsored changes too gradual to have occurred under the aegis of fully modern capacities, particularly linguistic ones. It is the innovation their taskscapes show compared to *earlier* ones that is important, not a proximity to fully modern behaviors.

Neither should we imagine some straight-line path from

Neandertals to musicking *sapiens*. Notwithstanding the recently detected traces of Neandertal-*sapiens* interbreeding, the evidence for cultural as well as genetic paths between these species is scanty. Neandertals, instead, offer the best-studied evidence we have for cognitive developments that seem to have followed a similar course in the Middle Stone Age of Africa, the crucible from which our direct ancestors emerged. The Neandertal mind elaborated older patterns of the material transmission of information by structuring them in hierarchic and discrete combinatorial ways. So, it seems more and more probable, did our direct African ancestors.[42]

Today these ways of structuring information are pervasive in musicking. Indeed if we take as historical starting point the emotive, gesture-call contours and loose social entrainments of the Acheulean taskscape and as endpoint modern music, it is not too much to say that the decisive steps along the way involved bringing hierarchic and combinatorial cognition to bear on the structuring of acoustic resources and perception. At a deep cognitive level we have already witnessed the results of hierarchic structural constraints in temporal aspects of modern musicking, specifically in the beat-based processing and metric entrainment introduced in Chapter 2. Organizing an isochronous pulse in any kind of higher-level regularity (i.e., any kind of meter) involves the perception of hierarchized nestings of longer and shorter durations related in small-integer ratios—a formulation neutral enough to apply across an immense range of musical experience. We perceive strongly marked, multilevel containment hierarchies in both musical meter specifically and musical rhythm more generally, and the best models we have for such perception posit hierarchies of neurons or neuronal groups oscillating in the same ratios. Both brain scans and psychological experiment have begun to provide an evidential basis for these models.[43]

The basic perception of pitch, meanwhile, seems also to involve a hierarchizing cognition. The human auditory system, from the ear to the brain's auditory cortex, shows a structural propensity to register frequency differences in sonic stimuli, with neurons all along this pathway attuned to respond to single frequencies or narrow bands of them. This seems to occur both in a "tonotopic" fashion, with local regions in the system attuned to vibrate at relatively specific frequencies (an organization particularly evident in the basilar membrane of the inner ear) and in a temporal fashion, with different auditory nerves locking into phase with the sinusoidal wave forms of particular frequencies. Pitch perception, however, involves much more than a frequency-induced neuronal firing, because musical tones are hardly ever made up of one frequency but instead comprise a number of frequencies related in small-integer ratios. The sensation of a pitch involves a process in which the lowest of these frequencies (the fundamental) comes into salience. The brain "analyzes" the interrelation of higher frequencies (overtones or partials) in creating this percept, a capacity most famously revealed by the "missing fundamental" phenomenon, in which we perceive a fundamental frequency that would give rise to a particular set of overtones even when it is absent. Though the nature of this cognitive analysis or calculus is not well understood, compelling models, as with metric perception, propose a Gestalt pattern-recognition created in a network of hierarchically related neurons firing in synchronized periods.[44]

At a more general level of perception, our abilities to distinguish the varied acoustical stimuli involved in most music might be the result of cognitive hierarchization. Albert Bregman describes how we separate the many sonic stimuli bombarding us into coherent streams as a basic aspect of our "auditory scene analysis." Even in relatively simple forms, this *stream segregation* can involve hierarchic ordering of the percepts thus distinguished. In music and other complex auditory segregation, it requires not merely bottom-up correlation and grouping of similar stimuli but an accommodation of these with correlations driven by top-down, learned or habituated *schemas*. The streams resulting seem themselves to rise into salience through hierarchic rankings of the schemas that can shift along with our changing attention to one or another aspect of the stimuli.[45]

While Bregman attends mainly to fundamental aspects of our auditory perception—in music, for example, the "emergent" perceptual qualities of melodic or harmonic integration—others have aimed to model the cognitive processing of full-fledged musical events. These models, like those for foundational musical percepts, have again and again relied on hierarchic structuring. Music theorist Eugene Narmour, for example, has explored the patterns of expectation and its fulfillment raised by his teacher Leonard Meyer—Narmour terms them implication and realization—in a wide-ranging theory of melodic cognition. Melodic coherence in his view arises from a hierarchized meeting, not unlike Bregman's, of top-down cultural learning and its stylistic patterns with bottom-up gestural archetypes generated by basic, Gestalt cognitive processes. All melody is a playing-out on many hierarchic levels of a small number of stylistic archetypes, and these are connected in our cognizing of them so as to imply further events that may occur or be delayed or denied. Narmour in effect extends Meyerian bifurcated systems of expectations fulfilled or not, which I have likened to patterns of engagement on the protodiscursive taskscape, into the world of hierarchic cognition.[46]

Linguist Ray Jackendoff, whose ideas on protolanguage came up in Chapter 3, has teamed with composer Fred Lerdahl to offer another approach to musical hierarchies, this one concerning the large-scale phrase shapes and balances of Western classical music. Starting again from certain general findings of Gestalt psychologists, especially grouping principles, Lerdahl and Jackendoff describe nested hierarchies of groups of musical events perceived against a background grid of metrical hierarchies of strong and weak beats. They adapt the tree diagrams of linguists to plot the importance of individual pitches or events at the several levels of their hierarchies and attempt to discern, in the manner of Jackendoff's teacher Noam Chomsky, the rules behind this music's "generative grammar."[47] The endpoint of Lerdahl and Jackendoff's analysis, though they follow a very different path than Narmour, is a hierarchic charting of binary patterns of expectation reminiscent of Meyer.

In more recent work they extend their model beyond Western music, in a direction that aims to highlight innate human musical capacities. This new path follows even more clearly in Meyer's footsteps, as Lerdahl and Jackendoff describe patterns of tension and relaxation, relate them to the kinship of motion and musical gesture that binds music and dance across humanity, and finally posit this connection of body and cognition as an important source of music's power to arouse emotional response. This work outlines a merger of their theory of hierarchic generativity in music with a deep phylogenetic history.[48]

The joining of evolutionary themes to Meyerian expectational and hierarchic models of musical affect and perception is made all the more explicit, finally, by music cognitivist David Huron.[49] Building from basic, evolved mechanisms of response and emotional arousal, he details the automatic, future-oriented structure of expectation, dissecting it into five different stages, both predictive and reactive in relation to the stimulus. He examines the grounding of expectations in mental structures shaped in relation to environmental structures and the roles of memory, learning, and habituation in forming them. All this elaborated expectation-and-response theory, then, he employs to analyze our responses to the large-scale hierarchies of music: the perceptions of pitch hierarchies that characterize tonality, of nested rhythmic periodicity and meter, and of musical schemas and the styles and genres generated from them.

These approaches to auditory perception, music cognition, and musical structure highlight the roles in them of hierarchy, and this hierarchization connects musicking, in a general way, to the innovations we have delineated in Neandertal culture. The approaches leave to one side, however, the more specific issue of combinatorial or compositional hierarchies, also evident in the

Middle Paleolithic toolkit. Metric perception, for example, creates containment hierarchies—nested sets of pulses, with durational patterns gauged against them according to more complex patterns of grouping and expectation—but there is no sign of the kind of combinatorial structuring represented in composite tools. Such hierarchies appear, instead, in music's building of discrete pitches into melodies.

As we saw in Chapter 3, combinatorial structuring is at work not only in language, where sentences are composed of discrete words and words themselves of combinations of phonemes relatively few in number in any language, but in melody also. In all three cases small, mutually distinct units, selected from limited sets, compose an in-principle limitless array of larger units. Component units may recur freely within a larger unit and also recur in any number of units. This makes possible the potentially huge proliferation of units at the higher level and explains an alternative name for such structuring: discrete infinity. In cognizing the compositional hierarchies of language and musicking we seem to attend to two functional levels. The effect of the organization does not accumulate across several levels, as in the containment hierarchies of musical meter, but comes about at a single shift between levels, as an effect akin to a phase transition: from phonemes to words, for example, or (a separate hierarchy, employing distinct cognition and production) from words to sentences, or from pitches to melodies.[50] Thus phonemes do not refer or bear displaced meaning, while morphemes and words do; and sentences present kinds of propositional meaning that isolated words cannot, except in special pragmatic contexts. Melodies suggest kinds of integrated coherence and hence raise expectational patterns and embody expressive forces that individual pitches cannot, again with the exception of special contextual circumstances.[51]

The musical instance is not quite the same as the linguistic ones, however. Our perception of melodic coherence in most musicking depends on many things: on metric and rhythmic concerns—both local durational and metric aspects and the larger containment hierarchies of phrases and subphrases—on the hierarchies of pitches themselves involved in tonality, on sheer proximity of one pitch to another, on timbral and dynamic changes, and more. It depends also on the aspect of our intonational perception whose evolution was reviewed in Chapter 3: the gauging of general pitch contours. The joining of these two systems of musical pitch perception makes melodic cognition a strikingly bivalent affair, with discrete pitch subject to hierarchization of several sorts in its effects and simultaneously building larger units cognized in a more general fashion.[52]

Another way of putting this would be to say that melodies are at once cognized in an ancient analog fashion, going back to the gesture-calls and their development in protodiscourse, and a more recent digital fashion, with the digital mode overlaid on the older, analog one. The combinatorial processing at the digital level reflects a kind of cognition that first appears, in the archaeological record, in the construction of composite tools.

Discrete Neandertals

New abilities to process information appear in Mousterian operational sequences, organizing it in hierarchic and combinatorial fashion. We can easily (if generally) imagine the changes associated with them, and not only in technology—for example, more flexible communication and more dependable decipherment of the signaled expectations of others. The reliable covariance always a part of information transmission was now coming to be elaborated in unprecedented ways. We know much less than we wish about the social structures of Neandertal groups, but it is certainly likely that they mirrored in some fashion the new informational patterns. At the least they must have elaborated orders of precedence and power in ways more complex than those witnessed in their predecessors or in today's nonhuman primates; at most they may have marked social hierarchy with body paint, constructed ornament, and more.

Meanwhile music theorists, cognitivists, and psychologists,

in their efforts to identify the structuring of modern musical expression at the most general level, converge on the ideas of complex acoustic information deployed hierarchically and organized discretely so as to arouse bifurcating expectations that may be fulfilled or thwarted. Even in the most optimistic estimates of Neandertal capacities, similarities and analogies between the patterns of their taskscapes and such modern human attainments must be drawn with caution. Their suggestive nature might be summed up as a question: Can we imagine that *music-like information*—not musicking itself, but rather the *kind* of information musicking would later exploit, complexly organized but independent of semantic reference and symbolic leaps—can we imagine that such information may have become a part of communication amid the growing intricacies and precision of Middle Paleolithic technosociality? If the suggestion were accepted, then the role of Neandertal evidence in the incremental histories of musicking and language would be to attest to further stages in the cognitive foundations for each, albeit before either one of them emerged fully into their modern forms. It would mark a new culmination in the gathering intricacies of societies of protodiscourse and extended (if not transcended) copresence.

By now in this study it might go without saying that any capacities sharpening hominins' regularities of interaction and the precision of their cognitive entrainment can be viewed as facilitating in a general way the ultimate emergence of musicking. There is a large gap, however, between the Neandertal capacities described here and communal activities governed by musical meter—the group drumming and dance I raised before, for example. We have little reason to think that Neandertals bridged this gap. True metric entrainment, in this scenario, emerged late, only with *Homo sapiens*, and not even with the earliest *sapiens*, at that. It is a recent development in an evolution of modes of social entrainment that are manifested at an earlier, advanced stage in Neandertal capacities, but that reach back very far indeed in more rudimentary forms. Nevertheless, we can at least say with confidence that the hierarchies later involved in meter and the procedural synchronies later involved in dance were not foreign to Neandertals' transmitted culture. These were hominins capable of perceiving the world and acting in and on it according to such structures.

For this there is one more tantalizing bit of archaeological evidence. From a few sites associated with Neandertals there survive bones incised with more or less regular, parallel lines or notches.[53] These reveal an operational sequence registering spatial regularities, and hence suggest patterns of action and cognition capable of the same. Beyond this they have inspired much speculation, some of it envisaging whole realms of Neandertal symbolism. A less extravagant speculation might see in the notches rhythmic information without referent, a spatial, material imprinting of the temporal experience of isochrony.

Less speculative still is the proposal offered here: that the innovations of Neandertals and our coeval ancestors who practiced similar technologies—the hierarchized cognition behind their procedures, the composite tools they came to make, their increasing distancing of thought, lengthening of operational sequences, and mediation of environmental affordances—all suggest a communicative sociality far more elaborate than that of earlier, Acheulean hominins. The new patterns apparent in the Neandertal record must have manifested themselves in the gestures of protodiscourse, most likely elaborating them in the same directions of hierarchic and compositional structuring, thus enriching them in ways that anticipate both musicking and language. This may have involved, in addition to the proliferation of acoustic signals, some extension of their referentiality beyond the intimate, deictic meanings of earlier societies of copresence. It may even have sharpened the emotive intonational shapes of vocal gestures, pushing them toward the production and perception of discrete pitch. On the Mousterian taskscape, operational sequences combining hierarchy and discrete combinatoriality met with a protodiscourse in which gathering complexities of design

171

answered to adaptive pressures for communicative efficacy and versatility. There is good reason to think that the gestures of the one affected in some fashion the other.

In other words: Neandertals did not sing as modern humans do, and they did not speak a modern language; but their fashioning of the material world preserves traces of powerful cognitive patterns at once protomusical and protolinguistic.

CHAPTER FIVE

100,000 Years Ago:
Symbolic *et non*

An Archaeological Conundrum

Far past the midway point of the chronological span of this book, we still have not encountered musicking. Instead, we have witnessed its incremental preformation, reconstructing the accumulation of capacities foundational for several distinctively human behaviors, musicking among them. These capacities carry us to the verge of human modernity. To witness its coalescence and to locate the place of musicking in it, however, will require coming to grips with another capacity ubiquitous in modern humans, *symbolic cognition*. This phrase and related words—symbol, symbolism—have appeared more than once in the preceding chapters, usually as a point of contrast to the capacities of early hominins. Exploring symbolic cognition more carefully here will involve a few other concepts also raised in those chapters: information, meaning, reference and referentiality, and representation. And it will add to this family a new set of concepts regarding the *sign* and its operation, that is, *semiosis*. For though the term symbol has many uses, it will for us assume its most productive form under the aegis of a broader theory of the sign.

Since at least the time of Cassirer and Langer, symbol-making has been understood to be a defining capacity of our humanity, one indeed that seems to be unique to our species in the world today. It could hardly help but figure prominently in attempts to discern the emergence of our modernity. Across the twentieth century, moreover, this prominence had a specifically archaeological stimulus. This was the uncovering of fascinating, even awe-inspiring remains of Paleolithic traditions that are, in any commonsense view, symbolic in nature: the representational cave painting and figural sculpture of Europe, with beginnings now traced back about 40,000 years. These practices, associated with the dispersion across the continent of "anatomically modern humans"—*Homo sapiens* as opposed to *neanderthalensis*—are still used by some archaeologists to mark off ancient Europeans from other humans and thereby set, in Eurocentric fashion, the border-line between Middle and Upper Paleolithic periods.[1]

For most, however, symbolic behavior is no longer seen as the exclusive province of early European *sapiens*. Important developments occurred in association with sapient populations in the Levant, long before they made it to western Europe. A rising star, African *sapiens*, has threatened to steal the show in recent years, entering from the wings with anticipations of European symbolism reaching back much more than twice as far, well into the Middle Stone Age (as this era is named in African periodization). Meanwhile, as we saw in Chapter 4, Neandertals have laid claim to a comprimario role through putative burials of their dead, red ochre or manganese dioxide "crayons" perhaps used for face, body, or other coloring, ornamental artifacts such as teeth or shells perforated for hanging on a necklace, and even bones incised with regular markings.

The symbolic heritage of the European Upper Paleolithic is for the most part a familiar one.[2] It includes "parietal" or wall work of many sorts, ranging from the animal depictions of Altamira, Lascaux, and (the much earlier) Chauvet to nonfigural finger fluting and other manipulations of soft cave walls. Numerous female "Venus" figurines, some of them dating back more than 20,000 years, rank among its most famous pieces, and the history of sculpture has been extended in a spectacular series of animal figurines (and one Venus) unearthed in southwest Germany, carved from mammoth ivory and reaching back to about the 40,000-year mark. From the same sites and the same era have come examples of pipes with carefully made finger holes, presumably for musical use, fashioned both from hollow wing bones of birds and from hollowed-out segments of mammoth tusk—a complex composite construction. These new finds are associated with the technology known as the Aurignacian, the earliest widespread European assemblage associated with *Homo sapiens*.[3]

Somewhat less familiar, meanwhile, are recent discoveries in southwest Asia and Africa that push back the horizon of symbolic behavior. Perforated shells probably fashioned for stringing have been unearthed in widely dispersed sites in Israel, Morocco, and South Africa and reach back as much as 100,000 years. Tanzanian and Kenyan beadlike artifacts carved from ostrich shell date from 40,000 years ago—and perhaps much earlier.[4] In caves in South Africa, meanwhile, numerous riveting finds over the last two decades have shifted thinking about symbolism: fragments of 60,000-year-old ostrich shell carefully incised, enough pieces of ochre scratched with geometric designs to suggest engraving cultures stretching from 70,000 to 100,000 years ago, and abalone-shell "paint pots" 100,000 years old, still containing dried ochre-based pigment and unearthed alongside hammerstones for grinding the ingredients and a bone stirrer.[5]

Archaeologists have reached a general consensus that all these Eurasian and African artifacts present evidence of symbolic behavior. But this litany of artifacts suggests no single kind of symbol, and in the face of it archaeologists have been hard-pressed to account for such remains by thinking carefully about symbolism in general. Their consensus recalls Justice Stewart's we-know-it-when-we-see-it reasoning, and it tends to start from seemingly indubitable examples—the lions or rhinoceroses of Chauvet or the animal figurines of Germany—and then extend the type to less clear instances—those European parietal flutings or the geometrical incisions from South Africa. Such implicit definition as emerges from this strategy links symbolism to the making of pictorial or figural likenesses—*iconic representation*, in other words—and indeed "symbolic representation" is a phrase that recurs often in these discussions. But the nature of the assumptions that permit us to connect representational to non-representational artifacts remains obscure, and even the bottom-line confidence that we can identify ancient representation when we see it has been questioned by art historian Whitney Davis.[6] His challenge is all the more effective because it issues from the discipline in which the search for the "origins" of representation has seemed most seductive at least since Henri Breuil dubbed Altamira the "Paleolithic Sistine Chapel."

Iconic approaches, being artifact-driven, are also limited in what they reveal of activities that might reflect symbolic capacity in less palpable ways. Take, for example, a human interment marked and ritualized in some measure by *Homo sapiens* or Neandertals. Whatever might be "represented" in the scattering of flowers or ground ochre around a grave, it is less clear than the depiction of an aurochs or a mammoth. And iconism, moreover, does not take account of the gorilla in the room: language, immaterial symbolic medium par excellence. Few archaeologists would maintain that pictorial or plastic representation arose before or independent of the emergence of modern language. This means that symbolic behavior took immaterial as well as material form from an early stage, and it underscores the need for a conception of symbolism much broader than iconic ones. Restricted to such representation, the symbol may seem to demarcate a starting point for human modernity but in reality poses only puzzles.

There is another, systematic difficulty posed by the emphasis on iconic representation: In limiting too narrowly the range of symbolism, it obscures its place in a wider biosemiotics. This will become clear when we take up a different approach to the problem in the tradition of Charles Sanders Peirce, for whom a distinction drawn between iconism and symbolism was basic. Locating symbols in this larger context allows us to view them as something other than miracles *ex nihilo* brought about by *Homo sapiens* and (perhaps) his closest relatives. It connects them to the coevolutionary flux of culture and nature that formed the hominin niche and, more broadly still, to the overarching informational flows that give rise to semiosis in all its varieties. To approach this other orientation we must slant our vocabulary away from the symbol as such (though we will finally return to it) toward symbolic cognition and behavior. We must also broaden our disciplinary purview to include not only archaeology but also a phylogenetic cognitivism conceived along biocultural and coevolutionary lines—to include, in other words, accounts of the emergence of the modern human mind more speculative than some archaeologists find congenial.

This move will help us, finally, to describe the underlying connections of the symbol to nonsymbolic modes of signification, including musicking. Here the terrain is challenging. At the beginning of Chapter 4, we saw that music stands in a relation to symbolism—in its basic sense of representation or reference—that is at least equivocal, wedded to it in some ways and divorced from it in others. Illuminating this relation can shed light on the different path along which music emerged. But the equivocation of musicking in regard to symbol-making is perennial and aboriginal; music may be described in the broadest sense as organized acoustic informational flows not in themselves symbolic but always constrained by the surrounding operation of symbols. An understanding of the coalescence of human modernity in its final form must take account of the inevitable entangling of a nonsymbolic musicking in symbolic webs, and this requires clear understanding of their nature and construction.

Regressive Symbolism

Some of the most perceptive recent approaches to the emergence of symbolic cognition blur the distinction between it and nonsymbolic or presymbolic capacities, thus suggesting a symbolism that can be seen to regress toward the ancient vanishing point of hominin culture. Evolutionary psychologist Merlin Donald, for example, whose views of early hominin mimesis we met in Chapter 2, considers symbolic thought an emergent byproduct of social and biological coevolution, unique to humans today but connected seamlessly to the long development of mammalian consciousness. The later stages of this development juxtaposed a number of special features of the hominin lineage with complex sociality, including expanded capacities for mimesis and theory of mind along with new forms of self-evaluating, metacognitive awareness—this last a kind of vast expansion of the rehearsal capacities he had discerned in earlier hominins. From this constellation arose the "cognitive communities" and "distributed symbolic systems" characteristic of humans, reliant on both language and the many technologies of external symbolic storage we have devised, from cave painting to cloud computing. Donald's argument is an aggressively continuous one, since he regards external networks of symbols as a late accretion on tendencies extending far back in the evolution of hominins and mammals more generally, and this is a strong point in its favor; but along the way he provides little specificity regarding the exact nature of symbolic cognition or the mechanisms of its emergence.[7]

The challenge that arises here is in essence one of demarcating categorical change along the line of a continuous history. It recurs in the coevolutionary views of theorists Eva Jablonka and Marion Lamb, encountered in Chapter 1. Symbolic information, for them, is one of four kinds of information in the biosphere, alongside genetic, epigenetic, and behavioral types. Like Donald, they consider it unique to our species, "a diagnostic trait of human beings," and they name several features that make it so. In the first place, symbols arise in systems or arrays, alongside other symbols, and take their meanings in part by virtue of their places in these arrays. This is an important feature, but we will see later, in treating discrete pitch, that systematicity is not limited to symbols and does not necessarily create referential meaning. Second, symbolic information can be "latent," transmitted without enactment, demonstration, or imitation, unlike the behavioral information of both human and nonhuman animals. This latency, third, is made possible by either referential language or technologies for the external storage of information in some material (or virtual) form. External symbolic storage thus looms large for Jablonka and Lamb, as it does for Donald.[8]

But can behavioral and symbolic types of information be so neatly distinguished? We have already witnessed, as early as Acheulean bifaces, modes of information transfer unique to hominins and externally stored, but not symbolic in Jablonka and Lamb's sense. The transmission of those operational sequences was an embodied, unmediated passage of information resulting from special hominin capacities—on the face of it, a clear instance of behavioral information. However, the bifaces themselves fixed cultural traditions in their crystalline forms long before a time when we have any evidence of the leap to language or referentiality. In this they can hardly be excluded from the category of external information-storage devices emphasized by Donald and Jablonka and Lamb. Also, it is by no means implausible that the immensely long Acheulean tradition, once established, took on some degree of latency in the transmission of this stored information, whereby the *observation* of the bifaces, in effect the external loci of cultural memory, could stand in in some measure for the *enactment* of knapping in instructing the neophyte.

Only one aspect of Jablonka and Lamb's symbolic information was surely *not* present in this tradition: the organization of discrete informational bits into larger, self-referential arrays that help to generate their significance. This systematicity is a crucial absence and will provide a starting point below from which to construct a nuanced definition of symbolic cognition. Otherwise, symbolic information as they define it must reach back in unbroken development to merge with the long history of behavioral information from which it derived.

Philosopher Kim Sterelny has recently offered a helpful set of distinctions in this long development, discriminating between different types of Paleolithic artifacts all often regarded, in we-know-it-when-we-see-it fashion, as symbolic. Cave-bear teeth or harvested shells perforated and polished for ornamental wear, he reasons, are symbolic in a different way than paintings or carvings of animals. Because the teeth and shells created little or no displaced reference of the sort involved in pictorial or figural representation, they made smaller "cognitive claims" on the perceiver. Instead, in their rarity, luster, or whatever other feature marked them as special, they posed a more direct expression of the difficulty or danger involved in gathering them. Rather than representations of other, separate objects, they were tokens of the labor, risk, and cost needed to acquire them. Sterelny thinks of status symbols and he jokes about "Middle Stone Age Ferraris"; but there is a serious, quasi-Marxian trajectory to the argument, in which objects come to be expressions of the labor—that is, the sociality—involved in their production.[9] There is also, in Sterelny's thinking, a collapse of the symbol into a different kind of sign, the *index*—to introduce terms from Peircean semiotic theory we will come back to.

This ancient symbolism arose not from some general system or array in which symbols found their places, in the manner of a military insignia that marks a rank in an overarching conceptual structure—a manner we will focus on in Chapter 7 as a primary reflection of a *transcendental* sociality. Instead the signification of these objects was produced by their proximity to the effort by which they came to be ornaments; by extension from this they could serve as tokens of other, related efforts and achievements. To put it in terms developed in Chapters 2 and 3, such symbolism marks the culling of environmental affordances or marshaling of them into a taskscape. It is a material sociality built from the bottom up.

The case is similar for ochre, collected by early *Homo sapiens* and Neandertals and possibly used for face or body painting. This putative painting should not be thought of as an independent symbol, according to Sterelny, but as an alteration of an already existing bodily sign. A painted face might exaggerate the features of a normal grimace, making it look more terrifying in an ambush-hunt than it could otherwise appear. This is signal enhancement and, again, distinct from symbols such as paintings of things or, for that matter, from words. In it we find an external medium of gestural intensification, an amplification of transmitted information, rather than an instance of modern displaced reference or representation. To indulge in an acoustical metaphor, the paint makes something *louder*. We mark a connecting and reorganizing of informational circuits rather than a symbolic leap.

If we follow Sterelny in thinking of tooth necklaces and ochre as symbols, we see that they narrow dramatically the divide or displacement between a sign and its object. But such narrowing of the distance of signification operates between the body and *any* artifact by which it is extended into the world; a stick or club amplifies an arm in the same way that face painting amplifies a grimace. So Sterelny's extension of the notion of symbolism must reach to all transmitted signs of labor and achievement. As in the cases of Jablonka and Lamb or Donald, a long regression of symbolism opens out. Since forms of production transmitted from generation to generation in the guise of stone tools reach back to the earliest Acheulean traditions we can trace, stone tool production itself—*culture* itself—comes from its first appearance to be pervasively symbolic.

Sterelny's symbolism, then, is not only regressive but also hugely expansive, and in this it veers toward classic models from cultural anthropology, though these were rarely couched in evolutionary terms. Marshall Sahlins, for example, examined both Marxist practical reason and a tradition of naturalistic, functional anthropology and found them to be wanting, unable to account for human systems of meaning in any but reductive ways. Symbolic webs of culture cannot be mediated outgrowths of material circumstance, he argued, because all human productivity and labor is suspended in these webs. Symbols are the social always-already in which systems of production take place, and there can be no one-way causality flowing from an asocial or acultural base of production up toward a cultural superstructure.

Sahlins imputes to Marx something like a definition of the symbol, though he puts it in riddling terms: "How can we account for an existence of persons and things that cannot be recognized in the physical nature of either?"[10] Marx provided a partial answer in his lesson that the objects of production are social through and through, though they can disguise or obscure this sociality—a lesson brought home famously in his analysis of commodity fetishism and recalled in Sterelny's Pleistocene Ferraris. Marx, however, could not fully incorporate this idea into his concept of use-value, which remained in his theory underdetermined, a generic notion of the answering of human needs. What spells out particular needs? Or, in other words, why *these* products rather than *those*? This question, Sahlins concludes, can only look for its answer to culture itself and its symbolic webs (and perhaps, though Sahlins does not say so, to a Freudian "narcissism of small differences" produced by those webs). But if he is right, we must conclude, the webs cannot be limited to modernity but must extend back to the socially conditioned modes of the earliest traditions of cultural production: Why *these* Acheulean tools rather than *those*?

In both Sahlins's and Sterelny's views, finally, the symbol appears even in the minimal displacement that is the distance between any situation of production, a transitory social circumstance, and the artifact—the scratch on the world, so to speak—it leaves behind. Symbolism is cultural production all the way down, and cultural production symbolism. Beyond this fundamental equation it is only a question of specific modes, greater or lesser displacement of symbol from object represented, and shifting technologies.

Here we have moved far from archaeologists' emphasis of representation or reference, from the stunning novelties of Upper Paleolithic Europe, and even from the recently unearthed African anticipations of them. The move suggests, among other things, that debates over Neandertal symbolic behavior have been engaged in too small an arena. The expansive view of symbolism also blurs helpfully Jablonka and Lamb's overdrawn boundary between symbolism and behavior. The bottom-line qualification

182

for symbolism comes to be something close to repetition itself, that is, the formal congruencies passed through generations that carry the replicated information of mimetic cultural traditions in the first place.[11]

This alternative approach also raises an issue identified in the preceding chapters as a basic one in the evolution of modern cognition and behavior: the interposing of increasing distance in copresent societies. We have already witnessed this in several forms, including the transport of raw materials or tools across ever-larger distances and the longer and longer curation of tools—which is to say, the lengthening of the *chaîne opératoire* itself. By the time of Neandertal industries, this extended sequence had developed new forms of internal organization, hierarchic and incipiently combinatorial. Now distance was extended through novel modes of formal and hence informational complexity in the transmission of cultural forms. Such distance would finally come to be expressed in displaced reference, starting modestly in the deixis of gesture-calls and protodiscourse but later fixed in conventional vocalized symbols approaching the status of words. In this deep history the displacement characteristic of referentiality is a late outgrowth of the move beyond copresence, of thinking-at-a-distance; it gives rise to a specific and recent kind of symbolism within an experience already symbolic in a broader sense.

The regressive symbolism sketched here has been advocated also by some of the archaeologists who have worked hardest to define this aspect of human modernity. Christopher Henshilwood and Curtis Marean, both at the center of recent South African developments, noted in 2003 the insufficiency of attempts to construct a list of defining markers of behavioral modernity. They understand aspects of behavior to be less schematic than such "trait lists" suggest, and they emphasize the behavioral response of hominins across their history to local environmental affordances and demands. These can lead in one circumstance to an intensification of the use of resources, entailing technological and social innovations, that remains absent in another. Operational sequences, in other words, may be extended for largely local reasons. Henshilwood and Marean retain "symbolically organized behavior" as a sine qua non of modernity; but the variable contexts they envisage help them to enlarge considerably what such behavior might comprise: styles of tool making, distinctive uses of space, and idiosyncratic group exploitation of resources all might function as "external symbolic storage."[12]

Closer still to Sterelny's expansive and regressive view is Paul Pettitt's recent "multiregional and multispecies" analysis of emergent symbolism. Taking off from Henshilwood and Marean's localism and their rejection of trait lists, he imagines a long, irregular, and sporadic emergence of symbolism involving multiple species of hominins and reaching back before *Homo sapiens*. This deep history was marked not only by the accumulation and dispersion of local innovations but by their frequent extinction and disappearance as well. And it involved categorical differences in different times and places in the manner of signification of similar actions; these distinctions harken back to Sterelny's judgments on the varying distances between sign and object. Thus an instance of body painting or ornamentation might function as a simple decoration ("for visual effect with no associated symbolic meaning"), an enhancement of another sign (cf. Sterelny's signal amplification), a node made meaningful by its place in a larger code read by others, or, in the most developed case, a marker of a participation in such codes delimited in time and space (or, as we might say, a *ritual*).

Treatment of the dead, the other long-term example Pettitt examines, needs to be understood along a similarly broad spectrum, one that extends well beyond *Homo sapiens* in the world today and must have done so in the past. This reaches from non-symbolic "morbidity"—special interest in or emotional response to a corpse—through opportunistic caching of bodies in natural formations (perhaps as at the Atapuercan "pit of bones" 400,000 years ago), to the self-conscious making of spaces for burial or other deposition. Here too the final stages of a long process might burgeon into the full-fledged ritual marking of places and times, in this case through association with the dead.[13]

Sweeping and regressive views like Sterelny's and Pettitt's include, under the umbrella of symbolism, many different length-enings of operational sequences. They highlight the importance of the "release from proximity" for any account of the evolution of language or other relatively recent features of humanity. At the same time, in looking back beyond these features they also order the deep history of symbolism into differing modes, if not deter-minate historical phases. If there is an overall historical trajectory in these accounts, it traces a path from a long period of sporadic appearances of proximate symbols with narrow displacement toward the late explosion of referential forms incorporating large representational distance. Through this period symbolism took on the aspect of cultural traditions embodied in the material replica-tion of forms—an aspect of a slowly elaborated, often failed, and irregularly accumulated Lower and Middle Paleolithic *formalism*.

Peirce, Deacon, and Emergent Symbolism

These regressive and expansive views generalize the deep his-tory of one important but not defining aspect of symbolism, its referential displacement, as a story of increasing release from proximity; and Sterelny's account, at least, has a good deal to say about how and why this occurred. At the same time, however, they have little to say about the systematization that is basic to the symbol, its participation (pointed out by Jablonka and Lamb) in an array of similar entities from which it derives its meaning. This feature is a foundational aspect of the symbol-making of modern humans, and we will see that it is foundational also for musicking, in an unexpected way that departs from symbolism. In order to move farther with this problem we need other understandings of the symbol than Donald, Sterelny, Pettitt, and the rest offer, and different conceptual tools with which to build them. Several approaches to the emergence of symbolism have recently found these tools in the semiotics of Charles Sanders Peirce.

From a Peircean vantage, Sterelny's and Pettitt's necklaces and painted faces are signs, to be sure; but they are not symbols. They function by means of proximity to, participation in, or causal relation with what they signify, striking up an indicative or "pointing-to" connection involving neither the duplicated likeness of icons nor the overleapt distance and transformative representation of symbols proper. Signs of this kind Peirce termed *indexes* or *indices*, their relation to their object *indexicality*. This is no mere terminological nicety but instead captures an important difference in semiotic operations at work in the biosphere. In its light, Sterelny's or Pettitt's differentiation of several kinds of Paleolithic signs can be seen to mark off stages in a history by which the indexical semiosis of earlier hominins and other animals was transformed into a human or near-human symbolism. The intimate relation of indexicality and symbolism in the archaeological record reveals semiotic processes that were reshaped across this history, leading without any revolutionary break from presymbolic signification to modern modes. The Peircean approach achieves, in other words, the marking of categorical differences in a continuous phylogenetic history. In the process, we will see, it opens a place for the transition from protomusicking to modern musicking.

Indexicality connects early stages of hominin semiosis to the kind of gesture-calls and protodiscourse introduced in Chapter 3. This may be put more strongly: Indexes show a fundamental kinship to the deictic taskscapes of both the late Acheulean (Chapter 3) and the Middle Paleolithic (Chapter 4) periods. This is because the deixis by which communication functioned on those taskscapes was itself indexical in nature. Deictic meanings are context-bound, managing their modest referentiality through their connection to the situations in which they arise and their proximity to what they convey: emotional stances, responses of acceptance or rejection, indications of simple, copresent actions, and so forth. Indexes likewise signify through their proximity to their objects and pointing relations to them. In this dependence on connection and context they differ from symbols and icons; because of this contextual imperative, in addition, they do not require for their meaning the systematic organization of symbols—that discreteness within a larger array characteristic of modern language but not of protodiscourse.

The strong circumstantial evidence for a deictic communication on those Paleolithic taskscapes is, then, evidence at the same time for a mainly indexical culture. It reveals a semiotic mode that came naturally to the inhabitants and makers of protodiscursive, protolinguistic, protomusical, and little- or nondiscretized worlds. By the Middle Paleolithic period, the index, like the gesture-call, came to be manipulated with unprecedented power.

The emergence of symbolic cognition that eventually followed on these developments—the emergence of symbolism from indexicality—has been traced in Peircean terms by biologist and anthropologist Terrence Deacon, whose general theories of coevolution we met in Chapter 1. Following his account in some detail will further clarify the continuities adduced above on the long road to symbolic cognition; pointing up some shortcomings of the account, conversely, will bring us back, finally, to musicking.[14]

We start with a general term, *emergence*, that highlights the central role of information in the intricacies of biocultural coevolution. Deacon distinguishes three orders of emergence.[15] Simple kinds of emergent organization characterize countless systems, organic and inorganic, in which aggregates show properties that are not predictable from the traits of their individual components—for example, liquidity in aggregates of certain molecules. (This amounts to a basic working definition of emergence in its recent usage.[16]) At a more complex level, stages of self-organization can condition and constrain further stages, as in the multistage formation of a snowflake. This characterizes for Deacon second-order emergence, in which organization takes shape on a prior platform of emergent organization. A different way of describing this would be to say that second-order emergence gives rise to *historicity*, since information resulting in one state of organization creates conditions defining the informational possibilities for later states. (Information itself, we remember from Chapter 4, requires nothing more than Fodor's "reliable causal covariance.") Second-order emergence, like the first-order variety, is widespread in nonliving as well as living systems.[17]

Deacon's third-order emergence is unique to living systems. Here coded units or bundles of information—as transmitted, for example, in DNA and RNA molecules—can be continuously reentered, more or less faithfully, into future systems, thereby constraining not merely single instances but whole lineages of future emergence. Historicity takes on new replicative possibilities. While second-order emergence involves one emergent state constraining a later one, third-order emergence involves also information isolated from and passed independent of an earlier state of emergent forces in which it took shape.[18] It involves, then, information *about* information, or *metainformation*.

Although Deacon does not carry his analysis in this direction, there is a huge arena of metainformational replication in the biosphere that is distinct if not disconnected from genetic codes: the arena of animal perception of and response to environmental affordance. Viewed as an informational dynamic, this arena forms a broad and ancient semiotics that has governed animate life for eons, a semiosis in which whole packages of animate responses to environments are passed through generations. Such *biosemiosis* was first theorized in ethological studies of the early twentieth century, especially those of Jacob von Uexküll, whose notion of *Umwelt* aimed to describe as an interpretation of signs the niche construction of animals as far removed from humans as ticks.[19] Viewed from the vantage of Deacon's categories, the regularities of these relations are instances of third-order emergence.

In more recent years, biosemioticians describing this far-flung *semiosphere* have exploited and extended Peirce's theories of signification. Peirce maintained that semiosis in all its forms manifests a triadic relation, a fundamental ontological category he termed *thirdness*. A sign relation comes about not merely as a connection of one thing (sign) to another (object); such *secondness* has no power to signify. Instead, semiosis is a product of the active engagement of a perceiver, which intersects with two entities so as to make one a sign in relation to the other.[20] In our terms this thirdness of signs means that they are always metainformational. Information itself, instead, exists and is transmitted already in relations of secondness, hence presemiotic, nonsignifying relations.

Extending the terminological thread, signs are not merely relational but *metarelational*, arising from a relation to a relation.[21] The perceiver's engagement is fundamental, and isolating it was perhaps the most important of Peirce's many contributions to semiotics. He called this element of thirdness in all signs *interpretant*. He saw also that the interpretant can only be, in its own relation to the sign/object unit, another sign, requiring its own interpretant and setting up an infinite regress in signification. In a more implicit way, Peirce recognized an affinity between the interpretant, with its causal action, and the index, with its semiotic relation of contiguity, proximity, touching, pointing, or causality. For this reason the index seems often to stand to the fore in his writings, more basic to semiosis than icon and symbol, the other two sign-types in his famous triad.

A specific case, fundamental to my account, of the metainformational emergence characteristic of biosemiotics is the compiling of the intergenerational archives that define hominin culture. These constrain future generations by contributing to the relation of individual and environment within which selective pressures are shaped, but they do this by passing on *accumulating* bodies of information from individual to individual and generation to generation. In these growing archives the pervasive, ancient biosemiosis swerves in a novel direction, reshaped according to a set of capacities more or less limited to the recent primate lineage and especially hominins within it. The capacities involve, minimally, features we have isolated in Chapters 2 and 3: deictic indication of objects in the world, joint attention to them, and mimicry or imitation. There will be much more to say in Chapters 6 and 7 about the extension of these and about accumulating cultural archives in late hominin evolution.

Deacon's achievement has been to describe this swerve in the hominin lineage from the vantage of Peircean biosemiotics in a way that illuminates symbolic cognition in *Homo sapiens*.[22] To do this he analyzes the informational dynamic involved in the emergence of the symbol from the more basic semiotic functions of iconism and indexicality. The perception of *iconic similarity* is shared by a wide array of cognizant species, in principal by any organism with a neuromuscular system. Its simplest form is a perception of the environment from which difference is absent, a default mode in which the intrusion of markings of difference looms as an interpretant-generating stimulus to action. Even this most basic semiosis remains an instance of Peirce's thirdness, a relation to a relation, and requires the interpretant. In bringing the presence or absence of difference to the heart of semiosis, ico-nicity can be seen to underlie systems of innate animal response to the world, whereby aspects of external stimuli are taken to identify food, predator, or mate.

Indexical association or proximity, instead, is a mode of per-ception found in far fewer species, mainly mammals and birds. It requires the capacity to learn from past experience to connect distinct perceptions—smoke and fire, in the famous example, or a moving shadow on the ground and a flying predator overhead. Through this learning, remembered connections can be applied to present circumstances. This results in a matching of pres-ent and past associations, even where the present perception is incomplete: smoke or shadow alone. This matching is as a whole iconic (the form, present shadow + its learned association, is an icon of past experience) and thus reveals the dependence of a semiosis involving learning on a prior, unlearned iconism. In effect, learning enables some species to kick iconic perception onto a higher level, yielding indexical association. Indexicality is iconism transcended and thereby transformed.

The emergence of *symbolism* requires an additional level and has been achieved in the world today only by humans and perhaps a few animals they have trained.[23] As associative indexes multiply and accumulate through learning, there occurs something like a phase transition in cognition. This is made possible by increased capacities for episodic memory and attention and for the learning of associations, and it functions in part as a mnemonic alleviation of the overloading of memory involved in all that indexical learning. At this threshold a categorical change in semiosis occurs whereby the accumulated indexes form and circulate in a system of their own. The elements in this system—symbols—point to one another in the manner of indexes; words, for instance, take their meanings from a system of differences marking them off from other, similar words. Thus indexicality is at work in symbolic relations, just as iconism works in indexicality. This self-sustaining systematicity of symbols governs their semiosis, opening a mediating distance between sign (within the system) and object (outside it); such mediation marks a kind of reference new in the biosphere. The distance is however filled in, again, by indexicality—a second order of indexicality operating within symbolism; and this second indexicality pins a symbolic system as a whole to aspects of reality external to it or, put differently, enables the symbolic system to be mapped onto that set of external aspects.[24] In language, for example, the *referent* of any word, however clear its *meaning*, remains ambiguous until some form of deixis, which can be linguistic or extralinguistic, points it toward something outside language.

A general feature of Peircean biosemiosis highlighted in Deacon's analysis is a hierarchical relation among the three kinds of signification, whereby indexicality depends on iconism and symbolism depends on both. Noting this relation is important, because it reflects the continuity of semiosis across the realm of animate life. Complex semiotic processes comprise and are founded upon less complex ones not only in the generation of signs—the making of interpretants—but also in phylogenetic history. Semiosis is always dynamic, in each of its modes a distinct stage, more-or-less complex, emerging from perception and interpretant.[25]

Several emergent aspects of symbolism arise from its systematicity.[26] Most generally, it introduces into semiosis the possibility of the kind of hierarchy discussed in Chapter 4, a combinatorial organization in which discrete individual components of the same general order are joined together in larger signifying units. The systematicity can also generate internal relations among the symbols that help to determine their meanings, and these can take several forms: typological or categorical distinctions among them, rules governing their juxtaposition, and hierarchical orderings of them. The parts of speech of language exemplify typological distinctions within a single class (words). We have seen another, nonsemantic instance of such a typology in the composite tools discussed in Chapter 4, with stone points or blades functionally distinct from wooden hafts or handles, adhesives, and leather straps. Rules of governance, instead, are represented by the syntax and grammar of language, while the general complexities of sentence structure represented in Chomskyan tree diagrams reveal hierarchical organization. In language, moreover, syntax and categorical distinction not only make possible the generation of larger symbol units, which carry more intricate and complex information than single words, but also enable symbols to form indexes within the symbolic system that point beyond it—deictic elements, for example ("*this* chair, not *that* one").

In the end, Deacon suggests that grammar-like rules are necessarily cocreated with symbols at least in some rudimentary fashion.[27] But we need to take a deep breath here, because his suggestion begs a few questions critical to accounting for the emergence of music. Do systematicity and combinatoriality require syntactic or grammatical governance? Are there more and less restrictive versions of such governance? In general, how close is the relation between systematicity and the symbol? Later on I will argue that tonality, a pervasive tendency if not universal feature of pitch organization in musicking, shows systematicity and combinatorial hierarchy, both characteristic of the symbol; but tonality shows neither categorical distinction nor a rule-governance tantamount to a grammar, and it symbolizes nothing. Neither are the individual pitches in tonal systems symbols. They are barely signs of any kind, but they still give rise to larger indexical units. This suggests a semiotic operation characteristic of music that Deacon, along with many others, has ignored: an *indexical systematicity*, that is, a high-level upstructuring with no symbolic outcome.

Symbolocentrism and the Indexical Challenge

In the light of this Peircean analysis, the coevolutionary epicycle of vocalized deixis in the late Acheulean period described in Chapter 3 takes its place in the broader course of hominin indexicality. It stands prior to Deacon's symbolism, which, for its part, we can see as a later, *symbolic epicycle* involving the three components symbol, syntax, and combinatorial generativity. Here, it will be evident, Peirce and Deacon together have carried us very far from the ill-defined idea of iconic symbols—mammoths on cave walls—with which we started.

For Deacon, as for the archaeologists, the emergence of symbolism marks a watershed in the development of human modernity, a leap in cognition that crucially defines our species. Its impact on human ways is wide and deep. Language is its most fundamental aspect, but it also undergirds most other distinctively human behaviors and cognitive and perceptual modes, including the capacity for humor, the conceptual structures of discovery, the spiritual or religious imaginary and its rituals, and what he calls the "aesthetic faculty." All these, Deacon argues, rely on an ability to blend concepts so they can be held in relation to one another and engender new, unanticipated concepts, an ability originating in the combinatorial generativity of symbolic cognition and the flexible distance that arises between a system of signs and the objects to which they refer. All these capacities, also, result in emergent affective valences, complex emotions that are themselves blended and probably unique to humans. Artistic experience in particular exploits these, holding them in an unresolved tension productive of further conceptual and emotive emergence.

Deacon founds even the experience of music without words or program on the bedrock of symbolic cognition, though he understands that it is not in itself symbolic. Our ability to follow complex sonic designs is for him an instance of our cognizing of individual patterns according to systems governing them, and this marks it as an outgrowth of symbolic systematization. And our ability to correlate sonic structures to blended emotional states and transitions among them—states in themselves dependent on the working of symbolism—requires the mapping of one systematization onto another.[28] Here Deacon's restricting of systematization to the symbolic mode of signification is clear; in the face of the indexical systematization mentioned earlier, his view of music requires revision.

However widespread the effects of symbolic cognition may be, its richest enactment, for Deacon as for many others, occurs in language. His nuanced hypothesis for the emergence of our language capacities involves all the processes of his multiplex biocultural coevolution described in Chapter 1, and we may name them more or less in the order of their cascading impact: increasingly intricate and self-defining systems of information, the feed-forward effects of these epicycles on niche construction, weakened selective pressure and the resulting dedifferentiation of genetic controls, cultural offloading of behaviors, and sociocultural diversification. With a nod to dedifferentiation in domesticated species, Deacon regards *Homo sapiens* as a species "self-domesticated" through symbolic culture. As the innate calls of our ancestors were loosed from genetic control and selective pressures, vocalization diversified through social and cultural transmission. Early on in this process the accumulation of signals resulted in the phase-transition to systematization described above. After this symbolic threshold was crossed, referentiality and grammar came to be connected to increasingly varied vocalization, setting up further communication- and culture-driven feedback loops and selective pressures.[29]

Here again Deacon discovers symbolic cognition behind the emergence of a complex human behavior—in this case flexible, consciously controlled, referential, systematized, syntactic vocalization. But the inhibiting force of his symbolocentrism is apparent, for his view pushes him toward the narrow mainstream of thought on the emergence of language and protolanguage described in Chapter 3. As we saw there, writers in this Chomskyan current have primarily sought to explain the emergence of semanticity and grammar. This agenda unites very diverse views, for example Derek Bickerton's lexicon-first, grammar-later model, Alison Wray's argument for the primacy of holistic semantic utterances, Ray Jackendoff's chronology of specific increments in the shift from protolanguage to language, and Stephen Pinker and Paul Bloom's general assertion, in the face of Chomsky's own doubts, that selective dynamics might explain the emergence of language.

All these views focus on the design features of human language that distinguish it from the vocalizations of other animals. Doing so, they tilt explanatory strategies toward a presumption of human exceptionalism rather than one of human participation in the broader semiosphere and evolution of communication. In aligning itself with these approaches, Deacon's symbolocentrism leads him to a position at odds with his own biosemiotic approach, which otherwise counters human exceptionalism and phylogenetic discontinuity in its extension of Peircean signification far beyond our species. Making the emergence of diversified vocalization dependent on symbolic cognition in effect retreats to a less encompassing position than this Peircean one. From a deep historical vantage, it is ill equipped to encounter the strong evidence for the development of varied and expressive gesture-calls *long before* symbolic cognition, as described in Chapter 3.

The aspects of modern language underemphasized in Chomskyan and Deaconian approaches to protolanguage include its prosody and pragmatics. These come front and center, instead, in focusing on protodiscourse. This was a medium dependent on pointing and deixis, constructed from intonational shapes, rhythms of articulation and exchange, and the other pragmatic elements of gesture-calls. From a semiotic vantage, we have seen, its deixis ties it closely to indexicality. At the same time, protodiscourse was not without order. It was a "sequenced communicative behavior," in Jill Bowie's phrase, and in it a nascent, rudimentary syntax of social interaction took shape, prior to and distinct from linguistic grammar.

The joining in protodiscourse of indexicality and incipient order returns us to the possibility, raised earlier, of the systematizing of indexes. In the analysis of modern language such systematizing has taken center stage in recent years in the *metapragmatics* associated especially with linguistic anthropologist Michael Silverstein. For him, the pragmatics of human language is fundamentally a question of the index, encompassing "the totality of indexical relationships between occurrent signal forms and their contexts." Since modern humans all deploy this pragmatics in frameworks that extend beyond mere contexts for discursive performance into *reflection* on such performance, indexical pragmatics plays itself out in mutual interaction with larger forces of ordering and organization—hence, *metapragmatic* forces. Indeed, no large-scale coherence or directedness of discourse is possible except in this interaction, which relates indexes to one another in aggregates at a higher hierarchic level. Such a metapragmatics shows systematicity to involve the indexes as well as the symbols of modern discourse. For Silverstein this ordering is particularly prominent in many manners of formalized discourse, and he singles out, among these, ritual forms, marked most profoundly not by semantics or grammar but by the complexly ordered configurations of the indexes involved in them.[30]

This metapragmatics carries basic implications for the deep history of discourse and the emergence of musicking with which it was bound. (I reserve the question of the emergence of ritual for Chapter 7.) Tracing the route along which the *reflexivity* of metapragmatics emerged is another way of exploring the path to more and more complex and recursive theory of mind—a path we have already begun to follow. The solidification of metapragmatics, meanwhile, points to the question of *systems of indexes*, and this carries us toward one of the fundamental design features of modern musicking: discrete pitch.

System without Symbol: A Phylogeny of Discrete Pitch

The defining of protodiscourse and indexical ordering reveals that narratives making symbolic cognition the preeminent, definitive feature of humanness finally overreach themselves, obscuring the appearance of behaviors not specifically symbolic and oversimplifying the history of our emergence. The missed opportunity looms large in the case of musicking.

The symbolic leap to language, in Deacon's view, was prepared in part by a decoupling of the manipulative meanings of earlier gesture-calls from selective pressures. In an analogous way, the foremost combinatorial aspect in musicking, pitch processing, could have emerged from the decoupling of prosodic intonational patterns themselves from their emotive correlates, as proposed at the end of Chapter 3. In the prehistories of both language and music, according to these hypotheses, distinct epicycles formed from earlier, selection-driven feedback cycles, and in each case the internal dynamics of these epicycles gave rise to combinatorial processing. In language this combinatoriality came to be embodied at two levels, in sets of nonreferential phonemes making up words (morphology) and in referential words making up larger utterances (syntax or grammar). In music, instead, the combinatoriality was constructed on a more basic set of percepts: discrete pitches.[31]

The perception of discrete pitch, the basic elements of which were introduced in Chapters 3 and 4, seems to arise naturally in normal human ontogeny and has no counterpart in the intonational prosodic structures of modern language. Though musicking can do without it—without pitch altogether, indeed—the vast majority of the world's musics exploit it. This point can be sharpened: It is probably true that *all* musical cultures rely on discrete pitch, if they do so with bewildering variety and need not do so in every act of musicking. Even so qualified a generalization as this will inspire cries of protest from certain quarters, so we must immediately qualify it further. What is at stake is not an assertion that all musical cultures conceptualize scales, or name pitches, or even articulate the presence of individual pitches as such, or, in performance, practice anything very close to stable pitch tunings. What is asserted, instead, is that any act of pitched musicking (except in some very recent, nontypical outgrowths of complex musical traditions) creates certain intonational points of attraction for the musical activity and that these are not arbitrary. Pitches in acts of musicking are sometimes like fixed frequencies (with associated overtones), as usually happens in the Western classical tradition. But in most practices they are freer than this, functioning as flexible centers of gravity along the spectrum of frequencies around which the musicking is elaborated, like attractors in a dynamic system; or acting, even more freely, as a set of intervallic behaviors, in which only local relations between adjacent points are determined, without any overall consistency of frequency. None of these freedoms challenges the perception of discrete pitch as here described; all of them, in fact, seem to be founded upon it.

Despite all this variety, musicking ramifies discrete pitch in ways that are consistent enough to suggest structural constraints built into the human auditory system. The ramifications include the general sense that melodies comprise smaller units, whether these are thought of as individual pitches or the intervals between adjacent points of momentary stability. They include also the capacity, ubiquitous but not well understood, to relativize pitch, witnessed in our ability to recognize the identity of a melody at different pitch levels—think of the arbitrary starting-pitch for the singing of "Happy Birthday" at a child's party.

Other complexities have to do with the interrelations of pitches. Most fundamental is the striking sense of similarity of pitches related in a two-to-one frequency ratio—*octave equivalence* or *duplication*, in the parlance of Western music. Aligned periodicities of neural firing, probably basic to the experience of pitch all told, might well underlie also this percept.[32] In effect it divides the continuous spectrum of pitches into repeating segments, and this division in turn gives rise to the exploitation of smaller intervals within the segments, creating the pitch arrays conceptualized in some musical cultures as scales.

Like the phonemes of language, the array of pitches exploited differs from one musical culture to another and within cultures as well. Even these culture-driven pitch choices, however, show general, cross-cultural tendencies, again probably reflecting general auditory structures and constraints. Very often they cluster around or emphasize pitches related through frequency ratios close to small integers (the fifth, 3:2, the fourth, 4:3, the major third, 5:4, and a few more); in this they may represent a perceptual extension of octave equivalence, less salient than it but founded in similar neural processes. They form aggregates of pitches that tend to be small in number, typically four to seven within each octave. They usually also mark off unequal intervals within the octave, an asymmetry that may abet the widespread perception of tonal hierarchies or *tonality*—here defined as the sense of greater salience or centrality of one or more pitches over others in a specific instance of musicking. This sense, also sometimes called *tonal encoding*, is far more widespread than some discussions of Western major/minor tonality suggest—perhaps, indeed, almost as ubiquitous as discrete pitch perception itself.[33]

Discrete pitch, in sum, seems to be a default mode in human perception of certain kinds of aural stimuli, formed in normal ontogeny and nearly ubiquitous in musicking. But how did it arise in our phylogeny? We have already connected this emergence to feedback patterns of biocultural coevolution, to the prosodic-emotive aspect of the ancient gesture-call system, and specifically to the hominin elaboration of deictic—that is, indexical—meanings associated with the general melodic shapes of the calls (see Chapters 3 and 4). Weakened selection played a role here, loosing formerly innate calls from strong selective pressures. As the calls were offloaded then to cultural transmission, brain areas long since fine-tuned for auditory scene analysis and emotive communication were recruited for novel activities, namely, the production and perception of vocalizations of increasing variety and informational precision; this created an epicycle of deictic or indexical vocalization. Cultural transmission in varied social contexts encouraged greater diversity in the calls. This diversification, working on the vocalizations and their ever more nuanced intonational contours, redirected the employment of established capacities, creating new pressures on them. Altered selection, finally, led to the refinement of the auditory system so as to build the frequency-tuned neurons and nascent networks involved in pitch perception.

As finer gradations came to be perceived along the analog spectrum of gesture-call prosody, then, another, distinct coevolutionary mechanism arose, a *discrete pitch epicycle*. This was driven in part by acoustical dynamics, especially the small-integer relations mentioned just now, and it created the cognitive foundation for the myriad cultural elaborations of pitch perception in musicking today. We have already proposed how rhythmic entrainment and the tracking of melodic contour emerged from patterns of early hominin technosociality, long before symbolic cognition. Similar mechanisms probably precipitated an incipient perception of discrete pitch from the indexical calls—an additional development, analogous to entrainment and tracking, but coming much later.[34] As in those other cases, the discrete pitch epicycle did not depend on the prior development of symbols, with their mediated distance and systematized reference.

The archaeological, paleoanthropological, and even ethological evidence for the emergence of discrete pitch perception
from such indexicality is suggestive, if indirect. The incremental
elaboration of hominin sociality through hundreds of millennia
outlines a general trajectory, albeit a slow and irregular one, of
increasing variety and precision of communicative gesture and
vocalization. This communication long remained indexical in
nature—no more than we would expect, since indexicality took
chronological priority over symbolism in the evolution of the animate biosphere all told and formed the semiotic means of protodiscourse. Within this realm of indexical meaning, hominins no
doubt commanded an unprecedented communicative richness by
the beginning of the Middle Paleolithic era, and probably even
farther back; but for hundreds of millennia and across at least
several species, the elaboration of indexicality toward greater
complexity, precision, and ordering predominated, with little or
no trace of symbols.

If the perception of *discreteness* in pitch coalesced out of the
deictic vocalizations in this communicative evolution, discrete
pitch *combination* into larger units—something like modern
melody—must have awaited additional attainments, especially
combinatorial cognitive processing. This development probably
occurred sometime in the Middle Paleolithic, near the appearance of Neandertals and our immediate African ancestors. From
this moment the linkage of the increasingly discrete signals of
protodiscourse in hierarchic and combinatorial arrangement must
have begun to form. Again, a background of symbolism was not
required for these rudimentary pitch hierarchies, and the archaeological evidence indicates that discrete combinatorial cognition
in general emerged on a taskscape without modern language or
representational artifacts.

Weak, nascent rule governance within assemblages of discrete signals was likewise not dependent on symbolism. It could
have emerged from tendencies within individual assemblages
themselves—as an outcome, for example, of inherent acoustical

relations among sets of signals and their associated indexical meanings, all in the context of cultural transmission and diversification. In his schema for the development of protolanguage, Ray Jackendoff has envisaged just such rule governance taking hold in sets of protosyllables, and it could also have coformed with emergent discrete-pitch arrays dividing the larger interval of the octave. Both could have resulted in a rudimentary metapragmatics featuring an ordering and governance of indexes. In the case of pitch, as the perception of octave duplication grew, itself a product of increasing precision of pitch perception in the new biocultural epicycle, it would have set in motion a cascade of novel capacities in pitch generation and exploitation, with the result of increasing complexity within pitch arrays themselves. The tendencies to associate particular pitches with, or dissociate them from one another would have been strengthened by the match or mismatch of the neural periodicities underlying pitch perception all told. Even hierarchies of pitch, tonal encoding or tonality, could have arisen as an emergent quality of such associations—that is, as a percept in effect ranking the strengths of association and dissociation within the pitch arrays.

During this combinatorial stage, the winnowing of discrete pitch from analog gesture-calls must have had another effect. The calls themselves, we remember, took their deictic, emotive meanings in some measure from their general intonational shapes. In relation to these broader contours, discrete pitches represented an atomizing of the shapes into newly perceived component units. Later, modern melodies retaining some of the general contour-indexicality of their ancient predecessors would be built from these components. From the first, however, the atomization of the old intonational contours created a new array of signals with little connection to the old, indexical meanings. The new component pitches were abstracted, distanced from the meanings of the calls, in their very generation from the increasing precision of indexical reference. And the abstract percepts gathered themselves into loosely governed systems, nonsymbolic but derived from indexical roots. In this process discrete pitch and combinatorial cognition might have not only separated distinct structural levels in the newly hierarchized vocalizations but also parceled out meaning unevenly to the different levels.

This development in pitch perception might well have coincided, again, with the first carving out of linguistic protosyllables; it seems closely analogous to it, at any rate. But in the case of protosyllables, we must imagine with Jackendoff a sequence of developments in which meaning was strengthened by the combinations of those phonemic units into words. Discrete pitches, instead, were never again so closely linked to meaning. To this day they carry little or no indexical association; they are signs only in extraordinary contexts, usually involving modern symbolism. This *abstracting of pitch from meaning* represents a momentous swerve in communicative means as, for the first time in the long development of hominin communication, a new ingredient appeared in vocalized gesture that *attenuated* meaning and referentiality rather than bolstering and specifying them. In Chapter 7 we will follow the far-reaching consequences of this swerve in a new kind of sociality, a transcendental sociality that could sponsor both ritual and religion—and tightly bind musicking to them.

In several basic respects, this description of the emergence of discrete pitch perception differs from the musical protolanguages advanced by Darwin, Brown, or even Fitch (see Chapter 3). First, unlike Brown's conception of "lexical tones," it does not grant semantic content to pitches before language, but only weak indexical reference to the gesture-calls from which pitches were abstracted and to the melodies they eventually produced. Discrete pitch perception, as it took shape, produced something closer to an antisemantic absolution than to a sung meaning before words. My description also suggests no counterpart to Brown's referential, "melodorhythmic" phrases anticipating language. Second, this account does not imagine in the first perceivers of discrete pitch the capacity to form melodies in the manner of modern musicking (cf. Darwin's gibbons, with their "true musical cadences"); instead, it regards the pitches as a coevolutionary consequence, far down the road, of ancient intonational calls. We may choose to term the initial, nondiscretized calls "melodies," but we should not confuse them with the constructive means of modern musicking. Fitch's conception of a "bare phonology" or phonotaxis preceding language, finally, comes closest to my model. But—a crucial difference—instead of his full, prelinguistic, weakly semantic melodies, the equivalent of birdsongs sung by our ancestors, it envisages a coevolutionary sequence whereby pitches arose from the gesture-calls, only gradually to be systematized by the nature of their own acoustical interrelations (and developing cognition of them) and then put to use in the melodies of musicking.

In general, this description does not give music any chronological priority over language, a primary feature of most hypotheses of musical protolanguage. It offers an alternative scenario in which *weakly rule-governed sets of signals of more than one type emerged from the advancing protodiscourse of late Middle Paleolithic taskscapes*. It suggests that discrete pitch perception formed alongside protolinguistic elements, and that both were abetted by nascent hierarchic and combinatorial cognition, before either modern language or musicking appeared. This conforms well to deep-historical evidence of hominin communication; whereas musical protolanguage hypotheses all disregard this evidence by assigning to ancient hominins a panoply of full-fledged, modern musical capacities.

In addition, the model has the advantage of distancing the first systematization and rule governance from the kind of referentiality characteristic of modern language and symbolism. There is no formal or abstract principle requiring that systematization be an all-or-nothing force, complex in the manner of language or else nonexistent. More generally, there is no requirement that indexes cannot be systematized, at least loosely; Silverstein's metapragmatics shows such systematization at work in modern discourse. Peircean and neo-Peircean conceptions of symbolism require only this: that the peculiarly human ability to marshal meanings invested in *symbols* demands a complex systematization and inter-referentiality within the symbol set. The weak governance envisaged here of *indexes*, instead, would have encouraged linkages of certain ones and discouraged linkages of others; but it would not yet have spawned any fully mediated distance between the system itself and the world referred to.

Arguments like Deacon's that make all our complex cognitive capacities dependent on a prior attainment of fully symbolic thought run afoul of deep historical evidence, since this indicates that complexities of behavior and cognition outstripping any non-human ones in the world today emerged in the hominin line long before the existence of language in its modern form. Symbolic capacities of the Peircean sort came very late in hominin evolution, after other, looser forms of systematization had sprung up; we need only attend closely to Middle Paleolithic, hierarchic and combinatorial technologies to establish this. Whatever models we construct and hypotheses we offer must allow for this presymbolic complexity in protolanguage and protomusicking as well as in material interactions with the world.

In the emergence of discrete pitch perception, finally, just as in the emergence of language, indexicality was not superseded, but preserved and channeled in new directions toward its roles in modern human communication. The mediated distance itself of symbol systems, Deacon shows us, is one of two forms of indexical function in them; this dependence of symbolism on indexicality for its operation is a reason to posit models in which hominins traversed a smooth development from the one to the other. Another reason is the fact that humans still employ in many aspects of communication remnants of the gesture-calls of our ancestors. It will seem demeaning of music's wonders only to those who have not attended carefully to the preceding chapters if I offer a general definition relating music to those vocalizations: *Musicking in the world today is the extended, spectacularly formalized, and complexly perceived systematization of ancient, indexical gesture-calls.*

Glimpses of Modernity

We cannot end here, for to do so would run the risk of exchanging the symbolocentrism of Deacon and most protolinguists for a likewise unjustified indexicocentrism. If discrete pitch was loosely systematized before fully modern symbolism and language, nevertheless this development alone did not bring about the final formation of modern musicking. Both the incrementalism of deep histories of complex human behaviors and the syncretisms among those histories suggest that this formation could only have occurred as one of many ingredients in the gathering perfect storm of human modernity. Other ingredients certainly included the falling-into-place of Deacon's symbolic systematization and the grafting of it onto the already considerable complexities of hominin sociality. They included also the final, dramatic extension of the (also complex) sociality of copresence through burgeoning capacities for thinking-at-a-distance. The possibilities of imagining invisible realms and of communicating by means of arrays of conventionalized vocal symbols coincided in this storm of development with the transformation of ancient, emotive, acoustical stimulus-and-response into the formalized shapes of all musicking in the world today; we will follow this development in Chapter 7.

From a narrowly musical vantage, the addition of discretized pitch leaves us still in the realm of protomusicking, if on the verge of these new, transformative possibilities. The further developments that would realize the transformation included the solidifying of discrete pitch as melodic building block, in part through tonality; the meshing of hierarchic pitch constructions with temporal patterns of entrainment, also hierarchized; and the sheer cultural investment in these complex, nonsemantic formalisms as a locus where the ancient arousal of expectation and emotion might be channeled to new societal and communicative ends.

These musical elements, again, can be understood best as coalescing *alongside* modern language and other markers of our modernity, not before them or in their wake. I asked at the beginning of Chapter 4: Can we imagine a scene of musicking produced on a Paleolithic taskscape *not* saturated with referential and symbolic distance? The question is valid even though, as will be clear by now, we have to distinguish musicking from such communicative modes. No: Forms of referential distance and forms of musicking cohabited, but not because symbolism is *required* before musicking can take shape. Hominin taskscapes became human taskscapes, on which symbolism, language, offline thinking of unprecedented reach, and musicking all conspired to mold one another into their modern forms.

Describing this turn requires an even finer sense of the complexities of incremental change, but, before walking out onto these Upper Pleistocene taskscapes, it is worth one more glance back at the protomusical heritage approximately 100,000 years ago. Alongside discretized pitch and combinatorial possibilities stood the older capacities detailed in earlier chapters: capacities for entrainment organized by now in temporal hierarchies, for the gauging of indexical and emotive meaning in broad intonational contours of utterance, and for the precise discrimination of myriad timbres and the intricate auditory scene analysis it abets. Alongside all these increments, also, were technological traditions of ever-increasing complication. Perhaps these had already begun, 100,000 years ago, to supply extensions of the body by which protomusical patterns could be projected out into the world—amplified, in both literal and figurative senses; if not, they would soon enough do so. These increments were of varying age and grew in prominence at varying rates. Many of them were very ancient indeed, and broadly dispersed among mammals; others first appeared in the hominin line long before our species, as focused cases of older capacities; and still others emerged rapidly in the last stages of our ancestry.

Archaeological, ethological, and cognitive studies all convince us of the communicative powers of protodiscourse, not to mention its wide dispersion beyond humans in the world today. Hierarchic cognition and behavior and their combinatorial outgrowths, meanwhile, appear already in Neandertals, a species all but certainly not endowed with language in the form all humans use today. The social processes whereby protodiscourse could become more and more focused, manifesting ever greater deictic precision, also come ever more clearly into view. Driving these developments was the complexity of hominin sociality in copresent interaction, and underneath this, finally—the foundation of all else—lay the coevolutionary and epicyclic dynamics I have described.

It remains to track the gathering storm.

CHAPTER SIX

100,000–20,000 Years Ago, I:
Homo sapiens and the Falling Out
of Modern Culture

The Fine Grain

As this narrative draws close to the present, the scale of its operation shifts in ways involving both observer and observed. For we, the observers, the grain of our pictures of the past grows finer with diminishing chronological distance. We see in more detail and intricacy as the evidence thickens, as methods for dating achieve narrower discriminations, and as differences in everything from climate to human behavior are plotted against time in smaller gradations. One recent account highlighting the question of scale across deep history has proposed that the new detail reveals anticipations, across the last 50,000 years, of innovations once thought to begin only 11,000 years ago with the advent of the Neolithic—"fractal" patterns duplicating one another at different times and in different local settings.[1] And, as our view sharpens, so do the historical constructions and accounts it affords. The chapters that follow will offer varieties of evidence and specificities of account that dwarf those of Chapters 1–5.

As to the observed: A compelling argument has recently taken shape in archaeological and other circles, responding to much new evidence, that the accelerating pace of human innovation was not limited to the Neolithic period or even the Upper Paleolithic/Late Stone Age but reaches farther back—at least 100,000 years and perhaps much more. This perfect storm of human modernity was not quick in the making. Rethinking the changing pace of change across this huge period confutes old-fashioned conceptions of seismic shifts in human behavior—the Eurocentric, Upper Paleolithic "revolution" we encountered in Chapters 4 and 5; for what can it mean to single out one moment in the midst of a vast period of gathering innovation? The long acceleration sets the emergence of human culture in a broad vista taking in all of Africa, a good deal of central and east Asia, and Australia, the latter more precisely a continent joining Australia, New Guinea, and Tasmania, created by low sea levels during periods of glaciation and now called "Sahul." According to some, as we have seen, the vista includes Neandertals as well.[2]

The finer grain of our picture reveals also that this long acceleration was not a smooth and uninterrupted one but unfolded in fits and starts. This discontinuous, sporadic history will occupy us later, but it is important to pause over some of its general features and implications. To begin with, a chronological caveat: behavioral discontinuity was no doubt not restricted to the last 100,000 years. For earlier periods in hominin evolution also, it is easy to predict, our sense of behavioral eruptions and uneven cultural accumulation will only multiply in coming years, as more evidence comes to light. Our coarse-grained picture of Acheulean and later hominins will resolve not into an image of smooth, progressive change but to one detailing episodic appearances of behaviors, their extinctions along with the populations that manifested them, and their reappearances in other times and places.

We have probably already witnessed instances of such earlier discontinuities. There is every reason to think that the 400,000-year-old wooden spears of Schöningen discussed in Chapter 4 are not a revelation of the *general* behaviors of *Homo heidelbergensis* (or early Neandertals) so much as they reflect a turn these behaviors took in a particular population, in specific ecological circumstances, and answering to specific needs: a microburst of early human innovation.[3] The spears manifest capacities of their creators—this much must be true; but those creators may well have exploited their capacities along pathways not taken by other groups of the same species. Something similar can perhaps be said also of whatever brought about the collection of human remains in the Atapuercan Sima de los Huesos.[4]

As the scale of our chronological catchment changes with passing time, the incrementalism that subtends the history narrated here is complicated by these discontinuities. Before 100,000 years ago, this history approximates a continuous development, as if the protomusical capacities involved formed an unbroken, accumulating sequence: first a growing rhythmic entrainment, then increasing precision and efficacy of protodiscourse, then hierarchic and combinatorial cognitive patterns, then discrete pitch and protolinguistic syllabaries. But this smooth continuity in the telling is an illusion created by sparseness of the evidence—something that should be obvious, given the several species of hominins, two or three continents, and million-year span involved.

Once we pass the 100,000-year mark and evidence mounts of several sorts, it becomes clear that some general principles are at play behind the discontinuity that is revealed. First, in the hominin lineage more than in any other, behavior is not synonymous with capacity. Hominins created their taskscapes according to local needs and affordances, not in some full-throttle demonstration of their potentials. They acted according to their cognitive and physical capacities, no doubt; but they did not reveal the full measure of these capacities at all moments. We can expect to see not only fits and starts in their deep histories but also idiosyncratic, even singular behavioral reflections of underlying capacities interacting with very local conditions. And, as we shall see, we should expect both of these to continue and intensify in the record of more recent hominins, as the increasingly intricate play of culture enlarges the spectrum of relations between genotype and phenotype and as wider-ranging movements of populations bring them into more and more diverse environments. Such localism is a basic reason why it seems wise, in trying to draw a general narrative of early hominins, to rely on the most widely attested evidences of their behavior, especially technological ones, and inferences drawn from them. But now we reach a point in the narrative where this strategy will no longer suffice.

Second, we must always bear in mind that the taskscapes hominins made operated as selective ecologies. They altered pressures on their makers over the long *durée*, and finally they reshaped the basic capacities themselves of their makers. Through this coevolutionary feedback, behaviors reflected in the archaeological record might not only reveal to us general capacities, in more or less exceptional ways; they might also have conduced to the formation of *different* capacities. Moreover, because of the fecundity of cultural accumulation and transmission among these creatures, the possibility arose that even the most singular of innovations might assume a more general currency, giving it an expanded potential to affect the selective alteration of inherited, genetically based capacities.

Recently, the episodic and discontinuous appearance, disappearance, and reappearance of behaviors akin to those of present-day humans have led some archaeologists to reject outright attempts to define any single or persistent behavioral modernity. John J. Shea, an eloquent convert to this position, adduces further reasons in its favor. He isolates the lingering Eurocentrism and teleology involved in archaeological ideas of modernity, not to mention their potential for racist and other abuse in popular accounts and the press, and he offers in their place a different model—not behavioral modernity but behavioral *variability*.[5] This set in, he argues, with the advent of morphologically modern humans some 200,000 years ago, armed with capacities for behavioral flexibility no different from those of Upper Paleolithic cave painters or, for that matter, from ours. Human behavioral differences over time were determined not by changing capacities, but by divergent strategies required for survival in different environments.

There is much to recommend this critique, which has been welcomed by many and seen by some as an emerging consensus among archaeologists, and we will take up below the ecological and demographic ingredients Shea highlights in the dispersion and behavioral strategies of *Homo sapiens*. It should be clear that I have tried in this book to guard against both Eurocentric and teleological biases in viewing the emergence of modern humans. The miracle of late hominin evolution is not that it led to us, but that it formed a cognitive panoply, probably not even restricted to our species alone, enabling an unprecedented versatility of interaction with the world.

Notwithstanding all this, Shea's shift from modernity to variability does not dissipate the fogs surrounding the emergence of present-day humans. In the first place, the appeal to unchanging capacities over 200,000 years—Shea calls it human "uniformitarianism"—only pushes the mystery of human uniqueness back to a period when many of its modern behavioral signatures had not yet appeared. The differences between the first sapient humans and those 160,000 years later are registered in the material culture preserved in the archaeological record; they suggest strongly that fundamental nonmaterial attainments of later humans, for instance fully modern language, did not yet exist in the first *sapiens*.

More important, Shea's variability does not take account of a fundamental feature of late-hominin cultures: their rich accumulation of archives of learned, transmitted materials. In ignoring this, his model is powerless to gauge the role of such cultural archives in the course of our evolution. Only by rejecting the basic tenets of biocultural coevolution can we imagine that the cognitive capacities of *Homo sapiens* were left untouched over 200,000 years of cultural innovation and sedimentation. The model we require to understand the deep history of our species is hardly one of smooth progress from Middle Stone Age tools to cancer research, but neither is it one of unchanged potential to act in changing environments—of biocultural coevolution at a magical standstill. Our model must weigh the strategic unfoldings of human culture in both their localism and their potential to exert a widening biocultural impact. The evidence, as problematic as it is to gauge, suggests that a human population in east Africa about 60,000 years ago had attained capacities more or less like ours, and then transmitted them by migration and interbreeding to other African populations and through the non-African world. Much as we might wish for it, the evidence does not suggest that this occurred 140,000 years earlier.

Migrations and Climates

The fine-grained evidence that has mounted concerning the last 200 millennia of human evolution comes from archaeological, paleontological, and, increasingly, genetic study, and it far exceeds what we have for earlier hominins. It has generally affirmed the hypothesis that the final dispersion of *Homo sapiens* across the globe involved recent migration out of Africa—an idea that took on the force of a consensus in the 1990s; but at the same time it has complicated this model in unanticipated ways.[6]

The move out of Africa, first, was not a single migration but comprised several or many. Humans repeatedly left the continent and at times may have returned to it, as populations relocated in response to changing climates and environments. In Southwest Asia, along the eastern end of the Mediterranean, populations of *sapiens* probably advanced several times beginning before 100,000 years ago—but then seem to have receded or died off, to be replaced in the same locales by *later* Neandertal groups migrating south during cool periods and glacial advances in northern Eurasia.[7] The migration or migrations that eventually populated the westernmost margin of Eurasia—the cave painters of France and Spain, for example—occurred relatively late. An earlier exodus had followed the south Asian coast and may have met late *Homo erectus* populations as it went. It found its way as far as Sahul between 42,000 and 45,000 years ago (some views put the date as far back as 60,000 years), in a migration that demanded marine technology adequate for island-hopping and crossing some forty-five miles of open ocean even at the lowest ebb of global sea levels.[8] *Homo sapiens* probably arrived there before they reached the far western regions of Europe.

A second complication involves the interaction of the new migrants with the indigenous populations they encountered. This was not a matter only of displacement or, more dramatically, of extermination; instead episodes of interbreeding occurred between old and new populations.[9] New genetic evidence has suggested some degree of *sapiens*-Neandertal interbreeding, leaving markers in most modern populations not of pure African descent. It seems to have been limited, and it may have occurred during those population replacements in the Levant, about 60,000 years ago.[10] Meanwhile the discovery in the last few years of human fossils at Denisova Cave in the Altai Mountains of Siberia has further complicated the picture. Analysis of the Denisovan genome suggested, unexpectedly, that they were remnants of populations that migrated out of Africa long before *Homo sapiens* but long after the first hominins to do so, *Homo ergaster/erectus*. They interbred later with both Neandertals and *sapiens*, and their genetic traces are found today especially in Melanesian populations—signaling further complexities in their dispersion.[11] This kind of evidence has forged a merger of sorts between the out-of-Africa consensus and modified forms of earlier "assimilationist" hypotheses, which had envisaged a full-fledged mixing across Europe and Asia of earlier populations with the new sapient migrants.

Africa itself, finally, source of the new and old migrants alike, should never be left out of the account. Here accumulating genetic evidence and careful computer simulations paint a picture of immense complexity, as might be expected in the continent where different taxa of hominins had always been most numerous. As climate and natural conditions changed over this immense body of land across the Middle and Upper Pleistocene, ecological barriers rose and fell between hominin populations. Groups seem to have dispersed within the continent and pursued independent fates, only to be brought back into contact tens or even hundreds of millennia later as climate and ecology ameliorated.[12] Imagine a map splotched with colors representing these populations, then animate it, fast-forwarding through the millennia: The ebbs and flows, the transits and retreats, and the blendings of colors would be too complex to follow. The pattern for early *Homo sapiens* itself, extrapolated from modern human genomes, bespeaks such divisions and meetings. One recent reconstruction distinguishes at least thirty-five independent lineages at about 60,000 years ago, only two of which were involved in the subsequent world-populating migrations out of the continent. In modern Khoisan lineages, at the southern end of the continent, this analysis discerns genetic traces of population divisions that occurred in east Africa as much as 150,000 years ago and lasted 50,000–100,000 years.[13]

As is true for any animals, the movements, sizes, and inter-relations of these various populations unfolded in intimate cor-relation with the ecologies they inhabited. These in turn were subject, across the late Pleistocene period, to changes in response to shifting climates. The drama of this climatic instability, more extreme than that of the earlier Pleistocene, is another point that has been brought home in recent years by the ever-finer grain of our knowledge. The late or Upper Pleistocene began about 127,000 years ago with an *interglacial*, a long period of relatively warm conditions in the otherwise cooler climates characterizing the Pleistocene as a whole. But most of the Upper Pleistocene, from about 114,000 years ago down to the beginning of the Holo-cene (11,700 years ago), was a long cold epoch marked by repeated glaciations. The Holocene, from this perspective, is merely the most recent Pleistocene interglacial; it has not yet endured as long as the one that initiated the Upper Pleistocene.

This 100,000-year span, however, brought not only cold, dry climates and expanding ice sheets, but also warmer, wet-ter periods; briefer than interglacials, they are called *interstadi-als*. Paleoclimatologists have since the 1950s tracked the longest interstadials, as well as the cold periods or stadials between them, in so-called Oxygen (or Marine) Isotope Stages, named after the ratio of two oxygen isotopes trapped in the shells of marine organisms, an indirect measure of global temperatures. These show major cold periods from about 71,000–60,000 and 24,000–11,000 years ago—respectively, OI Stages 4 and 2. Between them came OIS 3, a period of relative warmth lasting more than 20,000 years.

At a finer scale still, these OI Stages were interrupted by quicker climate changes, some of them staggeringly quick, as fast as a human lifetime. These resulted from forces that are tracked by means of various geological signatures but not fully understood. The fluctuations include for the Upper Paleolithic alone some twenty-five cycles of rapid warming followed by slower cooling, called Dansgaard-Oeschger or D-O Events. Bursts of abrupt cooling occurred as well, brought on by the breaking off and circulation of huge icebergs from glacial ice sheets, known as Heinrich Events; there were five major such events in the last 50,000 years. Finally, several "supervolcanic" eruptions, including those of Mount Toba in Indonesia about 74,000 years ago and of the Campi Flegrei near present-day Naples sometime after 40,000 years ago, may have brought on cooling of local or even global climates. How extreme and lengthy these "volcanic winters" were is a matter of debate, with some experts denying that they occurred at all, others going so far as to implicate Mt. Toba in the onset of OIS 4. In any case, the Italian eruption, named also after the mineral signature it deposited as the "Campanian Ignimbrite" event, must have disrupted local ecologies of human populations, Neandertal or sapient, in the huge area of its ashfall across south-central Eurasia.

It is tempting to correlate the migrations of hominins out of Africa, all the way back to *Homo ergaster* about 1.8 million years ago, with warm periods when the northeast corridor from that continent into Southwest Asia was wet and ecologically welcoming. For the early movements in this period we have too little precision of timing for this to be much more than speculation. We can be more precise concerning the final migrations of *Homo sapiens*, and a broad agreement has formed placing these generally in OIS 3, beginning about 60,000 years ago. The hypothesis is bolstered by evidence both archaeological and genetic. Studies of mitochondrial and nuclear DNA in modern humans point to the origin, at about the same time, of the two modern lineages that populated the non-African world.[14] Some see in this evidence signs of a bottleneck in the sapient population in northeast Africa about 70,000 years ago, estimating the sum of our species to have fallen as low, at its nadir, as a few thousand mating pairs. After this, the hypothesis continues, the population expanded, eventually quickly enough to create demographic pressures that helped to drive the migrations.[15] This would put the population from which modern humans stemmed in the right place at approximately the right time, from the vantage of climate dynamics. In addition, the earliest archaeological traces of *Homo sapiens* in far eastern Europe point to our dispersion there shortly after 50,000 years ago—again, as we might expect if these humans had made their way into the Levant in the preceding millennia. It is probably safe to say that the prolonged, warm interstadial OIS 3 was important in our ultimate movements out of Africa.

In the most recent analyses, paleoclimatologists have pushed the chronological precision of this hypothesis. A warm period in the changing climates *within* OIS 3 extended from about 55,000 to 49,000 years ago. This brought benign and wet conditions to northern Africa at the same time as mild climates prevailed through the Levant and Europe, and it may have allowed the final, enduring expansion of sapient humans into the latter areas. The favorable conditions did not last, however, but were cut short by a major Heinrich Event 48,000 years ago that brought centuries of cold and drought.[16]

We are reminded in all this of two truths. First, the cautionary tale of the fine grain must not be forgotten. The detail we have of this period is alluring, but as smaller resolution is achieved there will certainly be surprises in store, even major ones, in our tracking of ancient populations through specific times and places. Second: The modern humans who came out of Africa and inhabited areas that often quickly turned inhospitable managed to survive, against odds that brought down their resourceful and long-lasting cousins, the Neandertals. This truth begs an essential question: What enabled them to do so?

Population and Innovation

The short answer is: modern culture. But this in itself says little, for what counts is the long, episodic gathering of this modernity across the shifting challenges of Upper Pleistocene life. This formation was one of accelerating but also discontinuous change; the view that modern culture took shape, even as it quickened, not as a smooth accumulation but in piecemeal and uneven fashion is another reward of the finer grain archaeologists have achieved. Many variables feature in the course of this development, variables linked to human innovation itself in loops of positive and negative feedback. Two that may not immediately spring to mind, but that have loomed large in recent analyses of our deep history, are population size and climatic and ecological constraint.

According to computational simulations, the size of a human population is positively correlated to cultural innovation and development. Such simulations of cultural change are of course reductionist in nature, necessarily thinning out the thick dynamics of human interactions in order to be tractable; within these limitations, nevertheless, they model a striking increase in the likelihood that beneficial cultural change will appear and be transmitted and preserved in groups as their sizes increase. And the correlation is at first dramatic: The frequency of occurrence and the staying power of innovations rise exponentially with growth in group size from about twenty to eighty individuals, gradually leveling off after that. These benefits accrue regardless of whether transmission is modeled only from parents to offspring or, more realistically for early human groups, from small groups of individuals not restricted to parents. The advantages of larger group size include also a culling of nonbeneficial innovations that is more effective than in smaller groups. And—an important feature—the models apply both to population growth within a group and to the effect of growth created through contact between groups.

Stephen Shennan, a foremost advocate for this kind of modeling, sees the link of population size and innovation as a key to understanding the cultural development of *Homo sapiens* through much of the Upper Pleistocene. Starting from the presumed population bottleneck about 70,000 years ago, he sketches a scenario for the growth of sapient populations and their final expansion out of Africa that involves not only the straight line of causality but also the powerful nonlinear, looping effects of feedback. As the climate ameliorated after 60,000 years ago, the resources afforded by environments increased; in Malthusian fashion, human populations grew in response to these expanded "carrying capacities." Larger populations brought accumulating innovations in technology and behavior, which intensified humans' exploitation of resources, in effect further raising ecological carrying capacities. This, then, enabled more population growth, renewing the cycle. Along the way, larger populations brought about more contacts with other groups across longer distances, redoubling the cultural transmission and innovation, an additional feedback loop. Meanwhile, dampening forces were also felt: the negative feedback of resource depletion, brought on by overpredation in the wake of innovation and intensification—this force, again Malthusian, can be followed in some instances in the archaeological record—and new deteriorations of climate and environment.[17]

Another view of Upper Pleistocene human expansion, building on Shennan's model but pointing in rather different directions, has been offered by Peter Richerson, Robert Boyd, and Robert Bettinger. They argue that the extreme climate changes of the Upper Pleistocene may have joined with growing population to *drive* innovation. The deforestation and spread of grassy, steppe biomes during periods of glaciation were not in fact disadvantages for humans, given the technosocial means they had devised for bringing down the large herbivores that populated such environments. Forest ecosystems, in contrast, afforded these hunters much less big game. In these settings, cultural versatility enabled *Homo sapiens* to create innovative behaviors in response to rapid climate changes in ways not available to other top-of-the-food-chain predators such as big cats. Humans, in other words, could compensate for fluctuations in resource availability brought on by the "noisy," variable environment through complex technology and social organization, enhanced communication, and so forth.

To maintain this cultural versatility, however, required sufficient levels of population—or the effect of such levels. Since not all groups reached these levels, *Homo sapiens* probably existed through the Upper Pleistocene in diverse states of equilibrium with their different and changing environments, notwithstanding fundamental similarities in basic capacities extending across the species. Small groups tended to subsist with simple technologies and little cultural change, while larger groups or networks of small ones formed and were driven by demanding environments toward enhanced cultural innovation, exchange, and flexibility. In western Eurasia in particular, the larger groups and networks may have given *Homo sapiens* an advantage over Neandertals. Moreover, innovative technologies not only flowered in circumstances of population increase, but also withered where environments could no longer sustain sufficient population densities. In complex, changing equilibria such as these, humans "could well have imposed their own bit of chaotic dynamics on Ice Age systems."[18]

A third model advanced recently by a team of archaeologists paints a less rosy picture of human achievement, portraying a development of human cultures in Europe from about 50,000 to 20,000 years ago that was neither continuous nor consistent. These researchers offer a case study of the Iberian Peninsula in this period, one with broad implications. In it they combine several kinds of evidence: as precise a calibration of climatic changes as is presently available, scrutiny and critique of carbon-14 dating

reliability, careful census of many archaeological sites, and ecological models of population reaction to environmental stress.
Twelve relatively quick cycles of climatic deterioration and amelioration can be tracked across this 30,000-year period, but the
most extreme downturns occurred when the recurrent, cold stadials coincided with Heinrich Events after about 40,000, 31,000,
and 25,000 years ago. The worst deteriorations made western
Eurasia as a whole all but uninhabitable for humans; even regions
that served as refuges during less harsh cold periods, such as
northern Mediterranean areas, were reduced to freezing deserts.

These harshest periods, also, match transitions marked in the
archaeological record from one complex of lithic technologies
to another: from Middle Paleolithic tools to Upper Paleolithic
Aurignacian industries for the first, from Aurignacian to Gravettian industries for the second, and from Gravettian to Solutrean
for the third. But only for the last, most recent change does the
archaeological testimony support a shift *within the same human
population*. The evidence, then, points for these archaeologists to
the stark conclusion that human populations retreated from or
died off in Europe during the most extreme downturns of climate. The earliest of these brought the final, "macro-extinction"
of Neandertals. The second brought a collapse of sapient Aurignacian culture (the earliest widespread culture associated with the
Upper Paleolithic), involving either the micro-extinction of its
makers or the breakdown of their networks of cultural transmission and their reduction to small, isolated, technologically diminished groups. Each of these population collapses was followed
by an influx of new groups, with new cultural patterns, when
conditions improved. Only by the time of the third, Gravettian/
Solutrean transition were sapient cultural attainments sufficient
for their makers to endure the worst climatic downturns; hence
the signs that this shift in techno-complexes was a continuous
one.[19] Though these researchers do not adduce it, genetic evidence too might support their dramatic view. Analyses of both
Y-chromosomal and mitochondrial DNA point to two founding

populations for western Europe, and these might have been successively associated with the Aurignacian and later Gravettian techno-cultures.[20]

The impact of this kind of analysis on conventional views of modern humans' populating of Europe could hardly be more unsettling. It is all too easy for us to picture "moderns" progressing gradually but inexorably westward, even sweeping Neandertals before them. But it now seems likely that this swelling, Eurocentric, Upper Paleolithic "tradition" was no unified movement at all, not even the product of the same human groups. Habitation of the continent was broken off, completely or almost so, more than once by late Pleistocene climatic catastrophes. The Aurignacian painters of Chauvet or bead makers of Isturitz or carvers and musicians of Hohle Fels, Vogelherd, and Geissenklösterle—all groups we will encounter later—were frontiersmen in this grand scheme, not permanent residents. They subsisted in small groups subject to extermination by ecological disasters from which their cultures could not shield them.[21]

This analysis of the situation in western Europe is certainly not an archaeological consensus, but echoes of something similar have begun to be heard from other regions. The whole of northern Eurasia requires on one view a hypothesis of "multiple advances" to understand the record of modern human incursions there.[22] In the Levant, primary gateway out of Africa, we have already noted that early sapient habitation did not last and that the area saw later influxes of Neandertals from the north. Even after the ultimate sapient migrations of ca. 50,000 years ago, however, the area regularly turned inhospitable. It was probably "emptied...of human settlement hundreds of times during the Late Pleistocene," "less a corridor than a cul-de-sac" for populations stemming from Africa and other parts of western Asia.[23] North Africa too has revealed signs of this discontinuity, with Moroccan sites supplying evidence consistent with repeated cycles of habitation and abandonment timed to D-O and Heinrich Events.[24] Finally, recent findings from several sites near the southern tip of

Africa suggest that local cultures were cut off more than once by climatic deterioration; we will come back to these below.[25]

All these demographic models and conceptions of sapient life through the Upper Pleistocene involve population equilibria struck in relation with a number of other, shifting forces: climate, ecosystems and their affordances, and human dynamics of innovation and maintenance of cultural systems. These are, however, not the equilibria of old-fashioned thermodynamics, closed systems to which new matter or energy might be introduced, resulting in newly set balances. Instead, they are open systems characterized, as we have seen, by circuits of feedback connecting the various elements. If population growth spawns innovation, this intensifies the harvesting of resources and in turn enables further population growth. Innovation brings about more complex intragroup relations, nurturing further innovation; larger population densities themselves may bring about increased interaction of groups, inducing innovation through another channel. On the other hand, resource depletion brought on by intensification might lead in various directions, depending on particular environmental circumstances: to population decline or even collapse in local areas, to the loss of earlier cultural innovations, or to migrations of whole populations. Within a biome, these might feed back on surviving resources, allowing them to rebound and—unless their depletion had caused a human extinction—renewing human populations, innovation, and so forth. The migrations, in addition, might bring about new meetings between human groups, new channels of cultural transmission, and more innovation. Looming over the whole system is the possibility of regional or global climate shifts, some of them of catastrophic rapidity, with all their implications for every other element. They represent the one element not subject to significant feedback pressures from the others. They would retain this special position until our own age, which has come to be called the Anthropocene in order to mark the entry of climate change itself into feedback relations with human culture.

Repeating Epicycles: Engravings and Beads out of Africa

Given the role of culture in all these feedback circuits, Richerson and his coauthors are right to note chaotic human impacts on Ice Age systems—except that their nod to chaos theory is imprecise. We should instead link these human cultural effects to a related body of theory, dynamic systems or complexity theory, which describes the kinds of emergent organization that can be generated through feedback relations in open, nonequilibrated assemblages. This requires a *nonlinear* historiography of the kind Manuel de Landa has practiced for a much more recent period, one accommodating the spiraling interdependencies of such feedback circuits and examining the regularities arising from them: repeating patterns and tendencies (or attractors) in flows of matter, energy, and information that define emergent organization. These are not the result of control systems governing from the top down, but instead arise from the bottom up. They can be conceived as schematics immanent to the self-generating complexity of assemblages, and this is why de Landa, following Deleuze and Guattari, terms them *abstract machines*.[26]

Darwin's natural selection is the most fundamental such mechanism in the biosphere, a process that takes shape in the interrelation of the basic components it affects—and that warns us against assuming that the identifying of such a "machine" brings with it simplicity or predictability of outcome. Variation in reproducing organisms meets the feedback of environmental conditions and constraints, and a process favoring some forms over others spins into operation; combined further with changing environments, the mechanism generates a limitless array of forms and operations. As we steered this foundational process in the direction of the complexities of animals with intricate sociality and culture, in the model of biocultural coevolution offered in Chapter 1, we discerned another mechanism peculiar to cultural systems, the *epicycle*, taking shape from learned bodies of information and learned sequences of practice—cultural archives—transmitted through generations. Epicycles identify a basic difference between the evolutionary conditions of animal cultures in which transgenerational accumulation is shallow (for example, chimpanzees in the wild today or many songbirds), and those—perhaps unique to the hominin lineage—in which it is deep and abiding.

Cultural archives certainly feed directly back into the loops of coevolution and of affordance, demography, and innovation, in the manner modeled and theorized in the "innovations" of Shennan, Richerson and his coauthors, and others. But the idea of the epicycle captures a different, emergent dynamic, as the archives take on their own propulsive force or systematic organization for reasons having to do with their internal natures. This organization can arise in several domains: in patterns of interactions of energies and materials, such as the "technical tendencies" of Leroi-Gourhan; in the organization of informational signals—discrete, analog, modular, hierarchized, nonhierarchic, and more; and in semiotic modes arising from the differing relations struck up by an interpretant between signs or groups of signs and their objects.

Once these epicyclic systems take shape, they can alter the relations of transmitted culture to the feedback loops of the networks in which they arise. They come to function not as internal elements in the self-regulating influences of those loops but as elements standing outside them, feeding *forward* into the network as a whole and redirecting its course. Culture, in this way, creates systems that gain some independence from niche-constructive and demographic cycles alike. Examples of epicycles we have seen in early hominin societies include the material and ergonomic tendencies that could result in symmetrical bifaces without being guided from above by "mental templates" (Chapter 2), the tendency toward discrete segmentation along an analog spectrum of signs that arose in a society of vocalized deixis (Chapters 3 and 5), the self-generating hierarchies that resulted from lengthened operational sequences joining *façonnage* and *débitage* in new ways (Chapter 4), and the systems that spring up in arrays of indexes and symbols (Chapter 5). This list reveals that the division of material, informational, and semiotic domains adduced just now for the epicycles is heuristic only. In the play of culture the domains tend to mix and merge: Acheulean bifaces and Levallois hierarchies emerge from different intersections of material affordance and informational systems, the tendency toward discreteness of information is driven by the play of deictic semiosis, and so forth. Most epicycles will involve more than one of the domains.

The epicyclic mechanism is missing from the models of climate, ecosystem, and human demography discussed above. In these, cultural innovations and their accumulation function as no more than additional elements within the networks of feedback. The independent, external action of systematized cultural archives is not taken into account. Across the last 200,000 years, however, these archives played a generally expanding role in the evolution of *Homo sapiens*, their action illuminating its puzzling course, at once accelerating and sporadic. Two sapient archives at the forefront of recent archaeological discovery can exemplify this, at the same time clarifying further the working of epicycles in general.

The engraved ochres of Blombos Cave in South Africa, excavated starting in the 1990s, number among the most arresting archaeological finds of recent years. They are small pieces of compacted siltstone and other sedimentary rock enriched with hematite—particular examples of a general type common in Middle and Late Stone Age sites dating at least as far back as 250,000 years. Depending upon their composition and hardness, pieces of ochre functioned as crayons used, as is generally assumed, for body coloration or other coloring. Ground up they yielded another form of dry pigment, ground and combined with suitable liquids a paintlike mixture, and 100,000-year-old "paint pots" containing such mixtures have been unearthed at Blombos. Perhaps ground ochre was put to other uses as well, as an agent in tanning hides, in one hypothesis, as an ingredient in adhesives to make composite tools, in another, or even as an offering at burial sites.

Among the thousands of bits of ochre retrieved at Blombos is a series of sizable pieces with scratches carefully engraved in them. The engravings take several forms, ranging from fanlike, branching arrangements to cross-hatchings resulting in ladder-like designs. Careful analysis shows that the designs were not haphazard byproducts of other processes but instead primary, intended creations—though the purposes they might have served and the manners of signs they might have formed remain mysterious. One example showing ladderlike cross-hatchings, dated to about 73,000 years ago, has become the poster artifact for early human symbolism, notwithstanding the problems attendant on this concept as archaeologists deploy it (see Chapter 5).[27]

The latest analyses of the Blombos engravings suggest that they accumulated across a period of staggering length, some 30,000 years, from 100,000 to 70,000 years ago. The lead archaeologists at the site argue that this long accumulation records a human tradition that unfolded in the cave.[28] But here the cautionary lesson of the fine grain must again be invoked. We are easily lured into a sense of such continuity—the word "tradition" almost forces it upon us—where, were we privy to a closer view, we would likely see a series of discontinuities. The stratigraphy of the archaeological site allows only the establishment of a sequence of deposition, and it cannot attain a resolution sharp enough to warrant assertions of cultural continuity. The researchers themselves have pointed out that Blombos history across these thirty millennia probably saw episodes of habitation followed by abandonment and disuse, population influx to the area followed by exodus, climatic amelioration and the approach of the bountiful seacoast followed by deterioration, arid conditions, and the receding of the coastline to the distant horizon or beyond.

More generally, we must wonder what sort of human "tradition" could endure for the unimaginable period of 30,000 years, ten times the span that separates us from Egyptian pharaohs, China's early dynasties, or the Homeric epics. We need to move with caution in proposing a localized course of purposeful human signification surviving across a time that so dwarfs human society, memory, and lifespan.

Nevertheless, the etching of ochre at Blombos undoubtedly bespeaks behavioral consistencies that require explanation. How can they be reconciled with the history of discontinuities archaeologists see more and more clearly in our deep past? In order to understand these consistencies, we must look more broadly than to a single cave and the human activities within it. We need to take account, for example, of other, related markings on hard, portable surfaces from the Middle Stone Age of southern Africa. Some ten thousand years after the most recent deposits of Blombos engravings, humans were incising complex designs on ostrich shells four hundred miles to the northwest, at Howiesons Poort; there is no reason to suspect that these resulted from direct contact with the earlier engraving technology.[29]

More broadly still, we must suppose a congruent array of cognitive, physical and social capacities relating the many southern African sapient populations involved in these related behaviors—all members, if disparate ones, of a single species. (This is Shea's uniformitarianism, only extending across a much smaller time span than his.) This array must have included enriched forms of all the things we have named in earlier chapters: a protolinguistic communication probably by now verging in its complexity on syntactic organization; cognition capable of ordering the world in hierarchized formations; in technology, long operational sequences with distinct stages, ordered groups of actions, and combinatorial products; intricate social organizations within groups, perhaps with kinship structures generally resembling those in present-day groups; and increased contact among groups and the enhanced thinking-at-a-distance it required and fostered.

Assuming these general likenesses in the peoples that made them, the engravings at Blombos or Howiesons Poort take on the appearance of *related epicyclic formalisms* sprung from generally similar human cultures. And they are unsurprising formalisms, at that. Both technologies are incised regularities on hard materials, instances, if of a novel sort, of what hominins had practiced since the beginning of Acheulean industries. The complexities of such human marking of the world had long been growing in the hominin line, and in this perspective it is no great leap from the regularities of advanced Middle Stone Age tools to the most geometric Blombos engravings or ostrich eggshell designs.

Highlighting the proximity of these kindred gestures provides a corrective to the imprecise notions of symbolism at work in many archaeological analyses of the engravings—notions of the sort analyzed in Chapter 5. Such notions push hard to widen conceptual or cognitive divides between the engravings and lithic tools: the magic word "symbolism" opens the Sesame of a symbolic revolution, lately transferred to Africa. But we have no reason to suppose that this was a distance perceived by their makers, and every reason to think that their practices that can look revolutionary to us *could not* have appeared so to them. The engravings extended an already deep history of incised design, making a modest swerve in the relations of hominin body and mind to material substance. They represent a novel epicyclic outgrowth from older cultural patterns and their epicycles, no more or less.

Once formed, this epicycle might well have been transmitted from group to group along with increasing intergroup contacts. Given the ubiquity of the proximate technologies and the mimetic transmission of culture, long a habitus of the hominin lineage, it would have required but a glimpse of such workings in one group to stimulate something not dissimilar in another. Such transmission has occurred in countless circumstances over the last 100,000 years.

But a more intriguing mode of dispersion of the epicycle exists. This alternative suggests that the model of epicyclic formations does not rely on hypotheses of unique invention followed by cultural transmission, and it outlines an episodic and discontinuous working of cultural dynamics in keeping with the pattern of Upper Pleistocene human development archaeologists now perceive.

As basic formalizations of human culture and habitation, epicycles are at every moment on the verge of coalescence; and the fertility of early humans in generating them must certainly have increased with the enrichment of their cultural archives. The proximity of engraving like that at Blombos to an earlier technological heritage, then, would likely have prompted its invention many times over in separate populations and cultures, without the necessity of dispersion by contact or from a single origin. These independently invented cultural forms, also, could have met and merged in subsequent intergroup contacts, meetings that might not only have fostered rapid convergence of the related behaviors but carried with them explosive potential to generate new epicycles.

This likelihood of *repeated emergence* should be considered a general feature of the mechanism of cultural epicycles. It comes about not because the epicycles progress toward a telos or play out cultural destinies. The only "destiny" being played out across late hominin evolution is a deepening of the sedimented cultural archives. The iteration of an epicycle is likely, instead, because it is an attractor formed from cultural patterns at play among animals accumulating archives; where the cultural patterns bear similarities to one another, for whatever reasons of environmental affordance or earlier widespread behavioral patterns or even sheer coincidence, the same abstract systematization will be likely to arise. This likelihood marks, then, a defining proximity of an epicycle to particular cultural patterns or, as we might say, its *attendancy* on them.

This attendancy is clarified by another Upper Pleistocene technology, again involving Blombos Cave: the facture of beads. Archaeologists use this word to refer to any perforated object, including marine shells, shaped bits of ostrich eggshell, teeth, carved pieces of ivory, amber, soft stone, and more. The evidence is strong that these were threaded on straps or strings, and irresistible inference posits them then as body ornaments—necklaces, bracelets, and so forth—or perhaps pendants on clothing or in hair. Beads fashioned from marine shells seem to appear very early, very episodically, and very far apart. Instances in the Levant may date back 100,000 years and more; 5,000 miles to the south, examples from Blombos Cave are probably about 75,000 years old, and a site in Algeria preserves examples at least 35,000 years old and perhaps much older. Beads carved from ostrich eggshell reach back more than 40,000 years. In western and central Eurasia, bead traditions attained an impressive variety and sophistication more than 30,000 years ago. In both the Levant and Europe, bead making may be associated with Neandertals as well as humans; in Siberia it may have been practiced by late Denisovans.[30] This huge geographical and chronological dispersion of a general technosocial mode—and perhaps even a multispecies distribution of it—points again to repeated inventions, at different times and places, answering to broadly similar cultural ends. It signals the attendancy of a cultural epicycle.[31]

But what is the nature of its immanence to the technology? For those who produced and wore them, the beads must have been markers: of what? Social differences of one sort or another? This phrase "social differences" is intentionally vague. It could embrace everything from a position in an elaborate hierarchy of rankings signified in many ways to something much simpler, for instance the passing of a growth rite or the participation in a hunt. Some archaeologists urge us to think of the beads as markers of group identity or tokens of exchange and solidarity between groups.[32] Undoubtedly, across the huge spans just outlined, the beads took on a wide range of meanings; but it is hard not to think that they were always manufactured to be *signs*.

This semiotic cargo is a defining feature of the bead-making epicycle, and its pressure helps to account for the fact that the epicycle appeared and reappeared. Put another way: The creators of beads possessed rich systems of communication, at the beginning of the period a complex protolanguage at least, by the end full-fledged modern language. They deployed these semiotic modes in groups with many varieties of social organization, no doubt, but all involving complexities outstripping the nonhuman socialities around them. They possessed, moreover, composite technologies involving straps and probably stitched clothing; the notion of using looped strands to hang things on the body itself could not have been far off. The juncture of all these cultural archives no doubt again and again coalesced into an epicycle wherein material means could become a sign of social complexity, of whatever sort.[33]

Trackless Paths

These instances of cultural epicycles suggest not only how groups of late hominins could converge on one another in the repeated move toward epicyclic attractors but also how hominin evolution could feature cultural *dis*continuities. Groups might exist for long periods in something close to cultural stasis, only to erupt quickly into other, full-blown cultural modes as a new epicyclic mechanism took hold of coevolutionary feedback mechanisms and pushed them in new directions. The igniting of behavioral patterns into epicyclic flame—the moment when a member of a group first put around his neck a strap with a perforated tooth on it—was on the face of it no more than an inch-wise displacement in a cultural archive. Underneath, however, it afforded momentous possibilities for re-formation of biocultural and sociodemographic feedback patterns. Taken together with those demographic and ecological models, epicycles spelled the likelihood of large cultural divergences among different human groups at the same time.

The epicycles indicate also that such differences depended on the inner workings themselves of deep cultural archives. Modern human differences sprang from our capacity to sediment cultural accumulations to a depth unrivaled in the rest of the animal kingdom; from this depth arose also the attendancy of epicyclic forms. It could not arise from feedback processes of coevolution alone, or from the dispersal of populations into divergent ecosystems. These could lead to genetic difference and speciation, but in the

233

absence of the internal, independent organizations of cultural forms they could not bring about the kinds of differences human societies manifest.

The differences, discontinuities, and convergences enabled by cultural depth and epicycles defined the history of *Homo sapiens* over at least the last 100,000 years and perhaps over the whole life of the species. The differences could persist over long periods in separate environments with distinct affordances and demands, characterizing the particular ecological equilibria struck by separate groups. They could create, in the midst of sudden climatic and ecological change, advantages for one group or disaster for another. They could also, however, vanish in a geological blink of an eye, either through the attendancy of similar epicycles on congruent ecological and sociocultural circumstances—even far-flung ones—or through contact, with one group provoking a new epicycle attendant on patterns already established in the behaviors of another. Through this long period, the epicycles created, in interaction with the more general feedback networks of coevolution and demography, the uniquely human operation of *foundational sameness bringing about limitless difference.*

The epicycles help to explain another basic feature of late hominin evolution, which I mentioned earlier: the widening distance between genetic capacity and phenotypic behavior. In fact, the epicycles must have been a driving force in this widening. Their operation independent from coevolutionary feedback cycles pushed these cycles in culturally defined directions—not, to be sure, toward counteradaptive technosocial strategies (or at least not for long) but toward modes that would not have arisen without their independence. The epicycles provided a mechanism of acceleration in the cultural accumulation of *Homo sapiens*, one that was fertile in its proximity to behavior and hence its iterability.

But the mechanism determined no comprehensive cultural organization. Like natural selection itself, it could exert pressure but not aim for any goal or telos. The immanence of abstract

234

machines in the dynamic systems from which they arise guar-
antees this aimless impulse. The idea of human modernity, as
John Shea warns, has often enough been yoked to more or less
pernicious teleologies. But to avoid those it is not necessary to
jettison modernity itself—jettisoning at the same time, in Shea's
alternative of cultural variability built on unchanging capacities,
biocultural coevolution within our species. It is only necessary to
understand the natures of mechanisms that *could not* have generated goal-directed development.

If there was any teleology involved in the career of *Homo
sapiens* over the last 200,000 years, it was the tendency toward
deeper sedimentation of cultural archives. This tendency was not
ours alone; it arose from the complexities of hominin technosociality more than a million years before us and was, long before
sapient humans, hard-wired in the clade. For reasons that remain
ill understood, but that could have much to do with the redoubling of epicyclic generation as accumulated culture deepened,
it was carried farther in our species than in any of our relatives,
hence farther than in any other species that has existed on earth.
The twisted paths of *Homo sapiens* took off from this enhanced
accumulation, and here I agree with Shea in identifying a general
cognitive capacity that was present in the species from its start.
To follow these paths, then, is to attempt to describe the complexities of feedback mechanisms of both coevolution and demographic ecology and, further, the bearing on these of the forming
and reforming epicycles of culture.

Along the way we must remember the nature of the world
inhabited by these earlier humans alongside several other hominin species. It was a world prey to the most extreme climatic and
ecological fluctuations hominin species had ever encountered; if
demands of earlier Pleistocene environments had long selected
hominins whose genotypes enabled phenotypic versatility, this
pressure was now greater than ever. In this world relatively small
human populations might pursue largely independent courses
over long periods, developing technosocial innovations under

different, unique conditions of environmental affordance and constraint. Depending on local ecological circumstance, on population sizes and proximity to other populations, and more, these innovations might have long-lasting but strictly local effects, or linger for some period and then die off as the originating circumstances and population changed, or spread rapidly to other populations in a never-to-be-slowed, finally global dispersion. Sometimes, given the likelihood of similar epicycles arising, innovations could have multiple origins, later merging in the meetings of populations and setting off new epicycles and cycles of innovation. In general—across some hypothetical statistical census of these populations—we must presume that the sedimentation of cultural archives deepened, and that with it the pace of operation of epicyclic mechanisms quickened. And, if across the whole period gene-culture coevolution never ceased, its potential to create large genetic differences among human populations diminished by about 60,000 years ago, as the genotypes that characterize all modern humans began to spread from east Africa both within that continent and across the globe.

The perfect storm, long in the making, is upon us. From its volatile mix of elements will emerge the features that define a universal human modernity. The repeated inventions of beads and engravings are lightning strikes on the horizon, revealing to us a process that set humans apart in the workings of biocultural coevolution. Three crucial and intimately bound features of the modernity-to-come will be left in the storm's wake: musicking, speaking, and the ultimate, dramatic extensions in our lineage of thinking-at-a-distance.

CHAPTER SEVEN

100,000–20,000 Years Ago, II:

Musicking

How the Hunters Returned

The group moved up the Danube Valley with the new season and the herds. In number they were reduced now, at the end of a harsh winter, but still some fifty strong. The migrating animals that provided their dietary staples led them on—reindeer, red deer, horses, also mammoths and rhinoceros. For a far longer period than their collective memory could embrace, larger forces had granted their subsistence and the animals'. A relatively gentle climate sustained a varied environment in the hills and glens over which they ranged: in the valleys, rolling steppe grasslands—the favored habitat of their herding prey; sparse, taiga-like forests on the hillsides, which the deer preferred; and, at the unwelcoming highpoints, alpine tundra. They rarely ventured to the highlands with their cliffs, usually only to hunt ibexes, to snare birds or, in the springtime, to steal their eggs.

The landscape was broad and they and their kind few—like the big cats who preyed along with them on the herds—so they met other groups only occasionally. These encounters were happenstance and fraught events, always on the verge of turning sour, with the larger group effectively raiding the smaller. When they did not turn, they presented essential opportunities for peaceable exchange of materials and group members, and even for transitory alliances to mount herd drives and hunts more ambitious than usual. The other, different humans that had hunted these grounds in much earlier periods of mild climate were long gone. Of them the group knew nothing.

Their chief material needs, the weapons for the hunt, were portable and valued enough to be curated across their travels. These and the clothing they wore made up most of the material possessions they moved with—most but not all. Other needs could be gathered as they went: wood for fires; berries for food; grasses for lashes and woven containers; stones for new spear points, blades, knives, scrapers, and awls. Still other materials were supplied from the inedible parts of their prey. Bone and antler made fine points and awls, more flexible and less likely to shatter than those fashioned from stone. Sinews provided strong nonvegetable straps, and the cured hides themselves were essential for clothing and blankets, and for the lean-tos and wooden-frame tents they sometimes erected. The herds provided much.

The terrain itself granted one more resource. The low hills and cliffs around were riddled with limestone caves where refuge could be sought. Here, in front of the caves and in their entryways and antechambers, they set down their temporary camps. These took on a novelty with each new season, even when they were built at caves they had visited before. This was because the group's portable cultures had left little behind from previous years, really nothing but a midden, at a comfortable distance from the cave's entrance, that had been well-picked by scavengers by the time they returned. It was also sometimes because the caves had welcomed other inhabitants since their last visit—lurking predators, especially bears to be driven out or killed.

Whatever the danger and effort involved, inhabiting the caves was essential. They provided solid shelter for lives either too mobile or too engrossed in other activities to construct it; they formed a network of nurturing way stations as the group moved with the herds. The caves protected them from the cold nights, even wintry nights, as well as from the hyenas, wolves, and other four-legged scavengers and predators not satisfied with the remains of kills the group left behind at the hunting grounds.

The caves provided something else, less palpable than this but essential to the group's well-being. In a fashion not new in itself, but which the group pushed to new levels of intricacy, their shelters sharpened their lifeways. The group identity crystalized in the light and heat of the fires they lit in the entryways. With this came many things, good and not: reenactments and recountings of the day's activities, the laying of plans for subsequent days, assertions of leadership, resulting rivalries and fights, the furthering or fracturing of new and old liaisons ranging from strategic alliance to sexual bonding—and often including both. This was also a time when a chosen few made excursions deeper into the cavern, to explore there mysteries of a sort the human psyche tended more and more to project into the world. There also, sometimes, they revisited scenes of earlier rites—even traditions of these—that they had enacted in prior years and habitations.

These crystalizing moments were a specialized aspect of the taskscape of the group. From them arose modes of creation different from the more functional facture of tools and weapons—subtly so, for at base they were only modest variants of that facture. The most skillful of the makers were entrusted with prized materials: animal teeth, amber, mammoth ivory, or light, hollow bird bones. From these materials, while other, younger and less skillful makers looked on, they fashioned beads, or pendants shaped in the form of animals feared or hunted. The objects were esteemed for more than the skill involved in their making. Hung on a strap or bound to clothing, they betokened special status within the group. Some of them signified other things, too, gathering unseen powers; these were talismans that accompanied the few who explored the deeper caverns.

From this corner of their taskscape emerged also distinctive kinds of tools. These, like all the tools and weapons their ancestors had fashioned before them, were extensions of the body designed to ease a process, amplify a force, or in general fulfill a function. But the functions of the new tools were qualitatively different from the usual ones. A hollow bone from the wing of a large bird was scraped at intervals along it to create openings to the interior. With its ends sawn off, blowing into it at the right angle could produce a marvel of sounds, like high voices but without words. Or a section of mammoth tusk was cracked open lengthwise, hollowed out, and fixed back together with adhesives; finger holes drilled with a stone awl along one side of this tube made another versatile instrument. This was a more elaborate, effortful construction than the other, managed only by the most experienced and skilled makers.

These instruments were not fashioned to help in the hunt, the processing of a carcass, the cutting and gathering of grasses, the making of further tools and weapons, or other such activities. Instead they were put to other uses, gathering acoustical energies, like voices raised in chant or lullaby, fostering that tightening of bonds around and within the caves, and directing activity toward an entrainment uniquely precise in the life of the group. They were resonators, amplifiers, voice shifters. Sometimes they too were carried to the inner recesses of the cave, sonorous talismans that appealed there to unseen agents or forces.

On the instruments, players often used a flint blade to incise careful, tiny notches. These were different from the marks the makers scratched to assist in the process of construction—gauging the placement of finger holes and the like. These other notches marked the serial uses of the instruments, an incised, material memory of the special circumstances in which their powers stepped to the fore. The oldest instruments recorded many years' rites; these too, along with weapons and clothing, the group carried with them on their travels.

Differences over Aurignacian Difference

So might go a story of the earliest *Homo sapiens* in northern Europe. Or so it might not. There is no part of the above fiction that is not grounded in findings or interpretations of archaeologists, yet its overall accuracy might be meager or worse. The humans it describes were the producers of Aurignacian culture, named for the type-site at Aurignac in the middle-Pyrenees region of southern France. Aurignacian lithic assemblages and other artifacts are known from many sites scattered especially in north-central and northwest Europe. The type-artifact for the assemblage is a bone or antler point with a split base, presumed to have facilitated its hafting onto a spear handle, but other characteristic tools include scrapers and blades elaborately retouched by flaking many tiny "bladelets" off the edges.[1]

Some of the most famous Aurignacian excavations are those of the Swabian Jura of southwest Germany, near the source of the Danube River: Hohlenstein-Stadel, Vogelherd, Geissenklösterle, and Hohle Fels. From the first site, in early twentieth-century excavations, came one of the most arresting and intriguing pieces of Paleolithic figurative carving: the so-called lion-man, a foot-tall therianthropic statue carved from mammoth ivory. It was unearthed in fragments and only recognized and pieced together many years later. The other sites have continued to yield treasures down to the present day, under the recent supervision of scholars from Tübingen and Heidelberg. New finds have included animal miniatures carved from mammoth-ivory, bird-bone musical pipes, and even a human figurine, perhaps the earliest known. The region as a whole has been the focal point in recent years of a theory that, in its strongest form, posits human modernity taking shape in central Europe during *Homo sapiens*' migration up the Danube Valley from the east. Most archaeologists, including the lead researcher at Tübingen, Nicholas Conard, adhere to a weaker version that sees the region as the center of a particularly vibrant but not unique early human culture.

Aurignacian artifacts are considered by archaeologists to represent one of the earliest modern human cultures in Europe. Some still hold to a view that places them first among the contenders, but the analysis of new sites and the fine-grained resolution of different hominin lithic technologies from this general period have tended to weaken this claim in favor of greater nuance. Nevertheless, whatever the status of these other industries—Proto-Aurignacian, Initial Aurignacian, Fumanian, Bacho Kirian, Bohunician, Uluzzian, and more—"classic" Aurignacian still occupies a primary place in debates about fundamental issues: the dispersal of *Homo sapiens* through western Eurasia, the final fate of the Neandertals, possible meetings in Europe of the two species, and the precise natures of the techno-complexes created by the last Neandertals and the first European modern humans. The Aurignacian is the industry that more than any other has been associated with the idea of a modern human "revolution" in Europe, the industry thought to mark off the Early Upper Paleolithic from the Final Middle Paleolithic period.

It is all the more vexing, then, that we know so little about the creators of Aurignacian cultures. This is true, first and foremost, because the classic European sites have not yielded human fossils; fossils also remain exceedingly scarce from archaeologically related sites in eastern Europe and the Levant. For the sites at the heart of the Aurignacian industry, that is, we have as yet no confirmation of *Homo sapiens'* involvement of the sort archaeologists prize most: artifacts found *in situ* with human remains. The consensus inference is, to be sure, that modern humans crafted the artifacts and the culture around them. But it is in part a negative inference drawn from the strikingly different nature of most late-Mousterian industries solidly associated with Neandertals—even through the occasional co-occurrence of artifacts and human bones.

Also severe is the problem of dating Aurignacian sites. Archaeological stratigraphy tells us that Aurignacian cultures precede the Gravettian and Solutrean industries in northern Europe, making them at least 28,000–30,000 years old. This poses a chronology deep enough to challenge the reliability of carbon-14 (radiocarbon) dating technology, for two main reasons. First, 30,000 years amounts to more than five half-lives of 14C, a time when about 97 percent of the original isotope—present at the start only in minute quantities—has decayed. The vanishingly small traces left magnify the problems of modern contamination in the samples dated; the earlier the sample, simply, the greater the chance its radiocarbon age will be significantly distorted by contaminants. Moreover, because of shifting levels of 14C in the atmosphere, all radiocarbon dates need to be calibrated against other dating standards. Beyond about 12,000 years, however, those standards become ever harder to find and interpret, so the resulting calibration curves become generally less reliable with increasing chronological distance from us. Recent curves warrant high confidence up to about 26,000 years ago, still not quite enough to take us to Aurignacian times. The newest agreed-upon curve reaches back 50,000 years, but its degree of accuracy at its earlier end remains a matter of analysis and debate.

In these circumstances, and given what is at stake in Middle/Upper Paleolithic research—nothing less, for many, than the origins of human culture—it is hardly surprising that large differences of view surround Aurignacian humans. All agree that these cultures hover back somewhere beyond the 30,000-year mark; almost all agree in assigning them to *Homo sapiens*. Beyond this our knowledge remains fluid enough that even two very recent analyses of material from the same site have led to datings several thousand years apart. The site in question, Geissenklösterle, is important here, since it has yielded three of the eight musical pipes thus far unearthed in the Swabian Jura.

On one side are researchers who assign the earliest Aurignacian levels of Geissenklösterle to sometime shortly after 40,000 years ago; on the other those who put them between 43,000 and 41,000 years back. But what immense, global changes took place across this span! Warm, brief interstadials, each lasting about a millennium, set in about 44,000 and 42,000 years ago; another longer interstadial lasted from about 38,000–36,000 years ago. Each of these three episodes was a D-O cycle of very rapid warming followed by gradual, then quickened cooling. Between the first two and the third, however, came an extreme cold spell that endured from about 40,000–38,000 years ago. Its expanding glaciers and ecological shifts coincided with a Heinrich Event and, dramatically, the Campanian Ignimbrite supereruption near Naples, with all the disruption these brought. There is much reason to believe that human populations in northern Europe, sapient or Neandertal, were much diminished or even extinguished in this intervening stadial; we saw in Chapter 6 that one team of scholars sees the climatic deterioration at this time as a central factor in the final "macro-extinction" of the Neandertals.

In short, though a few thousand years' divergence at the distance of 40,000 years may not seem like a lot, it has immense implications for questions of modern human dispersal in Europe and the continuity of their habitation there. The two datings of Geissenklösterle lead to fundamentally divergent ideas about Aurignacian culture. In the later dating it is imagined to flood quickly across a newly warmed, benign Europe, carried by new sapient groups filling areas that earlier catastrophes had emptied of humans. A few much-debated earlier human industries in western Europe—particularly the Uluzzian of Italy and Greece—are judged to be Neandertal productions, cut off by the deteriorations about 40,000 years ago; still other, eastern European industries reflect incursions of other sapient populations into those areas from the east. The new populations of western Europe brought a new density of exchange, and with it a new concentration of cultural innovations. "Once set in motion," these authors conclude, "an accelerated flow of information led, not only to continued technological progress, but also, during the later Aurignacian, to innovative social adaptations in the form of art, music and, probably, religious beliefs."[2]

In the other, earlier dating of Geissenklösterle, Aurignacian cultures dispersed across northern Europe slightly later than Uluzzian cultures had moved along the northern Mediterranean coast; the Uluzzian, for these researchers, was produced by *sapiens*, not Neandertals. The first sapient humans crossed Europe early and quickly, starting about 45,000 years ago and reaching southwest England, then a peninsula rather than an island, as early as 2,000 years later (on the sole evidence of a maxilla unearthed in Devon long ago and recently reanalyzed and redated). The modern human populating of northern Europe predated by several millennia the deterioration of conditions after the 40,000-year mark. The authors (they include Conard) do not speculate on what became of the sapient populations during the cold millennia that followed; but the continuities and progress that they envisage from early to later Aurignacian cultures across a number of millennia clearly indicate that, in their model, the humans weathered the bad times: "The caves of the Swabian Jura document the earliest phase of the Aurignacian, and the region can be viewed as one of the key areas in which a variety of cultural innovations, including figurative art, mythical images, and musical instruments, are first documented." While these authors are quick to caution that all these innovations probably did not emerge *uniquely* in the Danube Valley, they see this region as a prime corridor for the movement of humans through, and development of modern human culture in, Europe.[3]

The conceptions of early *Homo sapiens* and cultural epicycles reviewed in Chapter 6 might well incline us to envisage a different history than either of these, in which the course of Aurignacian cultures was not continuous and progressive, but more episodic in nature. Such a history would assign a different significance than the other accounts to these cultures in the overall career of *Homo sapiens*. To emphasize discontinuity in this picture is not to doubt that common techniques of lithic and bone tool- and weapon-making characterize sites spread widely across the Danube Valley and farther west into central and southern France.[4] But it is a mistake to think that Aurignacian lithic remnants must reflect an overall homogeneity of culture across large geographical and temporal spans. To do so denies to these groups the special hominin capacity to generate large cultural differences through accumulated archives and threatens to resurrect the kind of teleologies that led in the first place to the idea of a European revolution at the Middle/Upper Paleolithic border. Cultural epicycles exert an impulsive but nonprogressive force which, as we saw in Chapter

6, can multiply the sphere of epicyclic effects: sometimes driving the creation of difference, sometimes reiterating gestures of difference in diverse local situations—in these together revealing the complex correlations of difference and sameness in human biocultural evolution—and sometimes facilitating the merging of distant but similar gestures in the meetings and migrations of peoples.

The most stunning objects unearthed at the Aurignacian sites of the Swabian Jura seem inevitably to elicit rhapsodies to teleology and progressivism, even from those who know better. Exquisite, small ivory carvings of horse, mammoth, bird, and big cat; the lion-man from Hohlenstein-Stadel; a bosomy female figurine, the earliest known Paleolithic "Venus"; and the several musical instruments of Geissenklösterle, Vogelherd, and Hohle Fels: these finds inspire speculations about the origins of art and music that often veer toward the exclamatory. Accompanying caveats (such as that of Conard and his associates: It probably was happening elsewhere, too) do little to calm the rapture. But the fact remains that the likes of these artifacts have not been unearthed in any of the two dozen or so other "classic" Aurignacian sites that share so much technological knowhow with the Swabian ones.

What are we to make of this absence? In the first place: That the actions of local or regional populations do not necessarily signal a Europe-wide or even northern European flowering of the techniques of figural representation, musical instrument construction, and counterintuitive, imaginary (not to say "mythical") figures. They could instead reflect no more than the epicyclic, local burgeoning of these gestures in circumstances not repeated for hundreds of miles around or thousands of years after them. It is unwarranted to assume that every cultural formation within a group reflects the behaviors also of every other group within the same techno-complex. Sometimes human gestures and families of gestures live themselves out in a single locale; we have seen, in the tendency of certain epicycles to recur, that this does not mean that similar developments cannot arise elsewhere.

In the second place, the absence of these special Swabian artifacts at other sites suggests that their appearance was not an originary moment but instead a local *movement of difference*. There can be no doubt that something extraordinary was going on in Swabian caves 35,000 years ago and more, but we cannot know either that it was the seed of later developments or that the like had not occurred in earlier circumstances. The nature of chance in the preservation of ancient artifacts such as these disallows such conclusions.

What we *can* know is that human capacities and cultural patterns, not new in themselves, were focused in *this* way at *this* particular place and time. What we can infer, in the face of this knowledge, is that this focusing bespeaks the attendancy of a cultural epicycle. Microbursts of innovation, we have seen, seem to be the natural product of deep cultural sedimentation and epicycle, and Schöningen, Atapuerca, Blombos and Howiesons Poort, and the Swabian Jura all suggest that we might need to see such microbursts as the rule rather than exception in the long-*durée* history of hominin culture. It is not the case that every human society that hunts large birds will end up fashioning from their bones pipes for musicking. But the reasons why one group does so while another does not cannot be understood simply as a measure of genetic capacity or through the operations of singular invention and cultural transmission.

If the rhapsodic, progressivist views quoted above assert a dispersion of cultural innovations not supported by the archaeological record, they also seem to assert sweeping diachronic continuities from Aurignacian cultures down to the later Gravettian, Solutrean, and Magdalenian cultures, a European series beginning about 28,000 years ago. The tendency is strong to assimilate the Venus of Hohle Fels to the many female figurines of Gravettian and later production, even though most of them are at least 10,000 years younger, some much more. It is likewise hard to resist associating the bird-bone musical pipes of the Swabian Jura with a series of such instruments excavated from the 1910s to the 1940s at Isturitz in southwest France, or with one more pipe unearthed in lower Austria in the 1990s. But these pipes are likewise much younger. The Austrian example dates back about 19,000 years, while the Isturitz pipes seem to be somewhat older, coming mostly from Gravettian layers.[5] All these other pipes stand at 10,000–20,000 years' distance from the Swabian instruments.[6]

The happy vision of long-term cultural continuities might be countered, categorically, by a possibility we explored in Chapter 6: that modern human populations were *replaced* in Europe between the Aurignacian and this later, continuous cultural sequence. True cultural continuities among European humans may start only with Gravettian cultures, not with earlier, thwarted habitations. Yet even if there was no wholesale replacement of populations, why should we see here a continuous technomusical tradition of ten or twenty millennia? This is akin to imagining a 30,000-year tradition of ochre engravings at Blombos Cave, except that here geographical separations of hundreds of miles are added to the immense chronological span involved. The mistake is to envisage human cultural accumulation in anachronistic ways: as the unbroken passing down and dispersion of a tradition, akin, say, to European painting since the Middle Ages, rather than as something distinct and impressively deeper in its function (something at work also in that painting tradition, no doubt, but almost invisible, given the short time-span involved). This different something concerns, again, cultural archives and epicyclic attendancies on them. Many rivulets of cultural innovation may have sunk into the sand of the same streambed before a river flowed.

The challenge here, as in the case of the Blombos engravings, is to avoid equating similarity with continuity. The bone pipes of Isturitz and the Swabian Jura resemble one another in many features, but the difficulty in ascribing these similarities to the workings of a continuous tradition arises even in considering the Isturitz pipes alone, if their insecure stratigraphy is taken to indicate that they were deposited in the cave over several millennia. Accepting this indication left Francesco d'Errico and Graeme Lawson at a loss in their careful study of the Isturitz pipes a decade ago. "Preserved in the forms of the instruments themselves," they wrote, "are suggestions of a long-term consistency in subtleties of design, which, considering the vast timescales involved is difficult to explain in terms of solely oral connection, or by imitating some preserved prototype, or indeed by independent invention."[7]

An explanation begins to take shape if instead of these alternatives we envisage the repetition of an epicyclic formation, and it involves just such independent invention, occurring outside any continuous cultural tradition. Material technologies grew more and more intricate and varied, in societies that were already musical and ritualized. With these preconditions, the likelihood grew that an epicycle would form fostering the production of *tools for musicking*. Add in hunting and trapping techniques that brought birds, with their hollow bones, into the family of species providing human sustenance—relatively new techniques: Neandertals seem not to have hunted birds—and the possibility quickly increases that blown pipes would appear, a specific outcropping of the epicyclic formation.

In such a scenario, the surprise is not that musical tools such as the Swabian ones exist as far back as they do. It is not even the sophistication of their construction, though this is considerable, for Aurignacian lithic industries demonstrate that their manufacturers possessed both skill and ingenuity. The question instead is why we have not found more such artifacts, and indeed earlier ones, produced as the musical-tool epicycle became more and more likely to spring up across many human societies.

But is this really surprising? The nonlithic materials from which musical instruments must often have been made—strings and notched branches for musical bows, perhaps, or percussion sticks, drum heads of hide, and wooden frames to stretch them on—are ephemeral at the scale of tens of millennia, doomed to decay and disappear. More than this: Do we always recognize musical tools when we see them, for example, airfoils made of bone for a bullroarer?[8] Our misrecognition might extend even to the lithic record. One recent hypothesis regarding the exquisitely thin stone bifaces fashioned by Solutrean cultures about 20,000 years ago and more recent Magdalenian blades sees them as too delicate for use either as weapons or as tools for scraping or cutting and proposes that they may have been produced as chimes.[9]

If the Swabian pipes suggest such epicyclic forces at work, can they indicate anything more general about the nature of these forces? More pointedly: If they are purely regional phenomena, playing no role in a continuous tradition attached even to subsequent European cultural formations, what implications can they carry for the general course of human musicking across the late Pleistocene? And finally: What is at stake in our desire to generalize from these artifacts?

What Aurignacian Musical Pipes Tell Us

Some specifics, to start. From three extensively excavated sites near the city of Ulm, Geissenklösterle, Hohle Fels, and Vogelherd, fragments have been retrieved of what seem to have been eight musical instruments. Only three of these are relatively complete; the other five are more fragmentary—in four cases, exceedingly so—their natures surmised from the similarities in material and workmanship of these fragments to those comprised in the more complete artifacts. Of the three relatively complete instruments, two come from Geissenklösterle, where they were excavated along with pieces of a third instrument in a layer associated with mature or late Aurignacian cultures. The other almost complete instrument, in contrast, was unearthed in 2008 in the deepest, "basal" Aurignacian layers of Hohle Fels; along with it were found two more fragments of instruments and the Aurignacian Venus mentioned above. (The several fragments of two pipes from Vogelherd were excavated under circumstances not permitting unambiguous stratigraphy.)[10]

The varying datings discussed above for the Swabian Aurignacian concern, precisely, Geissenklösterle. The earlier estimates would make the *late* Aurignacian instruments here as many as 40,000 years old; the later dates would assign them an age of 34,000–38,000 years. The earliest Aurignacian layer from Hohle Fels, if of comparable age to that at Geissenklösterle, would locate the instruments newly discovered there anywhere from 37,000 to 43,000 years ago. These are, by any measure, arrestingly ancient artifacts. They were created about three-quarters of the way back from the present day to the final, successful migrations of modern humans out of Africa and their first permanent incursions into many new territories. Perhaps, indeed, they were made within ten millennia of those movements.

The Swabian instruments were seemingly all of a similar general design, namely, pipes with finger holes arranged along them. It is difficult to imagine that they were devised for anything other than the blown production of pitches. Whether they involved reeds or some other embouchure aid is not known; to produce tones they would not have required them, or even built-in notches or fipples (in the manner of a recorder). While they are of similar design, however, the pipes show two very dissimilar approaches to construction. Four of the eight instruments were fashioned from wing bones of large birds, especially radii from swans and griffon vultures. These were hollow, so to fashion a pipe they required only the scraping and smoothing of the exterior of the bone, the sawing off of the ends, and the making of holes. The finger holes were created not by drilling with an awl, which probably would have cracked the delicate bones, but by scraping across the tube until the hole appeared. This left a characteristic beveling effect around the hole; whether it was intended to facilitate an air-tight stoppage of the hole with finger pressure or did so as a serendipity of engineering cannot be judged. Two of the nearly complete instruments are of this construction, one from Geissenklösterle and one the recently unearthed pipe from Hohle Fels; the latter is pictured in Plate I.

All these techniques of sawing and scraping, it is worth noting, must have been employed by these humans regularly in the treatment of other organic materials; there is nothing revolutionary in the toolmaking techniques themselves, no radical innovation on the taskscape.

The second construction was more complex. It employed mammoth ivory, broken longitudinally along the grain of the outer cementum or underlying dentine, hollowed out, and reassembled, probably with adhesive. Into this tube the finger holes were scraped, or perhaps, in this case, drilled. One of the relatively complete Geissenklösterle pipes is of this construction (see Plate II), and three other small ivory fragments that seem in their working to have belonged to similar pipes have been recovered from Hohle Fels and Vogelherd. The techniques here, if more elaborate, again show no innovations; adhesive manufacture must by now have been a regular part of the fashioning of composite weapons and tools, probably playing a role in a characteristic Aurignacian weapon, the spear with a split-end point fashioned from bone. The proximity of the techniques used in fashioning these pipes to other Aurignacian technologies counters the suggestion, made by d'Errico and Lawson in their consideration of the Isturitz pipes, that their sophisticated construction must point to a long developmental prehistory.[11] On the contrary, these musical tools are exactly the kind of outcropping one might expect as sedimented archives of material techniques came under the sway of attendant epicycles. Whatever the human musical behaviors that no doubt preceded them, the pipes do not necessitate an extended predevelopment of specifically musical technologies.

D'Errico and Lawson speculate also in another direction, taking up at some length the parallel notches cut into the Isturitz instruments perpendicular to the length of the tube. The enigma of these notches was discussed before them also by Dominique Buisson, also apropos of the Isturitz pipes.[12] These seem to have been incised at various times and with different tools. They have no obvious relation to the construction of the instrument, as for example in the gauging of the placement of finger holes; indeed Buisson shows that some of the notches can be seen to have been cut *after* the holes were abraded. Neither do they take on any of the regularities that might be expected of ornamentation. D'Errico and Lawson point to instances, instead, where their irregular spacing shifts from relaxed to squeezed as the end of the bone is reached, as if the engraver or engravers had run out of space in attempting to record a series of marks whose length was otherwise determined. These facts suggest to them that the notches were an "artificial memory system" recording—and accumulating, if they were incised at different times—some kind of information.

The Swabian pipes show markings of a sort generally similar to those on the Isturitz pipes. On the ones from Geissenklösterle the markings are regular and might have functioned in the construction of the instrument. The markings on the swan-bone pipe fall at more or less even intervals along much of its length, exactly as might a gauge for positioning the finger holes, while those on the mammoth-ivory pipe are more numerous and regular and are incised along the joint of the two longitudinal halves of the pipe—as if, Conard and his coworkers speculate, to help seal the joint.[13] One of the other ivory fragments, from Vogelherd, also preserves such notches.

The earlier Swabian pipes, that is, the Hohle Fels artifacts unearthed in 2008, two ivory fragments and the almost complete bone pipe, show rather different markings. All three have incisions less numerous and regular than the pipes from the other sites (though one of the ivory fragments also shows traces of the "sealing" notches along its edge). The idea that these somehow stored information, perhaps recording or counting events in which the pipe was used, is an appealing one. It might gain support from the enigmatic incisions, cross-hatchings, and dots found on the Venus figurine from the same stratum at Hohle Fels and on the animal figurines from Vogelherd. The markings on these objects seem not to be of iconic ("figurative") intent, but rather to serve a more purely indexical purpose (see Figure 7.1).

This speculation opens out onto the broad use-context of all these objects—their location, that is, on Aurignacian taskscapes. We cannot know the specifics; for that, there is only fiction, like the story that opened this chapter. The revelations of the artifacts must come at more general behavioral levels. The markings, whether for constructive purposes, decoration, or commemoration of some sort; the constructions themselves, requiring not new techniques but the swerving, even in lives of constant, hard challenge, of technology in the directions of figurines and pitch pipes; and the sheer attention and effort these artifacts commanded: all these bespeak some considerable importance invested in objects not of obvious pragmatic utility. They represent a sense of the usefulness of objects expanded toward new horizons—a usefulness taking a step beyond physical advantage to metaphysical benefit. In this they signal a hominin sociality of a kind nonexistent 500,000 years ago, probably not attained in the same degree by Neandertals, and perhaps not even fully manifest by the ochre-engravers and ochre-painters of Blombos 100,000 years back.

This is not to sing again an old rhapsody, the European Upper Paleolithic revolution, but instead to reaffirm a model of *epicyclic proliferation*. The early Blombos societies were no doubt different from Aurignacian ones, but subtly so. These subtle differences may have been largely effaced already 60,000 years ago, when, in nearby Howiesons Poort, designs similar to modern Khoisan designs were scraped onto the same materials the Khoisan would use—ostrich egg shells. The effacement might have begun as soon as the genetic stock that would eventually populate the non-African world took form in East Africa, beginning as much as 100,000 years ago. From that time the enduring dispersal of this population beyond Africa would await the passage of another 50,000 years, but it spread not only out of but through that huge continent, meeting and mixing several or many times with other populations of somewhat different genetic makeup. The humans

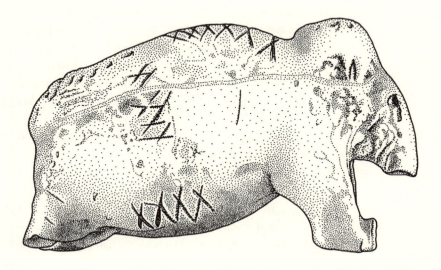

Figure 7.1 Mammoth figurine from mammoth
ivory with incised cross-hatching, Vogelherd.
Drawn by Virge Kask from a photograph by
Hilde Jensen, © Tübingen University.

encountered along the way must have been much like the new-comers in their capacities, and the final, intra-African genetic shifts incremental, not revolutionary.[14]

By the time of this genetic formation and homogenization, at any rate, the *behavioral* possibilities of late hominins, especially sapient humans in several or many independent populations, were unpredictable and volatile, spurred by the frequent operation of epicyclic mechanisms. Humans and their local societies and cultures must have been always on the verge of flowerings of cultural investment—in the sense of the Swabian investment in those figurines and pipes—that might lead in extraordinary directions. Sometimes nothing flowered. At other times the flowerings resulted in the paradoxical, repeated anomalies described above and in Chapter 6, which were not expressions of new genetic capacities but instead opportunities found and explored in specific circumstances on local taskscapes.

Never forget the power of feedback: A cultural gesture that arose could in turn alter taskscapes and selective terrains and eventually have some impact on humans' continuing biocultural coevolution. By about 50,000 years ago, however, the power of this feedback was lessened; it could create only minimal, not wholesale genetic difference in a humanity that was, across most of the Old World, essentially one group. The classic instance of the small genetic differences that could still emerge is lactose tolerance among certain African and European herding populations, selected since the beginning of the Neolithic period. But now the sporadic, rich behavioral flowerings were more important than such genetic microshifts. They could under the right circumstances contribute to sedimentations of cultural behaviors from which would stem both the commonalities and the staggering differences of human societies today. As we saw in Chapter 6, there is only one teleology at work in late hominin and particularly sapient evolution: the tendency for cultural accumulation to deepen. From this and from the resulting proliferation of epicycles, acting to accelerate the deepening, come all the rest.

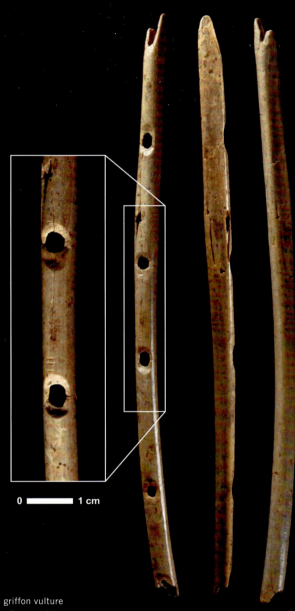

Plate I Pipe from griffon vulture radius, Hohle Fels. Photo: Hilde Jensen, © Tübingen University.

0 ▬▬▬ 1 cm

0 ▬▬▬ 2 cm

Plate II Pipe from mammoth
ivory, Geissenklösterle. Photo:
J. Liptàk, © Tübingen University.

This interrelation of general, hard-wired capacities and volatile behaviors is exemplified also in one of the features of the Swabian pipes that is both obvious and consistently overlooked. Within rather flexible limits involving lip adjustments, possible use of embouchure aids, and overblowing, the placement of holes *fixed the pitches* the instruments could play. Musical archaeologists tend to leap immediately from this fact to reconstructions of the instruments and questions of *what* pitch arrays they might have sounded—the "is it a C-sharp? A Phrygian scale?" debate. What is staring us in the face is a different question: What is the import of a technologically fixed array *in itself*?[15]

We have seen in earlier chapters that discrete pitch is no matter to be taken lightly in either perception or cognition. Under any hypothesis the complex, not fully understood apparatus employed in hearing and reproducing it required a complicated coevolutionary development. This included, in the area of hominin communication, the winnowing of discrete intonational signals from the analog gesture-calls, which resulted in the formation of a dualistic perception that simultaneously gauged broad (phrase-length) intonational contours and the pitches comprised in them. Meanwhile, perceiving discretized pitch is bound up with perceiving octave duplication and the weaker senses of pitch alliance probably related to it in cognition, for example the interval of a fifth. This complex of percepts seems to generate emergent hierarchies, a "tonal encoding" of pitches probably fostered also by asymmetries in the division of octaves into smaller interval arrays. Both the falling out of hierarchized pitch arrays and the dual perception of contour and individual pitch connect the perception of discrete pitch to capacities of late hominins for hierarchic cognition and its subset, discrete combinatoriality. These features of musicking emerged from the deep history of hominin communication, extending back before our species. Though they involved many turns around biocultural coevolutionary cycles of early hominin technosociality and communication, they were probably well established in *Homo sapiens* before the first traces of musical tools.

In this coevolution, at any rate, *Homo sapiens* came late and the Aurignacian pipes later still. It is far-fetched to think of the recent and straightforward technological swerve represented in the Swabian pipes as *initiating* evolutionary developments toward the complexities of discretized pitch perception. The instruments instead give us the first technological trace we possess *reflecting* this achieved perception; they must not be confused with its emergence. In fact, given the proximity of their technology to techniques deployed elsewhere on the Aurignacian taskscape and the sophistication of humans long before these cultures, it is probably only a matter of time before similar musical tools from another, separate epicyclic eruption are found—perhaps, indeed, an earlier one in Africa, from before the sapient incursions into Europe. But this is just the point: The Swabian pipes are remnants of such an eruption in the early Aurignacian, in which technologies, their cultural applications, and hard-wired percepts merged locally to incite novel human behaviors.

The pipes, in representing materially the perception of fixed pitches, have one more insight to yield. The winnowing of discrete pitches from the graded intonational contours of the calls of protodiscourse brought with it an abstraction, a distancing of the pitches themselves from meaning (see Chapter 5). While broad pitch contours continued to convey emotive and even semantic content, the pitches underwent an absolution from signifying. Music was from the first, in this sense, *absolute*. Discrete pitch arrays have in fact ever since maintained this distance from signification. Individual pitches within them become signs only in extraordinary contexts, usually involving accompanying language, not as an inherent function of their deployment in musical designs. This abstraction was momentous, marking a point at which, from within the selective pressures for effective communication, there arose an element (or assemblage of elements) *resistant to signification*.

The abstraction involved was, I think, related to growing hominin capacities for abstraction of all kinds—to, in other words, the increasing ability of late hominins to think at a distance. I have mentioned several times this capacity and the "release" it enabled from the constraints of copresent sociality. It is a hypertrophied aspect of all humanity today; and, while it arguably extends in the modern biosphere beyond our species, to some birds and other mammals, this extension is not large, and no other species carries it as far as humans. Early hominin societies show little sign of the capacity (see Chapter 2), but its increase is apparent by the era of Neandertals and presumably our immediate ancestors (Chapter 4). With the clear intimations of rule-governed indexicality and symbolism in early *Homo sapiens* (Chapter 5), the span of thought beyond copresence approaches modern dimensions. I will return below to some of the social implications of this final extension.

The neurological coalescence that enabled perception of distinct pitch and abstraction of pitch from signification seems to fall into the same cognitive developments that enable thinking-at-a-distance in general. Symptoms of these developments include the move from palpable copresence to something less palpable, and with it a vast expansion of the human imaginarium. They include also more schematic elements of thought, especially its hierarchic structuring and the rule-governance that can order these structures. Discrete pitch assemblages carried these formal elements of cognition into new territory. Through immensely intricate cognizing of perceived stimuli, the assemblages formed hierarchic structures according to constraints of frequency, overtone, duplication and affinity of tones, and, finally, tonal encoding—all this in the process of abstracting an acoustic phenomenon to a nonsignifying level. The crystallization of discrete pitch hierarchies may have represented one of the most dramatic instances of all of thinking-at-a-distance.

This brings us back, finally, to the Swabian pipes. Their form is remarkable not merely because they fix pitches, but because they visualize, spatialize, and finally materialize a ubiquitous human capacity for cognitive abstraction. These pipes are *measuring devices*, perhaps the earliest we have yet found, and all the more remarkable for measuring material acoustical phenomena. But at the same time, they are registers of the immaterial; they use material forms to structure sound elements into an immaterial system. The Hohlenstein-Stadel lion-man is frequently and rightly cited as a stunning product of the modern human imagination. Its impossible mixture of two familiar animals is seen as a "minimally counterintuitive" construction of a sort that might be basic to the imagining of gods or metaphysical perception all told (I return to this notion below). But if the mixing of two familiar, all-too-palpable animals in one statue is such a feat, what are we to think of the mind that contrives to represent in bone and ivory sonic systems known nowhere outside itself?

Musicking

In this and the preceding chapter I have expanded on the concept of the cultural epicycle, introduced in Chapter 1 and exemplified several times in Chapters 2–5. A synopsis will take us at last to the heart of musicking's coalescence.

The deepening of cultural archives is a basic feature of hominin, and especially late hominin, coevolution. These archives include repertories of behaviors, assemblages of activities, articulated group memories—everything, in short, involved in the elaboration of a taskscape, learned, and passed on to succeeding generations. As archives deepen, they generate cultural dynamics that operate independently of the niche-constructive feedback cycles that sedimented them in the first place. These are the epicycles. Their relations to the archives—how they originate in them, how they accelerate their operation, even how they control them—was defined as the attendancy of the epicycle.

The epicycle can form a general propulsive force, or it can take on a more systematic self-organization, arising from the natures of the archival ingredients that spawned it. Examples of the first are the Lower and Middle Paleolithic epicycles of entrainment and vocalized deixis I described in Chapters 2 and 3: tendencies inhering in technosocial synchronies or deictic gesture-calls that pushed them toward greater control and precision (in the first case) and increasing diversity and specificity of signification (in the second). Examples of the more systematic kind of epicycle include the rule-governance that crystalized in a protophonology, generating weakly meaningful, syllable-like gestures (Chapter 3; cf. Ray Jackendoff); the phase-transition in which multiplying indexes assumed the layered, dual indexicality of a symbol-system (Chapter 5; cf. Terrence Deacon); and the hierarchic ordering of discrete pitches according to degrees of acoustic affinity, starting from the percept of octave duplication (Chapters 3 and 5). Beneath each of these systematizations, not only the last, lie the general capacities for hierarchic and combinatorial cognition, highly developed already in Neandertals and also, it is reasonable to assume, in the earliest *Homo sapiens* (Chapter 4).

The deepening of cultural archives brought with it greater potential for the generation of epicycles, and this led, probably not before late hominins, to epicyclic proliferation. This accelerated the rate of cultural change and increase in social complexities of *Homo sapiens*; it is even possible that Neandertals were endowed with capacities not very different from ours but, for various reasons of climate, environment, population density, local extinctions, and more, never reached the tipping point of epicyclic proliferation. Epicyclic proliferation led sapient humans in many directions, sponsoring in independent groups a vast array of cultural constructions, which could also converge when populations met and mixed. Given basic similarities of cultural attainment across the species and the nature of epicyclic attendancy on them, the proliferation often resulted in the independent formation of similar epicycles. We must expect, in the deep history of humankind, the independent rivulets whose whorls took on similar forms.

Genetic, archaeological, and paleoanthropological evidence indicates that the African humans we left at the end of Chapter 5, about 100,000 years ago, were quite close to us in general *capacities* but profoundly different from us in *behavior*. The behavioral changes since then define modern humanity and span its whole range in manners that cannot be accounted for by simple additive cultural development, which would model the emergences of musicking and language with mechanisms like those that gave us the internal combustion engine. Continued, if slowing, operation of the feedback cycles of biocultural coevolution over the last hundred millennia—that is to say, the genetic modification of the capacities—played a role in the changes, but one that must have been reduced already early in this period, when the homogenization of the human genome began. In itself, genomic alteration cannot plausibly account for both the huge changes and the sweeping commonalities that exist today. Neither, though these too played a role, can the complex trajectories we examined in Chapter 6 of the many human populations that must have existed then and in the intervening millennia—their migrations and meetings, flourishings and extinctions. Over and above all these forces we must adduce also the epicyclic mechanism to construct a reasonably full account of the emergence of human modernity.

Those African humans at the 100,000-year mark possessed complex modes of social organization. The excavations at Blombos Cave alone are enough to indicate this, but the additional evidence gathered by McBrearty and Brooks and others, from different parts of the continent, is conclusive and continues to mount. It indicates moreover that, in some populations at least, the complexity was not new at this time. Bound up with increasing hominin capacities for thinking-at-a-distance, the complexity must have involved an extension of sociality well beyond immediate copresence in several directions. One was an intergroup dynamic that enlarged the taskscape so that both transport of materials across longer distances than before and exchange with other groups were feasible. This involved communication across what Andrew Shryock and Daniel Smail have recently called the social "middle distance," a space where recognition of gestures and cultural forms was possible in the absence of personal knowledge.[16] Sociality was extended beyond copresence also within the group itself, structured now with clear rankings of power and status and using technology to supply indexes of rank—ornaments hung on the body or affixed on clothing, or painting, coloring, and other alteration of the body itself. As a foundation for such social orders, kinship relations must have reached a point in their development adumbrating the complexity and variety of modern human systems.[17]

The maintenance of this social complexity required supple and precise communication. We have followed the emergence of this from a stage of protodiscourse to a set of communicative means that was bifurcated along certain lines. The means included, on one side and starting from something like Jackendoff's protophonology, a growing array of signifying vocal gestures. Hierarchic and combinatorial cognitive processes brought these into more and more intricate juxtaposition, generating a rule-governance of them at first weak, later strengthened. *Homo sapiens* about 100,000 years ago probably did not possess fully modern language; sapient protolanguage by then probably had developed to a communication like that of late Neandertals, perhaps well beyond it. It is unlikely, however, that the final move from this near-language to language required the lightning strike of genetic mutations enabling dramatic new capacities. The basic, hard-wired armature was already at hand, the product of long ages of hominin communicative sociality. The move to language instead needed the propulsive force of an epicyclic formation. Perhaps Deacon identifies a crucial element in his phase-transition to a full symbol system, in which a new framework for an array of signs fell into place as a mode of organization, fostering a strengthening of combinatorial rules.

This is not to depict Deacon's emergence of symbolism or the appearance of modern language in which it was involved as purely cultural events. Both relied, after all, on the panoply of sapient cognitive capacities, and, once an epicyclic impulse had created a symbol system and its advantages on the taskscape were evident, weak coevolutionary pressures would have selected those brains that, though minimally different from others around them, were best at assimilating the system during their ontogenetic development. Insofar as the emergence of symbolic arrays *was* an epicyclic event, however, the likelihood was great that it would arise again and again from advanced protolanguage, in many contexts and populations, and, moreover, that it would spread quickly as populations exploiting it met others. Language in its final coalescence may have been analogous to the independent, multiregional development of bead-signs discussed in Chapter 6, if of immensely greater complexity.

Alongside this linguistic path ran the second fork of the bifurcated communication system about 100,000 years ago, the second path stemming from the legacy of deictic gesture-calls. This comprised a sequence of developments. First there was the emotive and manipulative heightening of indexical intonation contours. Then, epicyclic development led to diversification of the contours quickened by a culture-driven decoupling of them from selective pressures. And finally, there was a Rubicon: the abstraction from the contours of elements perceived and cognized as discrete pitches.

The emergence of discrete pitch, along with the persistence of phrase-length contour processing, brought about a dualistic perception: a focus at once on general shapes and the specific elements comprised in them. This relied, like linguistic rules, on hierarchizing and combinatorial capacities of mind. We have already seen the evidence and reasons to conclude that early *Homo sapiens* possessed this dualistic perception, evidence that goes back to the earliest formation of protodiscourse and to the hierarchic and combinatorial technologies of Neandertals. We can see that epicycles leading to modern musicking must have hovered low over our species, attendant on many aspects of increasingly intricate hominin communicative behaviors. Like linguistic epicycles, they could have arisen often and spread quickly through meetings of populations.

In those Aurignacian pipes we encounter traces of the final, epicyclic push toward the coalescence of discrete-pitch musicking.

Discrete pitch arose as a mode of abstraction of information from meaning. Its hallmarks, octave duplication, hierarchic ordering (tonal encoding) of individual pitches, and combinatoriality of design, probably reflect the firing of low-integer synchronies in neural networks; whatever their neural substrate, however, they are closely related to other abstractions that were new in late hominin sociality. Discrete pitch, in other words, is an informational system ordered in ways congruent with the fundamental capacities that enabled complex sociality: hierarchy and abstraction. The coevolutionary developments that resulted in it and in social complexity were in each case many and of long making, and any model positing one of these two as a new offshoot of the other cannot take account of those histories. Instead, we must conclude that the systematization of discrete pitch in modern musicking and abstract sociality *formed together*, the products of intersecting histories and similar cognitive capacities.

This falling in place of pitched musicking, however, is only one aspect of the coalescence of musicking all told. The second aspect is temporal in orientation and revolves around entrainment. The complexities of human societies culminated a long history not only of growing communicative sophistication, but also of synchronies of hominin interaction on the taskscape. We know that these reach back to the Acheulean beginnings of mimetic technology, and their history could be followed much further than this, to primate gesture-calls, mammalian social interactions in general, and beyond. Entrainment, as we saw in Chapter 2, takes forms that widen vertiginously, finally reaching beyond the biosphere. In this wide perspective, the advent of Acheulean mimesis marks a small but important event, a sharpening of enacted synchronies and the cognition behind them in a tiny corner of the animal kingdom, the hominin clade. It is preserved in material traces that indicate a prelinguistic pedagogy and shallow cultural archive.

The synchronies would have continued to sharpen in techno-sociality of all kinds, including the exchanges of protodiscourse.

And the tendency persisted in the final coalescing of both language and music. Modern speech pragmatics must be far more ordered and intricate than the exchanges of protodiscourse, involving, as we have seen, whole metapragmatic levels. Musical pragmatics, on the other hand, requires a different protocol, combining behavioral simultaneities with successive discursive gestures. Musical pragmatics assumed levels of synchronized precision beyond those needed for language. The advent of musicking marked a station in hominin entrainment that entailed simultaneities more precise than any others on the taskscape.

What kind of epicycle could have driven this extension of synchrony? As the internal structure of human groups became more complex, it gave rise to moments of group activity more frequent and organized than before. A band of *Homo heidelbergensis* 500,000 years ago, gathered for the butchering of a carcass at the scene of the hunt, created a transitory taskscape affording rich opportunities for the unfolding of communication of many kinds, from the persisting gesture-calls to the deictic interactions of protodiscourse, and even involving some momentary division of labor. *Homo sapiens* at 100,000 years ago, instead, processing a carcass or gathered foodstuffs in a space removed from the hunting ground and protected from scavengers, reflected in the organizing of activities the complex structure of the group itself. Supervision, division of labor, and ordered parceling of spoils were likely all parts of this taskscape, and through them it came to mirror the abstract structure that governed the group. As the structure was enacted, it rhythmicized the taskscape in ways more fixed and predictable than ever before. Belonging to late hominin groups was a matter of a thinking-at-a-distance extended enough to lead to the enacting of structures and facts not evident in the material world. We are close, here, to a working definition of ritual, and we will soon narrow the remaining distance.

The temporal synchronies and simultaneities that characterize modern musicking accord well with such organized activities—this

266

goes almost without saying. But the circumstantial evidence of the long growth of both protodiscourse and synchronized technologies argues for a stronger thesis than this. Like discrete pitch, the entrainment of musicking must have taken its modern form alongside all these new ways of structuring the taskscape, fostering them as they fostered it. Musicking has powerful potential to organize the taskscape so as to mirror social complexity in a new, sensually rich way, and in doing so it enabled the orderings themselves to solidify and grow. While the rhythmic structures of linguistic exchanges hover close to situational pragmatics, musical entrainment, loose or strong, constrains normal discourse to a different degree of formal rigor. In this abstraction it was congruent with the novel social designs of sapient groups; whether an elaborated kinship structure or a set of ranked statuses, they were bringing an invisible formalism to copresent interaction. Moreover, musical entrainment enabled the communicative *performance* of social design. Complex sociality, juxtaposed with the musical side of the ancient bifurcation of communicative means, fostered group-structured synchronies and formed taskscapes of an abstract sophistication never before seen.

Once we think in terms of this epicycle, the many accounts suggesting that music formed *in order* to achieve or facilitate social bonding seem not wrong so much as superficial and out of sequence. They cannot trace the incremental path that laid the foundational capacities required for such musical bonding, but instead assume the existence of these capacities, at hand and ready to be exploited: Time to march! Time to dance! In this they are like all unilateral causes proposed to explain the adaptive emergence of music: lullabies, courtship displays, sheer entertainment (whatever this may be), and so forth. None of these can describe mechanisms from which emerged the immensely complicated capacities needed to sing the simplest lullaby or wooing song, or play an "entertaining" drum cadence. Positing them as causes of music is akin to thinking that the making of Aurignacian pipes created the perception of discrete pitch.

This is not to deny that these proposals invoke uses to which modern musicking is regularly put, or even that these uses are ancient ones. It is only to insist that the uses came to musicking very late, at the earliest along with its final coalescence. We can imagine a sing-song comforting of an infant even during the protodiscursive stages of hominin evolution—protomotherese, so to speak—but a full lullaby is inconceivable until discrete pitch perception was formed and linked to the temporal hierarchies we call meter. Many capacities had to take shape between the one stage and the other, and a simple enhancement of the comfort offered to the infant is a dull tool for building them. Similarly, we have described social synchronies that existed on hominin taskscapes long before a group dance at the campfire could have taken place; it required other capacities than they did. One more example: Sexual display is an ancient heritage of the hominin clade and many others, but it could not be a *musical* display until diverse forces created and finally melded the capacities exploited in musicking; and such display in itself is hard-pressed to model the forming of discrete pitch perception or metric hierarchy. All these uses of musicking are impressively widespread symptoms, not causes. The futility of the adaptationist proposals they have served is the futility of all monocausal modeling of complex histories—and of all superficial descriptions of symptoms.

With the coalescences of pitch hierarchy and measured entrainment came other, less abstract aspects of musicking, carried along as expressive ingredients in the new communicative and social modes. The most basic of these, tempo and dynamics, were pure *energetic indexes* (in the Peircean sense): the approximate indication of emotional arousal through, on the one hand, pace of movement and, on the other, signal amplitude. Both of these had always been fundamental components of hominin protomusic, protolanguage, and protodiscourse—of all hominin communication, in fact. The protomusical, singsong comforting of a baby imagined just now, for example, no doubt never occurred at the decibel level of a shout. In this indexical, premusical capacity, of course, both of these indexes extend far beyond our clade.

The perception of musical timbre, for its part, intricate and poorly understood, must be related to discrete pitch perception, since it also involves a cognitive construction based in part on blends of frequencies. Nevertheless, it too has a broad premusical and extramusical application, forming an ingredient of all auditory scene analysis of hominins; it too came naturally, then, into the coalescence of musicking. But as we saw in Chapter 3, it formed also an aspect of the communicative bifurcation of protomusic and protolanguage, in that its musical perception moves along a graded, analog spectrum of limitless possibility, while its linguistic perception generates forms more discretized and, in individual languages, constrained. The appearance of musical instruments in the course of the final coalescence of musicking must have answered to needs to heighten emotive indexes, and we can think of these instruments as tools devised to amplify somatic gesture in many different ways. But we need meanwhile to keep in mind their exploratory function, their use to discover or imitate nonhuman sounds and traverse new sonic realms. Instruments did acoustical things voice or body alone could not. In this function—in the sound of a bullroarer, for example, or of those Aurignacian pipes—instruments began to move toward a recreative or even creative dimension of timbre. They provide one more instance of thinking-at-a-distance involved in the final coalescence of musicking.

Musicking on the Transcendental Taskscape

I have connected the hierarchies of pitch and temporality involved in the emergence of modern musicking to characteristic modern patterns of human sociality. Musicking, in this proposal, coalesced from a range of cognitive and perceptual capacities alongside a coalescing social complexity; the two formed together and were fundamentally tied to the emergence of abstract, formalized thought. To name this thought and the forms it takes, here and in the previous chapters, I have borrowed several expressions: thinking-at-a-distance, offline thinking, the release from proximity, the superseding of copresence, theory of mind, recursive mindreading, and more. All these phrases aim to approach from different vantages this most fundamental expansion of the cognitive capacities involved in advancing hominin sociality. We need now to examine one final analysis of this expansion, elaborating its link to musicking.

For anthropologist Maurice Bloch, modern human sociality is characterized by a double structuring, which we can liken, in first approximation, to the dual, bottom-up and top-down structuring described in Chapter 3. The bottom-up structuring we share with all social animals, though Bloch uses the social intelligence of chimpanzees as his favored example. Because it emerges from the transactions of copresence, "a process of continual manipulations, assertions and defeats," he calls it the *transactional social*. The top-down structuring is unique to us, according to Bloch, but could be extended at least to Neandertals, who must have evinced it in some significant degree. It arises from our foundational "capacity to imagine other worlds," in itself closely related to our advanced theory of mind. These foster a separation of conceptualizations from sensed realities and the flux of transactions, and this separation enables us to create essentialized social roles assigned to people and groups. These roles exist apart from the individuals assuming them; notions of a chieftain, for example, or a descent group, or a nation all give to individuals identities not physically present in them, "invisible halos" around them that determine much about how others interact with them. The roles also establish a permanency reaching beyond, often far beyond, individuals and events; a king may die, but a kingship (in principle) does not. Such roles transcend the identities we structure through face-to-face transactions, creating what Bloch names the *transcendental social*.[18]

Beyond their invisibility and relative permanency, the essentialized roles of the transcendental social are tokens in imagined systems of related types, and this systematicity is a defining feature of human sociality. The role of a tribal elder, for example, takes its meaning from a system of other, likewise transcendental roles such as tribal junior and ancestor. Kinship categories present similar systems of types, providing, at any distance from the most basic parent/offspring relations, an abstract (and very variable) "map of social location." The expansion in complexity of human social orders across the history of *Homo sapiens* has depended on such abstraction at many levels, "simplified formats" that reduce "large numbers of people to a small number of types."[19]

Bloch's transcendental systematicity is the source of the special complexity of interaction humans have managed to construct, since it creates the hierarchies that guide social practice and the lasting, invisible structures that inform fleeting transactions. This connection of transactional and transcendental pervades human sociality, but it is manifested most powerfully in ritual of all sorts. Here copresent encounters are formalized. This formalization deflects the moment-to-moment intentionality that humans so adroitly read in one another away from the enactors of the rite, and onto a higher plane—onto the plane, in fact, of those transcendental systems of identities.[20]

The systematicity of Bloch's transcendental social will seem familiar to us, because the systems we have analyzed in semiosis, language, and musicking are nothing but instances of it. A conjuncture appears here in particular between Bloch's transactional/transcendental dualism and Michael Silverstein's pragmatics and metapragmatics, discussed in Chapter 5. For Silverstein, we recall, pragmatics is a matter of the indexicality inhabiting language, and metapragmatics is the ordering of linguistic indexes that enables effective discourse. This ordering of indexes comes to the fore in formalized discourse, and especially in ritual in all its varieties. Through the lens of Silverstein's metapragmatics, Bloch's connection of his two social modes, especially in ritual, can be seen to be a question in part of ordered indexicality. For both Bloch and Silverstein, *ritual conveys systems of indexes that point by virtue of their ordering toward the transcendence of their (transactional) performance.*

In modern human sociality these *indexical* systems and the transcendentalizing performances they foster take shape in the context of *symbolic* orders. Nevertheless, in them the indexicality so fundamental to ritual and discourse finds its transcendental métier and its distinctively human outline. But, as we know, this indexicality is the semiotic mode native to musicking. In the most general way, musicking came about via capacities that enabled the formalization of the indexes of protomusic, protolanguage, and protodiscourse all told. This formalization of indexes, we can now see, was tantamount to a transcendentalizing of the transactions in which they were deployed. A deep, abiding, historical backdrop appears here to the more recent coalescing of musicking and of ritual behavior, and indeed to the inevitable connection of the two in human sociality. And we can go farther still: In musicking, *formalized indexes enter the sphere of the transcendent without symbolization.*

There are further implications of Bloch's transcendental systems, these involving religion rather than ritual. Since the systems are built from essentialized qualities, their extent is in principle limitless, reaching all the way from the least empowered individuals to gods. Bloch's transcendentalism enables the movement of mind upward and downward, as well as outward through lateral expansion of the hierarchies. It creates, in its vertical extension, all the special features of what we might call the *metaphysical imaginary*, and it enables us to posit a source for all supersensible percepts. Once the transcendental social takes shape, the capacity to imagine other worlds burgeons with possibilities of realms beyond material experience, beings inhabiting them, spirituality, and religion. Religion is in this way a direct outgrowth of our transcendentalizing tendencies. It "is nothing special but is central," as Bloch says, because it arises spontaneously from the basic patterns of mind that characterize all human sociality and make it unique in the world today.

This view of the transcendental, social foundations of religion runs athwart the many recent proposals of evolutionary psychologists and of some religious cognitivists as well, who prefer to trace gods to the workings of the individual, adapted mind. They propose mechanisms such as an "agency-detection device," the hyperactive operation of which explains why humans discover human-like actions behind unexplained events, invisible forces, and mysterious phenomena. (This is a time-honored explanation; you can read something like it in Giambattista Vico's *New Science* of 1744.) To account for the special natures and powers of supernatural beings, they imagine the adapted mind taking recourse in "minimal counterintuitions," a notion I alluded to in describing the lion-man of the Swabian Jura. The concept behind a cultural product like the lion-man is *counterintuitive*, they propose, because its mixture of species cuts across categories for biological recognition that are deeply wired in our brains (for example: predator/nonpredator; similar/dissimilar to me). At the same time, it is *minimally* counterintuitive because it violates those innate categorizing intuitions in only one way: its mixing of distinct animals. Otherwise it conforms to our recognition devices, its lion aspect easily discernible, its human aspect familiar, and its identity as an animal clear.[21] This sort of psychological explanation for the invention of gods, metaphysics, and religion has attractive ingredients. It is easy, for example, to imagine the selective advantage for our hominin ancestors of an agency-detection module in overdrive, in effect a hard-wired radar locating a predator behind every swaying branch. Some such capacity probably reaches very deep indeed in our phylogeny and in those of many other, nonhominin clades.

As usual with adaptationist explanations invoking unilateral causality, however, such accounts tend to be too weak to capture essential elements. Whatever the mental capacities for biological recognition that made possible the therianthropic mixture of the lion-man, it was not only an individual creation but also the product of a sociality that was relatively new in the hominin lineage at the time of its making. We can think of it as a shifting upward along Bloch's hierarchies of something akin to bead technologies, in that it did not merely indicate the otherwise invisible "halo" of a group member, as beads must have done, but materialized an otherwise altogether invisible being. The society that produced it must have conceived reasons for mixing animals in this way, for choosing *this* minimal counterintuition rather than another, and for giving it material form. These probably endowed the animal portrayed with special status or powers and organized patterns of action around it—performances indexing its powers, that is, *ritual* performances. These, in sum, located the counterintuition on the taskscape—but a taskscape now transcendentalized so as to express the hierarchies mapping the society's metaphysical as well as physical spaces and to formalize these in metapragmatic orders.

The model advanced here emphasizes these social dimensions, missing from narrowly adaptationist explanations. Late hominin evolution created a sociality constructed according to, and at the same time elaborating, a cognition of abstraction, hierarchy, and diverse, insensible localizings of status, power, and even being. As this imaginary took shape, it worked reciprocally to reshape the social patterns of action on the taskscape in ways akin to those pictured above in the wake of a hunt or in actions revolving around the lion-man. Rites, rituals, and institutions emerged as the expression in social praxis of this imaginary, according importance to their enactors as warranted by their locations in invisible hierarchies. The reciprocity here is basic: The hierarchic imaginary could only have arisen from a deep history of indexical interactions on the taskscape; once formed, it had to cast its patterns back onto those interactions, reshaping them in a feedback loop of yet another kind.

Missing also from the evolutionary psychologists' approach is consideration of the elements of communication that coformed with such sociality as it emerged across millions of years of hominin evolution. Agency detection devices and the like will only carry us so far toward this communicative sociality, but language and musicking can hardly be ignored in an account of features of modern humanity as basic as supersensible realms, gods, religions, rituals, and institutions of power. And this is particularly true of musicking. In the ethnographic and historical records, from ancient times down to the present, it is connected ubiquitously to religion, rituals, and the institutions associated with them—so regularly, in fact, as to suggest the connection as a kind of default setting of human behavior.[22] Like musical meter or tonality, this setting can be abrogated; but, unlike those specifically musical features, it extends *between* two broad realms of sociality, associating them and shaping the behavior that results from both.

The reasons suggested above for this abiding connection involve the congruency between the ordering indexes in all formalized human sociality, especially pronounced in ritual, and the formalization and abstraction of indexicality basic to musicking. Metapragmatic analyses of ritual, however, tend to be grounded in language, not music, so there is a danger here of lapsing back into banal linguocentrism, pervasive in accounts of human evolution. In fact, two recent, suggestive proposals to explain the connections of music, ritual, and religion, though they point along productive paths, suffer this lapse. We must revisit, one final time, the connections and distinctions of music and language, now in the era of the final coalescing of each.

Stephen Mithen, at the close of *The Singing Neanderthals*, broaches what we might call the "leftover theory."[23] As language became referential and propositional late in our evolution, he suggests, it removed itself from channels communicating with supernatural realms, emptying out a space that music filled. Music assumed its modern communicative function, in other words, only when language focused its powers elsewhere. Aside from raising questions as to why propositionality is ineffective in communicating with gods, Mithen's view assigns priority to modern language in determining after-the-fact adjustments in music and metaphysics. But we have seen that there is no reason to grant this priority. One burden of this book has been to show that any carefully considered incremental view of music's emergence will extend it far back into the history of protodiscourse; and the course of this emergence provides, finally, ready explanations of the deep link of musicking and ritual. Likewise, any nuanced view of the formation of transcendental sociality and the metaphysical imagination must reach far back, coinciding with or antedating the shaping of modern language; the beads of Blombos as well as many other lines of evidence tell us as much.

Mithen also proposes that music was connected to religion because it offered a "cognitive anchor," easing the difficulties we have in conceiving of the supernatural. In this he turns topsy-turvy the arguments on the underpinnings of religion of both Bloch and the evolutionary psychologists. The latter demonstrate, if anything, why supernatural, minimal counterintuitions are so *easy* to conceive; while for Bloch the emergence of the metaphysical imagination is an inevitable outgrowth of his hierarchized transcendentalism, itself inevitable in a sociality involving advanced theory of mind. Religion, again, is nothing special, and metaphysics calls for no mechanism easing the strain.

Nevertheless, Mithen's second proposal is productive in this: It offers the image of a musicking somehow congruent with the cognition involved in thinking at a (religious) distance. Helping us further along these lines is the suggestion of Ian Cross that the fundamental semantic indeterminacy of music is basic to its human uses. He calls this feature of music its "floating intentionality," and he proposes that it played a role in a deep, incremental emergence of human communication. It gives to music a signifying flexibility or "polysemy" ideally suited to all social situations of uncertainty or ambiguity, allowing multiple constructions of meaning along a generally trustworthy communicative channel.[24] Cross's idea makes more specific Mithen's cognitive anchor and gestures toward the ubiquitous connection of musicking and ritual. To close the gesture we need only interpose an extra link. This is the formalized, performative nature of ritual in its

276

negotiation of situations of liminality and uncertainty. It is this formalization that highlights the centrality of nonsymbolic semiosis in ritual and indicates the deep-historical bond to musicking.

In Cross's suggestion, however, linguocentrism again rears its head. He conceives the place of musicking in human evolution according to aspects of language that musicking lacks, namely, semantic specificity and propositionality; musicking is seen to assume its social functions only through its insufficiency in the face of language. But why should semanticity thus control the judgment of deep-historical performances on the task-scape? The many differences between musicking and language stem from long histories with deep, pre-sapient roots, and if the only advantage musicking offered was the *absence* of linguistic features—if, to make one more turn of the screw, music's *insuf*ficiencies needed to await full linguistic meaning in order to come into their own—then it would be implausible to propose cognitive capacities basic to musicking arising and persisting across the long period between the first bifurcation of protomusic and protolanguage and the emergence of ritual and transcendental sociality. These capacities would, simply, not have existed to be gathered in music's final coalescence and related to ritual and the rest.

The indeterminacy of meaning Cross points out is an important feature of modern musicking, rooted in its modes of synchronized formalism, indexicality, and the abstraction of discrete pitch from deictic meaning that I have traced, which brought intonation into juxtaposition with emerging hierarchic cognitive possibilities. His floating intentionality is probably even a widespread feature of the social deployment of music. But it could only have come into being once communicative intentionality *stopped* floating in other arenas and was pinned down by other means, a development that intersects relatively late with the long histories of both musicking and language. Like the lullabies and wooing songs discussed above, it is a symptom of a deeper condition.

This deeper condition is a formal one rooted in the processes of human brains and, probably to a lesser degree, in the brains of our closest extinct relatives. The role of musicking in the emergence of sapient modernity as it took shape during the Upper Pleistocene was a reflection of the structural aspects of the cognition that made it possible. The connection of musicking to ritual, religion, metaphysics, and the institutions they fostered came about as an unfolding congruency between this musical cognition and the similar cognition that made them possible. In each case it essentially involved hierarchies of several sorts and (an outgrowth of these) combinatoriality within type-sets. Across tens of millennia, minds capable of formalized abstraction and immersed in cultures of epicyclic proliferation linked transcendentalized sociality to musicking in a dance coforming the two.

If language also exploits this kind of cognition and was therefore a third partner in the dance, it does so differently than musicking. These differences were crucial in determining and separating the roles of each in the consolidation of our modernity. They encourage, in reaction to the usual, linguocentric priorities, a *musicocentrism* that can overturn all the terms of its counterpart. Language does not offer, except in league with musicking, modes of entrainment precise and hierarchized; its intonational structures remain analog in nature even in tonal languages, offering no developed hierarchies such as discrete-pitch combinatoriality; and its timbral limitations do not afford the boundless explorations of the soundscape available through musical tools. These are the features that *constrained* the role of language in the coalescence of human modernity. They are the musical absences at the heart of language.

CHAPTER EIGHT

Afterward

The promissory notes at the end of Chapter 1 have been largely repaid, yet I have succeeded only in reaching a point that many will consider a beginning, not an end. So it is; it would be flippant to suggest that everything that happened in the history of musicking after about twenty thousand years ago amounted to no more than endnotes to the great text that preceded it. Across these millennia human musicking, like human culture in general, never ceased its motions of change: accumulation, diversification, convergence, invention, transmission. We cannot doubt this, even if for the first eighteen thousand years of this period the history of musicking is known to us in little more detail than in the earlier periods I have followed. Only about three thousand years ago does this history grow much more legible, as some very few societies begin to record in material and written forms a development that will finally accelerate toward a "modernity" measured as historians customarily do—that is, across the last four hundred years, not the last sixty thousand.

Why, then, do I end my story twenty thousand years ago, just before the Last Glacial Maximum began to loose its grip on the world's ecosystems? In part it is because of that other, longer scale of human modernity that has been my object. The scant Paleolithic evidence pertaining directly to musicking suggests that about forty thousand years ago some humans were engaged in behaviors we would immediately recognize as musical. Together with genetic evidence this suggests that the capacities founding these activities reach back at least another ten thousand to twenty thousand years, to the world-populating lineages that were then present in East Africa. Older archaeological evidence not directly related to musicking, but redolent of sophisticated societies, extends the potential for similar capacities and behaviors even farther back, reaching a point where their coalescing forms merge into the long earlier history, sketched in Chapters 2–5, of protomusic, protolanguage, and increasing social and cognitive complexity.

Whether or not to extend modern musicking—or modern language, for that matter—back to the 100,000-year mark is a choice as speculative as any I have entertained here. Our positions vary, probably, in proportion to the deep-historical *optimism* of our general outlooks—not strong grounds for argument. I suspect that musicking and language in their modern forms were not general features extending across all populations of *Homo sapiens* in Africa and the Levant at this time, or for a long time after. Nevertheless, epicyclic mechanisms could engender sudden developments and large differences in the behaviors and even the capacities of different human populations. Unstable ecological circumstances, as we have seen, helped to kick-start the operation of the mechanism in some groups but not in others. Were evidence to be unearthed for essentially modern musicking in one or more of them, even as far back as 100,000 years, I would not be surprised. The incremental history traced here puts *Homo sapiens* at this time on the verge of such possibilities, and at a tipping point where the attendancy of epicycles could play itself out in varied, proliferating ways.

However far back we might extend this near-modernity, it is clear that the humans who emerged from the last major glaciation were in all essential capacities identical to one another and to the humans who crowd the world today. Steven Mithen, whose views of the emergence of music I have noted and sometimes taken issue with, has written also an evocative and playful history of human cultures from 20,000 to 5,000 BCE. After fifty chapters surveying more than that many local societies known to archaeologists, he cannot but conclude that the histories of all these groups, emerging, thriving and disappearing across fifteen millennia, reflect a single set of capacities. Fundamental among these was a "creativity" of mind like our own, something related to the cultural accumulation and thinking-at-a-distance I have dwelled on; without it, "there would have been no human history but merely a continuous cycle of the adaptation and readaptation to environmental change."[1]

These local populations lived out their histories in the face of changing ecological affordances, just as earlier populations had done. They continued to enjoy the boons and suffer the hardships of climatic instability. The most dramatic episode of this after the Last Glacial Maximum set in 12,800 years ago and abruptly ended several millennia of warming weather. This was a stadial called the Younger Dryas period, and it brought many centuries of cold, drought, dust, and reglaciation, especially to the northern hemisphere. When the warmth returned 11,500 years ago, ushering in the Holocene, it arrived in an even more abrupt shift: a rise of about 3°c in global temperatures over little more than a human generation.

Archaeologists used to perceive several human "revolutions" at the outset of the Holocene, revolutions thought to mark the turn to new human ways gathered under the term "Neolithic." At the center of the new developments were the rise of stable settlements and villages ("sedentism"), the domestication of animals and plants, and, above all, agriculture. All three were thought to be causally bound, if in different arrangements according to the archaeologist consulted. This was yet another revolutionary narrative, like the European Upper Paleolithic revolution, and like that one it has been challenged in recent years from several quarters. The emergence of agriculture, it is now clear, was not one development but many, spaced around the world from the Oaxaca Valley to the river basins of China, involving many different plant species, and beginning in several places almost simultaneously about 10,000 years ago.[2] This independent emergence of similar

behavioral tendencies is not captured well in any sweeping revolutionary model; as a global development it instead shows the
earmarks of a repeated cultural epicycle of the kind discussed in
Chapters 6 and 7.

Another challenge to the Neolithic revolution is the recognition that domestication of plant species and agriculture need to
be considered as separate developments.[3] If this is so, we need
also to entertain more flexible views of the domesticators, sedentary farmers as well as foragers. Felipe Fernández-Armesto and
Daniel Lord Smail have emphasized the continuities between
plant foraging and plant breeding. For the border between them
to blur, they point out, takes only a bit of modest replanting by
a forager or a setting aside of seeds for times of need—or, to
mention one more mechanism, a fire intentionally set to burn
out unwanted plants. Given the breeding practices involved in
the late Paleolithic domestication of dogs—itself a process that
occurred in several places, recent evidence suggests—it is easy to
imagine that human populations harvesting certain plant species
were engaged also in incipient breeding of them for thousands
of years before the organized farming of the Neolithic began.[4]
The distance can be small, in other words, between farming
and an ancient niche-altering symbiosis of plant and (cultural)
animal; and this small gap, like that between complex bone tools
and musical instruments, was probably easily and frequently
stepped over.

Meanwhile, the idea that sedentism was connected to farming,
an aspect of its revolutionary impact, has also been undermined
by the realization among archaeologists that many past societies fit into neither of the traditional molds, sedentary farmers
and mobile foragers. A whole new class of societies, sedentary
hunter-gatherers, has emerged. The early Natufian societies of
the Levant exemplify the type; they arose about 14,500 years ago
and thrived until conditions were dramatically altered by the
Younger Dryas cooling.[5] But even then the type was not new. As
many as five millennia earlier, mammoth hunters on the steppes

of the Ukraine and Russia built small clusters of dwellings out of the tusks and bones of their kills with hides stretched over them—certainly not temporary or casual constructions.[6]

If shifts in agriculture and sedentism look to us less revolutionary and more incremental, episodic, and dispersed than they once did, so also does the emergence of the institutions that have characterized all large societies over the last few millennia. The putative egalitarianism of hunter-gatherer groups, in the first place, long ago came to be understood as a complicated matter, not a plain absence of social differentiation. A sheer contrast between it and the stratification of sedentary agriculturalists is at best an oversimplification. Archaeological evidence projects such differentiation far back into our history, at least to the shell beads of Blombos Cave, and I have already speculated that the hierarchic cognition evident in Neandertal technologies manifested itself also in aspects of their sociality. Faced with the increasing prominence of signs of elite status in Upper Pleistocene artifacts, with the signatures of ritual behavior that these and broader circumstances constitute (marked burials and painted walls of deep caverns, for example), and with the final extension of the hominin release from proximity in the nascent transcendental social—faced with all this, it is hard to imagine that some societies were not socially differentiated and even stratified in certain ways a very long time before the Neolithic began. In the context of such layered sociality, then, formalized behaviors probably brought about institutional structures much earlier than we tend to think. Like plant domestication, these might have begun with small gestures, no more perhaps than modest transcendental roles for individuals: the restriction to chosen members of the tribe of access to a certain area (that deep cave, for example), or the assigning to specified individuals in specified circumstances of the playing of a bird-bone pipe or whirling of a bullroarer.

From the recent end of the timescale also there are indications that the institutionalization of ritual power may extend back into the Paleolithic, even in monumentally structured ways. The

excavations since the 1990s of Göbekli Tepe in southeastern Tur-
key have uncovered a project of staggering scope of stone quarry-
ing, carving, and building that resulted in a long-lasting center of
activity starting about 11,000 years ago. With little sign of on-site
habitation yet found, Klaus Schmidt, the lead archaeologist, and
others posit this as a sacred locale for groups of foragers in the
surrounding areas, periodically gathering to celebrate essential
rituals. It is, to say the least, not the kind of project hunter-gatherers have usually been thought to mount. For Schmidt it points
to a new, ideological stimulus for the beginnings of the transition to sedentism: religious ritual and institution. In this view
it is metaphysics that drove settlement patterns and eventually
brought about farming, not the reverse.

A recent revisionist account has taken issue with this interpretation, seeing in it an anachronistic distinction of shrine from
house and envisioning Göbekli Tepe as a sacred settlement, along
the lines archaeologists have now and then perceived elsewhere.[7]
(Inca Cuzco is a much more recent example.) This new interpretation suggests that the real message of Göbekli Tepe might
instead be that what counted most for early Neolithic humans
was life integrated with incipient ritual, not separated from it.
It is hard not to imagine this as a repeating of earlier, Paleolithic
lifeways.

Whatever our interpretation of the site, however, we are left
with the construction of a special center, built and used across
centuries and involving daunting technological challenges—all
some seven millennia before Stonehenge or the Great Pyramid of
Giza. We must contemplate that arresting date in prospect, so to
speak, from the vantage of Paleolithic developments, not merely
in retrospect. It places the earliest monumental construction at
Göbekli Tepe closer in time to the painting of Lascaux than to
the building of the pyramids. The famous decorated caves from
the end of the Paleolithic propose themselves to us as ritual spaces
just as eloquently as Göbekli Tepe does; this similarity is inescapable. To entertain it is, however, to locate Göbekli Tepe in a

history of the making and use of such sites reaching far back into the Paleolithic period, if on smaller scales. This history includes not only Lascaux, Altamira, and many other sites from after the Last Glacial Maximum but Chauvet also, painted much earlier, in Gravettian or even Aurignacian times; and it includes many open-air and enclosed sites of rock painting and sculpture from Africa, the immense antiquity of which has only recently begun to be appreciated. All these ritual spaces, from the Later Stone Age and Upper Paleolithic to the nascent Neolithic, come to appear as similar products of repeated, separate epicyclic mechanisms.

No one doubts the importance of the transformation of much of the world's population from a hunting and foraging existence to a farming or pastoral one in the period between the end of the Younger Dryas and about five thousand years ago. Its sweeping consequences for human subsistence and sociality shape the vast majority of human lives today. What is in question, instead, is the focused revolutionary force of the change. Every effort we make to demarcate basic behavioral ruptures across the last twenty thousand years founders on the reefs of earlier, anticipatory histories. These become visible only as the grain of our view grows finer.[8] As they appear, they reveal that human ways of engaging with ecological affordance and with each other, at the most basic level, changed across that period locally, sporadically, and incrementally, not in the great leaps of the revolutionary narratives. They show, in other words, that these changes occurred in ways not qualitatively different from manners of human change reaching far back into the Pleistocene.

The weakening of Neolithic revolutionary narratives provides, then, another rationale for my stopping point about twenty thousand years ago; for if we are no different in basic capacities from humans at that moment, wherever they lived, we are also not separated from them by successive, revolutionary shifts of behavior. What separates us, instead, are the unceasing cultural accumulations and the proliferating epicycles as they have played out their effects against multiple, shifting backdrops of ecological affordance. It is a salutary exercise to think of ourselves, caught up in a thickening web of megacorporate farming, overpopulation, and environmental degradation, in these late Paleolithic terms. Our centers of sedentism gather groups numbering in the tens of millions; our ritual life has gone viral.

At this foundational level, not only basic capacities for musicking but also the general social uses to which it is put probably assumed familiar forms farther back in our deep history than we have thought. Musical behaviors have changed, to be sure; but can we discern much fundamental social difference between a church choir singing today and the musicking that must have resounded at Göbekli Tepe? And, once we have recognized this similarity across ten thousand years, can we avoid extending it across another thirty thousand, to caves near the source of the Danube? These, once more, are *similarities*, not continuities; the specific lineage of *Homo sapiens* that left traces of musicking at Hohle Fels may, after all, be long extinct. They are congruencies brought about by reiterated cultural gestures, which themselves manifest deeper patterns laid down across long epochs in hominin history. The repetition starts in general fashion from the dynamics of biocultural coevolution, in which patterns of hominin sociality bring cultural change into the flux of selective pressures and thus into a relation of mutual formation with biological change. The repetition, that is, bespeaks the fundamental truth that our musicking capacities and the place of them in our sociality assumed their modern shapes together.

The development of capacities and behaviors I have traced over the last million years has involved many aspects of hominin communication and sociality. No one of these can take priority as the guiding force shaping all the others, unless we step back to a vantage so broad as to empty our terms of heuristic force. (For example: These developments could not have taken place but for the brute fact that all hominins have been social animals.) In the narrower and far more productive view, we are brought again and again to face systems of mutual developments related in feedback cycles, systems building always incremental difference, never new beginnings. In such a circumstance, it is worth saying once more, a unilateral causality does not explain much. The linguocentrism that mysteriously grants lexicon and syntax priority in the evolution of hominin communication, the specific adaptive advantages (sexual selection, social bonding, and so forth) so many see as the stimulus for a Music writ large: As explanations they are vast and alluring, but they fail.

If, then, several abstract machines are at work, and if no single term can take priority in that operation, then any explanation of our modernity must try to take account of the coformation of its basic aspects. This is why, even while highlighting certain proto-musical increments in each chapter, I have taken pains to set them alongside other major aspects relating to them. In communication narrowly conceived this has involved protolinguistic elements as well as the gesture-calls and their emotive, deictic semiosis. In a wider social frame it has included theory of mind, copresence, incipient thinking-at-a-distance, and the technosociality of the taskscape.[9]

In focusing on these things we have arrived, perhaps unexpectedly, at an understanding of the interrelated emergences of musicking, language, and the cognitive release from proximity. The interdependency of these, I have argued, is aboriginal. It grew from protomusical and protolinguistic communication on a taskscape of sheer copresence. From this, across a gradient of incremental differences and in the fits and starts that the epicyclic mechanism helps to explain, emerged the features of our modernity: language and symbolism; musicking; the hypertrophied technology nascent already in the Middle Paleolithic period; a transcendental sociality gesturing toward metaphysics; social differentiation; ritual; and institutional structuring.

Chapter 1 began with the statement that humans today make music. But what we should really say is that humans today make music *because they have no choice.* ("Now must we sing, and sing the best we can," wrote Yeats, and it is a more ancient comfort than Cuchulain could have suspected.) To ask why humans are musicking creatures is tantamount to asking why they are speaking creatures or why they imagine and perceive immaterial, even unreal things. Humans today must do all these things because of how they came to do any one of them. Our sociality took on its modern complexities in constant interaction, across evolutionary timescales, with the coalescing of musicking. Neither could have come to be what it is without this tangled coformation, and each hovers even today in near proximity to the other.

Language too hovers close, and it shared in the coformation; but language and musicking played distinct roles in it, intersecting in different ways with the emergence of the abstraction that characterizes all human sociality today. In summary form, the systematized abstraction of the symbol came to inhabit language, while musicking came to be governed within a loose assemblage of formalized performative abstractions and systematized indexes foreign to normal linguistic usage. These differences are fundamental, and they shape to this day what societies everywhere recognize, in tacit practice or explicit formulation, as the special powers of musicking. Linguists may rightly tell us of sovereign mysteries of language structure and process; but only *lift a voice in song*, and all humans are struck—enthralled, seduced, threatened, made, or unmade—by these powers. One lesson of the foregoing chapters is that, however these differences appear in our developing understanding of them, they will be best understood from the context of a deep-historical interrelation and coevolution. The distinctive abstractions and formalizations of musicking, language, and social transcendentality were built together from the ground up.

The history traced here has dwelled on the emergence of cognitive abstractions involved in musicking, and it might be read as advancing a defense of Paleolithic beginnings for musical *formalism*. But that puts things backwards. It is not that ancient humans anticipated modern musical formalism, but that all the formalist conceptions of musical effect generated in Western discourse over the last two centuries—and in many other times and places as well—have been groping their ways toward basic, ancient truths about musicking and its difference from language. The full measure of musical formalism too needs to be taken from the perspective of a very deep history indeed.

At its deepest, long before musicking or language, this history is a question of stones chipped on a taskscape of transitory, copresent sociality and, of course, a question of what this knapping reveals to us of other behaviors. This is a Lower Paleolithic/Old Stone Age formalism of the most embodied sort—technosociality. Although the embodiment would come, far down the road, to be attenuated in a growing abstraction of cognition and the behaviors it sponsors, the attenuation would always remain less for musicking than for language. This is not to advance a *disem*bodied view of language; there can be little doubt that it retains in its pragmatic structure the rhythms and emotional flux of hominin protodiscourse. These ancient elements, however, are more evident still in musicking. For this reason musicking should occupy a special place in the effort that has recently coalesced from various disciplines to analyze and describe the embodied aspects of all our modes of consciousness. Musicking is a human activity unique in the degree to which it highlights somatic experience while structuring it according to complex, abstract, and relatively recent outgrowths of our cognition; this again can only be fully understood in deep historical perspective.

The artifacts left by our Paleolithic predecessors are, as cognitive archaeologists like to say, proxies for the behaviors we impute to them. But the behaviors themselves that created stone tools are not proxies for musical behaviors; they were instead part of the matrix from which musicking arose. A further lesson of deep history, then, is that the material entailments of musicking are part of a heritage that preceded and shaped it. These include, of course, the rhythmicized, entrained movements of bodies. I have throughout this text resisted the temptation to write "musicking *and dance*" only because of its tautology. I take it for granted that this entrained movement is a default ingredient of musicking, a physical experience of it muted only in special institutionalized contexts.

The material entailments include also, however, all the artifacts that extend the musicking body out onto the taskscape. This inclusiveness has its own history, extending back far beyond musicking itself: the history of the material crudescence of the heritage of musicking in Lower Paleolithic technosociality. A focus of this sort on musical materialities might also be a helpful step *reconnecting* musicking at a moment such as our own, in an Anthropocene already grown late (the Upper Anthropocene?): a moment when bodies still dance and musicking has not lost its grip, but when we are enticed to believe that the music can be delivered from a cloud free of implications for failing copresent musical interactions, for the breakdown of our sociality, and for the degradation of our environment.

The conceptual burden carried by terms such as taskscape and technosociality is that the actions of hominins, rather than reflecting fixed cognitive patterns, were a decisive force in shaping those patterns through the niche-constructive pushback of the material world. In cultural animals such as hominins, as we have seen, this mechanism must take on new dimensions in its operation; coevolution becomes biocultural coevolution. Finally, in animals that accumulate deep archives of culture—here we can cite only a few late hominins, perhaps even only *Homo sapiens*—these new dimensions carry potential for explosive development, change, and transmission. Deep human history is crucially a story of the outgrowth of this generation of cultural forms from biocultural coevolution and the runaway, epicyclic momentums it gathered. The momentum is not slackening today.

If, on the pessimistic side of the ledger, the coevolutionary model I have offered points to the powerlessness of musicking to rescue us from such momentums, on the optimistic side it models also the limitless diversification of musical behavior. What biocultural coevolution fixed in place in regard to musicking—what it fixed regarding the coalescence of human modernity all told—was a set of capacities that ensure the production of behavioral variety on a scale that dwarfs that of any other living or, undoubtedly, extinct species. This too is crucial in our deep history: The fixed features of our cognitive and perceptual makeup are unique exactly in determining diversification as our inescapable métier. If humans are music-making, language-making, and symbol-making creatures, we are also, constitutionally, makers of difference. Musicking can be seen in deep-historical vantage as a force pushing from the beginning toward this difference making. Perhaps this makes easier the affirmation, even *celebration* of musicking in this role.

In words that today can only seem an exercise of overweening modesty, Darwin concluded his *On the Origin of Species* by taking the measure of his great abstract machine, Inheritance-Variability-Selection. "There is a grandeur in this view of life," he wrote, in which "from so simple a beginning endless forms most beautiful and most wonderful have been, and are being, evolved." Famously, he contemplated this diversity in "an entangled bank, clothed with many plants of many kinds, with birds singing on the bushes, with various insects flitting about, and with worms crawling through the damp earth," and reflected "that these elaborately constructed forms, so different from each other, and dependent on each other in so complex a manner, have all been produced by laws acting around us."[10] The question of humankind had barely been raised in the book, but Darwin would return to it in his second great work, *The Descent of Man and Selection in Relation to Sex*, setting the terms and outlines for hundreds of books that would follow, including this one.

Any humanist today can substitute for Darwin's bank the unending diversity and fecundity of human cultural productions. Indeed, to savor the lush entanglements of cultural banks across large swathes of human experience has been the hard-won achievement of Western academic humanism over the last half-century. There is grandeur in this vision, too. But a different kind of grandeur, closer to what Darwin sensed in surveying the whole spectrum of life, emerges from contemplation of our deep-historical roots. In this we uncover the mechanisms that have generated the very possibility of our diversity, some of them the "laws" envisaged by Darwin, others conceptions of more recent vintage. We see that the much-feared determinism of evolutionary views of humanity is, rightly conceived, a determinism of nothing other than this boundless difference. And beneath all this we sense historical forces that have, in forging such diversity, made us one.

Evolution, Emergence, and History:
A Final Note

"Hypothesis," Hans Jonas once wrote, "implies the construction of at least a mentally workable model."[1] The situation I have modeled in this book concerns the late stage of hominin evolution: It is, as my subtitle has it, *the emergence of human modernity* all told—which is to say that the hypothesis claims relevance beyond the musical instance that exemplifies it.

The general mechanisms driving this evolution include, first, the role of biocultural feedback in the coevolutionary niche construction of hominins. This idea has been a staple of many accounts before mine, reaching all the way back to Darwin. Second, there are the altered selective pressures created by hominin behaviors and the resulting "offloading" of innate behaviors onto cultural transmission, described by Terrence Deacon. Next comes the hominin capacity to accumulate archives of cultural practice, evident in the archaeological record long before the appearance of *Homo sapiens* and emphasized by Kim Sterelny. Early on in hominin evolution, these were sedimented to depths unknown in any other lineage.

Finally, there is the propensity of these deepening archives to form, in certain no doubt numerous circumstances and in many areas of culture, independent congeries of arrangements among their parts. These are the cultural systems or formalizations I have called epicycles. They can be understood as emergent dynamics within hominin cultures, rendered likely by deep cultural accumulation but not wholly predictable from it. They take shape from the interactions of the particular material, social, cognitive, and informational aspects they involve, and I have suggested how several instances related to musicking and other human attainments might have formed.

In the epicycles, the concept of emergence surpasses vernacular usage and points toward large issues. Questions concerning the nature of emergent phenomena are pressing in many areas these days, from physics through life sciences to cultural and social studies. They raise the possibility of dynamics at odds with much conventional scientific explanation, including built-in unpredictability, outcomes irreducible to their causes and component parts, and reversed or "downward" lines of causality running from complex arrays to their simpler constituents. These new questions are not easily framed, let alone answered. There are some who regard emergent phenomena as illusions, or at most as incomplete descriptions of situations that eventually will (or ideally could) admit of explanations that trace causal paths from their components and earlier stages. Others see emergence as a qualitatively new way of accounting for phenomena unanalyzable in reductionist scientific method, phenomena such as the origins of life or the appearance of high-mammalian consciousness or the human mind. But most of us sit somewhere between these positions, engrossed in careful observation and modeling of possible situations of emergence and wary of the foreshortening of method that overconfidence in reductive explanation might bring. The emergentist/nonemergentist edge broached in this book concerns the complexities of biocultural evolution and hence is limited in scope to cultural animals. But as a productive, cutting edge for generating competing models in the life sciences, it reaches from culture all the way to the molecular levels of cellular ontogeny and phylogeny.

Although my position on emergence lies somewhere in the middle of the spectrum, I have found myself drawn toward its emergentist end. I do not think that reductionist modes of explanation will be able to answer satisfactorily the basic questions we pose about the appearance of human modernity. (For reasons I have made clear, I have still less confidence in the alternative explanations of evolutionary psychology or magic-bullet accounts of "language genes" and the like.) Something extraordinary—or, rather, many extraordinary things—occurred across the recent stages of hominin evolution, and these coalescences are not well described by tracing linear causal pathways from before to after, from simple to complex culture.

My account, then, urges that questions of emergence be further explored, in specific ways, in order to illuminate matters at the heart of human evolution. The loci of emergent dynamics are the epicycles. Many of these must have been something like phase switches from nonsystematic to systematic organization in behavior, perception, and cognition (as in the formation of a self-referential set of symbols) or from analog to discrete cognition, perception, and production of information (as in the precipitating of discrete pitch from analog pitch communication). Others might not have involved phase transition–like shifts. The move from a purely transactional sociality to one involving transcendental elements, for example, was evidently a gradual one, and the growth in prominence of the transcendental elements may finally have brought about strikingly innovative human social elements through many incremental epicycles, but without sudden, revolutionary demarcations.

This possibility of gradualism suggests why it might be difficult to distinguish an epicycle from any coherent set of cultural behaviors and percepts transmitted across generations. In Chapter 6, for instance, I included the behaviors involved in fashioning an Acheulean biface in a list of epicycles; but is this too rudimentary a collection of behaviors to constitute a system and exert feed-forward influence? If so, where in the growing complexity of hominin cultures do we draw the line between nonepicyclic and epicyclic behaviors and cognition? A list of necessary and sufficient features or criteria by which to define epicycles will be elusive. I have suggested some such criteria in the course of this book: They include a self-generating, self-perpetuating complexity and consistency of interactions among social behaviors, cultural forms, and material and informational substrates. But these general criteria can only nudge us along the path to modeling specific biocultural histories. Because the epicycles themselves form from the particulars of the histories, any general definition of them will fly high above those particulars—so high that it might cease to characterize their specificity.

What holds for the epicycles might hold also for emergence more generally. The shock of burgeoning novelty might not always accompany it; it might more often show subtle nuances of novel formalization. And, if there is a unified field theory of emergence to be discovered, it might involve the most general nature of emergent organization and little more, a generality playing itself out differently in individual cases reaching from deep cultural archives to autopoietic molecular systems.

Perhaps there appears here the edge of an *epistemological* divide, alongside the ontological emergence/nonemergence one. While it is safe to say that scientists will be debating questions of emergence for some time to come, the debate will need to be engaged beyond the sciences, since, insofar as it concerns human cultural attainments, even across evolutionary time scales, humanists will have a central role to play. For the humanist, however, the question of emergence cannot help but resolve itself into one of history—or, viewed at the meta-level, of *historicity*, the general presence and effects of historical dynamics. Historicity lives at the heart of emergence of any complex sort, as Deacon's useful taxonomy of emergence shows (see pages 187–88). And history itself resists necessary and sufficient definition, perhaps *any* definition. "Only that which has no history can be defined," says Nietzsche; historicity is unruly in the face of reductive explanation, and history proliferates in luxuriant growth that is better described than defined.

It will be quickly appreciated that I am thinking here of *certain kinds* of histories, not all phenomena to which the term could be applied. We might, for example, think justifiably of the coming-to-equilibrium of a simple heat gradient, or the dissolving of sugar in a cup of coffee, or the decay of 14C as "histories." But they are stochastic histories whose outcome can be accurately predicted from starting conditions, at least in statistical terms; they are histories of aggregates of undifferentiated individual entities, without modes of persistent self-organization or formalization—without (the emergentist would say) any sign of emergent system or process. Other histories, for example those of hominin evolution or of life on earth, are of a different kind than these stochastic ones. It may be that some scientists are resistant to recognizing the role of emergence in evolution precisely because the term betokens, above all, an unruly and causally indeterminate change across time. But this is just the kind of history—the way of encountering historicity—that has long been humanists' bread and butter.

It is possible that, in the fullness of time and knowledge, all these unmanageable histories might turn out to be nothing more than hypertrophied versions of simpler, statistical ones. They might turn out to involve no processes foreign to those simpler histories and to be explicable through nonemergent models—*predictable*, even, in a fullness approaching the capacity of Laplace's demon. In that case, emergentist explanations would turn out to have been placeholders, explanatory modes that had been, at one point, the best we could do; and in this they would have served useful ends. Description would retreat before an on-marching definition. My wager, however, is that this will not turn out to be so: that such definition, were it achieved, would in each case be so weightily elaborated as to collapse toward a particular description without generalizing power. It is a wager that there have been at least two categorically different kinds of history in the unfolding of the cosmos, and that this difference has much to do with the nonlinearity of feedback and feed-forward systems that characterize histories of one kind and enable them to evade statistical norms.

The cosmos may be destined to wind down to a point of maximum entropy and to an unarticulated dispersion of matter/ energy. It seems probable, however, that the systems and histories that are maintaining it far from that point across billions of years cannot all be explained by linear thermodynamics alone. The *systems* that present the brightest evidence of this are living ones, the *histories* evolutionary and—at a late, incandescent moment—cultural ones.

Notes

CHAPTER ONE: SOME FIRST PRINCIPLES

1. Christopher Small, *Musicking: The Meanings of Performing and Listening* (Middletown, CT: Wesleyan University Press, 1998).

2. In keeping with recent (though unsettled) taxonomic practice, I use "hominin" to refer to humans and their most closely related ancestors, in place of "hominid," now usually taken to include, among extant genera, chimpanzees, gorillas, and orangutans as well as humans.

3. See Jerry Fodor, *The Modularity of Mind: An Essay on Faculty Psychology* (Cambridge, MA: The MIT Press, 1983). The literature on cognitive modularity is large; for developments since Fodor's book, see, for example, Kim Sterelny, *The Representational Theory of Mind: An Introduction* (Oxford: Blackwell, 1990); Dan Sperber, *Explaining Culture: A Naturalistic Approach* (Oxford: Blackwell, 1996), ch. 6; and, for the view of evolutionary psychologists that mind is an adapted and "massively" modular structure, Steven Pinker, *How the Mind Works* (New York: Norton, 1997) and Peter Carruthers, *The Architecture of the Mind* (Oxford: Oxford University Press, 2006). For Fodor's response to Pinker and rejection of adapted modularity, see *The Mind Doesn't Work That Way* (Cambridge, MA: The MIT Press, 2001), chs. 4–5. An important evolutionary view limiting the role of modularity is philosopher Sterelny's; see *Thought in a Hostile World: The Evolution of Human Cognition* (Oxford: Blackwell, 2003), esp. chs. 10–11, and *The Evolved Apprentice: How Evolution Made Humans Unique* (Cambridge, MA: The MIT Press, 2012). I am grateful to Sterelny for allowing me to read the latter before publication.

4. Cross features such an approach in his introduction to *The Oxford Handbook of Music Psychology*, ed. Susan Hallam, Ian Cross, and Michael Thaut

(Oxford: Oxford University Press, 2009) and in other writings; see also the contributions of collaborators in his circle such as Iain Morley, "The Evolutionary Origins and Archaeology of Music," PhD diss., University of Cambridge, 2003; and John Bispham, "Rhythm in Music: What Is It? Who Has It? And Why?" *Music Perception* 24 (2006), pp. 125–34. For an especially speculative incremental approach, see Steven Brown, "The 'Musilanguage' Model of Music Evolution," in *The Origins of Music*, ed. Nils L. Wallin, Björn Merker, and Steven Brown (Cambridge, MA: The MIT Press, 2000), pp. 271–300 (for Brown's views, see also Chapter 3).

5. See *Cognition* 100 (2006), special issue on "The Nature of Music," ed. Isabelle Peretz; also two issues of *Music Perception*, 23 (2005) and 24 (2006), the first containing two target essays, Timothy Justus and Jeffrey J. Hutsler, "Fundamental Issues in the Evolutionary Psychology of Music: Assessing Innateness and Domain Specificity," pp. 1–27, and Josh McDermott and Marc Hauser, "The Origins of Music: Innateness, Uniqueness, and Evolution," pp. 29–59. The second contains commentary by nine scholars and a response by McDermott and Hauser (pp. 79–116).

6. Steven Mithen, *The Singing Neanderthals: The Origins of Music, Language, Mind, and Body* (Cambridge, MA: Harvard University Press, 2006); see p. xx.

7. Charles Darwin, *The Descent of Man, and Selection in Relation to Sex*, facsimile of the 1871 edition (Princeton: Princeton University press, 1981), pp. 53–62. For an especially explicit recent incremental hypothesis, see Ray Jackendoff, "Possible Stages in the Evolution of the Language Capacity," *Trends in Cognitive Sciences* 3/7 (July 1999), pp. 272–79; revised in his *Foundations of Language* (Oxford: Oxford University Press, 2002), ch. 8. Jackendoff's stages are elaborated by Robbins Burling, *The Talking Ape: How Language Evolved* (Oxford: Oxford University Press, 2005), ch. 9. See also Derek Bickerton, *Language & Species* (Chicago: University of Chicago Press, 1990); Steven Pinker and Paul Bloom, "Natural Language and Natural Selection," *Behavioral and Brain Sciences* 13 (1990), pp. 707–26; and Philip Lieberman, *Toward an Evolutionary Biology of Language* (Cambridge, MA: Harvard University Press, 2006).

8. For examples, see Sterelny, *The Evolved Apprentice*; Merlin Donald, *A Mind So Rare: The Evolution of Human Consciousness* (New York: Norton, 2001); and Philip J. Barnard, David J. Duke, Richard W. Byrne and Iain Davidson, "Differentiation in Cognitive and Emotional Meanings: An Evolutionary

Analysis," *Cognition and Emotion* 21 (2007), pp. 1155–83. For an incremental, deep-historical account of the emergence of human kinship, starting from modes close to today's nonhuman primates, see Bernard Chapais, *Primeval Kinship: How Pair-Bonding Gave Birth to Human Society* (Cambridge, MA: Harvard University Press, 2008).

9. Sally McBrearty and Alison S. Brooks, "The Revolution That Wasn't: A New Interpretation of the Origin of Modern Human Behavior," *Journal of Human Evolution* 39 (2000), pp. 453–563.

10. See, for example, Richard G. Klein, *The Human Career: Human Biological and Cultural Origins*, 3rd ed. (Chicago: University of Chicago Press, 2009); and Paul Mellars, "The Impossible Coincidence: A Single-Species Model for the Origins of Modern Behavior in Europe," *Evolutionary Anthropology* 14 (2005), pp. 12–27. I will have much more to say about these issues in Chapters 4–7.

11. See also Justus and Hutsler, "Fundamental Issues," p. 4. This signals a very long (if not infinite) regress, of course: the evolution of human capacities is a current in a continuous historical stream reaching back to the beginnings of life on earth, with no nonarbitrary starting point in midstream.

12. For the coining of the term, see Stephen Jay Gould and Elisabeth S. Vrba, "Exaptation—A Missing Term in the Science of Form" *Paleobiology* 8 (1982), pp. 4–15. For a different conceptualization of related issues in cognition, see Sperber, *Explaining Culture*, ch. 6. For Sperber, working from a Fodorian, modular stance, a cognitive domain is *proper* to the informational inputs it was selected to process (i.e., its adaptive constraints), though its *actual* inputs may include other information different from these selective determinants.

13. Pinker, *How the Mind Works*, pp. 528–38. For a far more nuanced view positing music as a "transformative technology of mind," but one that did not enter into any coevolutionary "modification of our brains," see Aniruddh Patel, "Music, Biological Evolution, and the Brain," in *Emerging Disciplines*, ed. M. Bailar (Houston: Rice University Press, 2010), pp. 91–144. Patel first sketched this theory in his important book *Music, Language, and the Brain* (Oxford: Oxford University Press, 2008), ch. 7. My difference with Patel's position is not that I deny the technological status of musicking, at least from the particular, deep-historical vantage on technology I will elaborate, but that my conception of the interaction of technology and hominin coevolution is different from his. The fundamental importance of this issue will become clear across the

chapters that follow.

14. For overviews of adaptationist approaches see David Huron, "Is Music an Evolutionary Adaptation," in *The Cognitive Neuroscience of Music*, ed. Isabelle Peretz and Robert Zatorre (Oxford: Oxford University Press, 2003), pp. 57–75; Ian Cross and Iain Morley, "The Evolution of Music: Theories, Definitions, and the Nature of the Evidence," in *Communicative Musicality: Exploring the Basis of Human Companionship*, ed. Stephen Malloch and Colwyn Trevarthen (Oxford: Oxford University Press, 2009), pp. 61–81; and Iain Morley, *The Prehistory of Music: Human Evolution, Archaeology, & the Origins of Musicality* (Oxford: Oxford University Press, 2013), ch. 11. For a collection of mainly adaptationist explanations, see Nicholas Bannan, ed., *Music, Language, and Human Evolution* (Oxford: Oxford University Press, 2012). An early and particularly important statement of the social bonding hypothesis, with an emphasis on group dancing, is William H. McNeill, *Keeping Together in Time: Dance and Drill in Human History* (Cambridge, MA: Harvard University Press, 1995), chs. 1–3.

15. Jonathan Kramnick, "Against Literary Darwinism," *Critical Inquiry* 37 (2011), pp. 315–47; followed by six responses and Kramnick's rebuttal, *Critical Inquiry* 38 (2012), pp. 388–460; see p. 443.

16. For an overview of the issues not limited to hominin evolution but extending from the genome to organismal societies and beyond, see Kim Sterelny and Paul E. Griffiths, *Sex and Death: An Introduction to Philosophy of Biology* (Chicago: University of Chicago Press, 1999).

17. See Stuart A. Kauffman, *The Origins of Order: Self-Organization and Selection in Evolution* (New York: Oxford University Press, 1993); Kauffman, *Investigations* (Oxford: Oxford University Press, 2000).

18. The fundamental study is F. John Odling-Smee, Kevin N. Laland, and Marcus W. Feldman, *Niche Construction: The Neglected Process in Evolution* (Princeton: Princeton University Press, 2003); see esp. the introduction and chs. 6 and 9.

19. For recent reappraisals of the Baldwin effect, see *Evolution and Learning: The Baldwin Effect Reconsidered*, ed. Bruce H. Weber and David J. Depew (Cambridge, MA: The MIT Press, 2003).

20. Justus and Hutsler, "Fundamental Issues," p. 4, have suggested distinguishing such post-exaptation adaptations as *secondary adaptations*, but this may

only set up categorical distinction where none is found in the fluid historical relation of exaptation and adaptation.

21. See Bert Hölldobler and Edward O. Wilson, *The Superorganism: The Beauty, Elegance, and Strangeness of Insect Societies* (New York: Norton, 2009); the term reaches back to the 1920s and the entomologist and ethologist William Morton Wheeler.

22. R. C. Lewontin, Steven Rose, and Leon J. Kamin, *Not in Our Genes: Biology, Ideology, and Human Nature* (New York: Pantheon, 1984). For later, less polemical statements and elaborations of the position, see Richard Lewontin, *The Triple Helix: Gene, Organism, and Environment* (Cambridge, MA: Harvard University Press, 2002) and Richard Lewontin and Richard Levins, *Biology Under the Influence: Dialectical Essays on Ecology, Agriculture, and Health* (New York: Monthly Review Press, 2007). For a dramatic recent extension of this position from the vantage of semiotic anthropology, see Paul Kockelman, "Biosemiosis, Technocognition, and Sociogenesis: Selection and Significance in a Multiverse of Sieving and Serendipity," *Current Anthropology* 52 (2011), pp. 711–39. He dubs the organism/niche unit the *envorganism*.

23. Peter J. Richerson and Robert Boyd, *Not by Genes Alone: How Culture Transformed Human Evolution* (Chicago: University of Chicago Press, 2005), p. 190, their emphasis.

24. Eva Jablonka, "Information: Its Interpretation, Its Inheritance, and Its Sharing," *Philosophy of Science* 69 (2002), pp. 578–605; also Eva Jablonka and Marion J. Lamb, *Evolution in Four Dimensions: Genetic, Epigenetic, Behavioral, and Symbolic Variation in the History of Life* (Cambridge, MA: The MIT Press, 2005). *Genetic* information is passed down in the genome and determined by the sequences of nucleotides in DNA molecules; its information is varied through sexual processes and mutations. *Epigenetic* information stands alongside the workings of the genetic code and involves various molecular and intracellular processes that biologists are only beginning to understand, including some autocatalytic chemical systems, self-maintained by positive feedback loops; alterations of DNA molecules by chemical groups attached to them, arising within an organism's ontogeny and tending to be passed along in DNA replication; and the templating of three-dimensional molecular architectures so as to produce offspring molecules without genetic intermediaries. These systems in effect pass information from generation to generation of cells; in

some cases (for example, autocatalytic loops) they may be even more basic than genetic coding. Stuart Kauffman in particular has argued that the emergence of autocatalytic loops provides an alternative to that of replicating molecules in explaining the origins of life on earth. See Kauffman, *The Origins of Order*, pt. 2; for a summary statement, Kauffman, *Investigations*, ch. 2.

25. *Symbolic* information, for its part, depends for its transmission on either referential language or technologies of external information storage—symbols in some material (or, today, virtual) form. This type of information is, for Jablonka and Lamb, a "diagnostic trait" of our species that seems to them to encompass all the uniquely human modes of information and its transfer—an inadequate conception, in my view, to which I return in Chapter 5. See Jablonka and Lamb, *Evolution in Four Dimensions*, p. 193.

26. Sterelny, *Thought in a Hostile World*, ch. 8; and Sterelny, *The Evolved Apprentice: How Evolution Made Humans Unique*, chs. 2-3.

27. See Terrence Deacon, "Multilevel Selection in a Complex Adaptive System: The Problem of Language Origins," in Weber and Depew, *Evolution and Learning*, pp. 81-106. For more on Deacon, see Chapter 5.

28. Terrence Deacon, "A Role for Relaxed Selection in the Evolution of the Language Capacity," *Proceedings of the National Academy of Sciences* 107 (2010), pp. 9000-9006.

29. Implicit in this statement is a general difference between the transmission of information in genetics and in culture. In the first, faithful replication is the rule and variation (through, for example, mutation) the exception. Human culture instead fosters a proliferation of variation that can probably be traced, at least in part, to the flexibility and systemic mediation of symbolism itself. (Note, however, that such variation characterizes other, nonsymbolic animal cultures as well, if in far smaller measure.) This difference between a tendency to faithful replication and one toward diversified reproduction undermines attempts to assimilate cultural to genetic change and to define meaningful analogies between genes and replicating cultural units—"memes," as they are usually termed, following Richard Dawkins, *The Selfish Gene* (Oxford: Oxford University Press, 2006 [1976]), ch. 11. The relation of nature and nurture should be modeled not as analogy but as ceaseless interplay.

30. Deacon, "A Role," pp. 9004-9005.

31. See Richard Dawkins, *The Extended Phenotype: The Long Reach of the*

Gene (Oxford: Oxford University Press, 1982).

CHAPTER TWO: 1,000,000 YEARS AGO

1. For surveys of Oldowan and Acheulean technologies, see Richard G. Klein, *The Human Career: Human Biological and Cultural Origins*, 3rd ed. (Chicago: University of Chicago Press, 2009), pp. 249–61 and 372–96; a briefer and older synopsis is Thomas G. Wynn, "The Evolution of Tools and Symbolic Behavior," in *Handbook of Human Symbolic Evolution*, ed. Andrew Lock and Charles R. Peters (Oxford: Oxford University Press, 1996), pp. 263–87. For the "archaeology of cognition," see Thomas Wynn, "Archaeology and Cognitive Evolution," *Behavior and Brain Sciences* 25 (2002), pp. 389–438; for a sampling of approaches to the topic, *Philosophical Transactions of the Royal Society B* 363 (2008), special issue, "The Sapient Mind: Archaeology Meets Neuroscience," ed. Colin Renfrew, Chris Frith, and Lambros Malafouris, hereafter cited as "The Sapient Mind."

2. For a confident assertion of standardization, see Wynn, "Archaeology and Cognitive Evolution"; for an argument on the side of weak standardization at most, John McNabb, Francesca Binyon, and Lee Hazelwood, "The Large Cutting Tools from the South African Acheulean and the Questions of Social Traditions," *Current Anthropology* 45 (2004), pp. 653–77.

3. For detailed discussion, Wynn, "Archaeology and Cognitive Evolution."

4. For the latter view, see Klein, *The Human Career*, pp. 378–79.

5. Thomas Wynn, response to McNabb, Binyon, and Hazelwood, "The Large Cutting Tools," p. 672.

6. Ian Davidson and William Noble, "Tools and Language in Human Evolution," in *Tools, Language and Cognition in Human Evolution*, ed. K. R. Gibson and T. Ingold (Cambridge: Cambridge University Press, 1993), pp. 363–88, quotations at p. 365. For a more recent summary of their position, see Iain Davidson, "The Finished Artefact Fallacy: Acheulean Hand-axes and Language Origins," in *The Transition to Language*, ed. Alison Wray (Oxford: Oxford University Press, 2002), pp. 180–203.

7. Clive Gamble, *The Palaeolithic Societies of Europe* (Cambridge: Cambridge University Press, 1999), esp. pp. 129ff; also Davidson and Noble, "Tools and Language in Human Evolution"; William Noble and Ian Davidson, *Human Evolution, Language and Mind* (Cambridge: Cambridge University Press, 1996).

8. For the phrase "release from proximity," see Gamble, *Palaeolithic Societies*, p. 40; Gamble elaborates it from L. Rodseth, R. W. Wrangham, A. Harrigan, and B. B. Smuts, "The Human Community as a Primate Society," *Current Anthropology* 32 (1991), pp. 221–54, where it describes the extending of social relationships beyond copresence and immediate contact.

9. Gamble, *Palaeolithic Societies*, pp. 41–42, 63–64, 129–35, and 171–73.

10. In general, see Michael L. Anderson, "Embodied Cognition: A Field Guide," *Artificial Intelligence* 149 (2003), pp. 91–130; and Robert A. Wilson and Lucia Foglia, "Embodied Cognition," in the *Stanford Encyclopedia of Philosophy*, accessed online at http://plato.stanford.edu/entries/embodied-cognition. For the connection to hominin evolution, Fiona Coward and Clive Gamble, "Big Brains, Small Worlds: Material Culture and the Evolution of the Mind," Lambros Malafouris, "Between Brains, Bodies, and Things: *Tectonoetic* Awareness and the Extended Self," and Chris Gosden, "Social Ontologies," all in "The Sapient Mind," 1969–79, 1993–2002, and 2003–10, respectively.

11. See Dorothy L. Cheney and Robert M. Seyfarth, *Baboon Metaphysics: The Evolution of a Social Mind* (Chicago: University of Chicago Press, 2007); also the Excursus following Chapter 3. For the complexity generated in primate societies from bottom-up performance, S. S. Strum and Bruno Latour, "Redefining the Social Link: From Baboons to Humans," *Social Science Information* 26 (1987), pp. 783–802.

12. Rodney A. Brooks, *Cambrian Intelligence: The Early History of the New AI* (Cambridge, MA: The MIT Press, 1999).

13. André Leroi-Gourhan, *Gesture and Speech*, trans. Anna Bostock Berger (Cambridge, MA: The MIT Press, 1993).

14. Anglo-American archaeologists and anthropologists embracing Leroi-Gourhan's *chaîne opératoire* in the 1990s include, in addition to Gamble: Randall White, introduction to *Gesture and Speech*; Marcia-Anne Dobres and Christopher R. Hoffman, "Social Agency and the Dynamics of Prehistoric Technology," *Journal of Archaeological Method and Theory* 1 (1994), pp. 211–58; and Tim Ingold, "'Tools for the Hand, Language for the Face': An Appreciation of Leroi-Gourhan's *Gesture and Speech*," *Studies in the History and Philosophy of Biological and Biomedical Sciences* 30 (1999), pp. 411–53.

15. See, among many examples, the material, technological, and gestural anthropology of Pierre Lemonnier, the analyses of lithic techniques of Eric

Boëda, and the journal *Techniques & Culture*, founded in 1982 under the sponsorship of Leroi-Gourhan.

16. Bernard Stiegler, *Technics and Time, 1: The Fault of Epimetheus*, trans. Richard Beardsworth and George Collins (Stanford: Stanford University Press, 1998), esp. pt. 1, "The Invention of the Human." I return to Stiegler at the end of this chapter.

17. Jacques Derrida, *Of Grammatology*, trans. Gayatri Chakravorty Spivak (Baltimore: Johns Hopkins University Press, 1974), esp. pp. 83ff.

18. Gamble, *Palaeolithic Societies*, pp. 86–87; Tim Ingold, "The Temporality of the Landscape," *World Archaeology* 25 (1993), pp. 152–73.

19. Leroi-Gourhan had understood as much, in strikingly similar terms: "Rhythms are the creators of space and time, at least for the individual. Space and time do not enter lived experience until they are materialized within a rhythmic frame. Rhythms are also creators of forms.... Manufacturing techniques developed from the beginning in a rhythmic setting—at once muscular, visual, and auditive—born of the repetition of impact-making gestures." *Gesture and Speech*, p. 309.

20. Gamble, *Palaeolithic Societies*, p. 130.

21. See also M. J. White and P. B. Pettitt, "Technology of Early Palaeolithic Western Europe: Innovation, Variability and a Unified Framework," *Lithics* 16 (1995), pp. 27–40, at p. 32. White and Pettitt see little preplanning in the manufacture of Lower Paleolithic bifaces, but instead "the rhythmic repetition of [a]...technological repertoire" modestly adaptable in immediate response to the potentials or affordances of the raw materials at hand.

22. For this point, see Craig T. Palmer, Kathryn Coe, and Reed L. Wadley, "On Tools and Traditions," and Derek Hodgson, "More on Acheulean Tools," *Current Anthropology* 46 (2005), pp. 459–63, 647–50, and the replies to each, included in these pages, by John McNabb.

23. Davidson, "The Finished Artefact Fallacy," pp. 190–98; also the responses to Wynn, "Archaeology and Cognitive Evolution," by Kenny R. Coventry and John Clibbens, p. 406, and J. Scott Jordan, p. 412.

24. See, in addition to Leroi-Gourhan's *Gesture and Speech*, his *L'homme et la matière* (Paris: Albin Michel, 1943).

25. Jeffrey B. Wagman, response to Wynn, "Archaeology and Cognitive Evolution," pp. 423–24.

26. Whitney Davis, *Replications: Archaeology, Art History, Psychoanalysis* (University Park: Pennsylvania State University Press, 1995), pp. 114–16.

27. J. B. Deregowski, response to Wynn, "Archaeology and Cognitive Evolution," pp. 406–407.

28. Leroi-Gourhan, *Gesture and Speech*, p. 310.

29. This model and its cognitive implications have been described from the vantage of dynamic systems theory by J. Scott Jordan, "Wild Agency: Nested Intentionalities in Cognitive Neuroscience and Archaeology," "The Sapient Mind," pp. 1981–91.

30. I summarize from a number of sources. A good overview of points of both agreement and debate can be gained from two important target articles already cited and the sets of responses they elicited; see Wynn, "Archaeology and Cognitive Evolution," followed by responses from twenty-eight psychologists, cognitivists, and archaeologists and a counterresponse by Wynn; and McNabb, Binyon, and Hazelwood, "The Large Cutting Tools," with six respondents and McNabb's counterresponse. Further responses to McNabb et al. and by McNabb followed in *Current Anthropology* 46 (2005), pp. 459–63 and 647–50. Also see Jane Hallos, "'15 Minutes of Fame': Exploring the Temporal Dimension of Middle Pleistocene Lithic Technology," *Journal of Human Evolution* 49 (2005), pp. 155–79; and Mark White and Nick Ashton, "Lower Palaeolithic Core Technology and the Origins of the Levallois Method in North-Western Europe," *Current Anthropology* 44 (2003), pp. 598–609.

31. Dietrich Stout, response to Wynn, "Archaeology and Cognitive Evolution," p. 421.

32. For this point, see White and Pettitt, "Technology of Early Palaeolithic Western Europe."

33. McNabb, Binyon, and Hazelwood, "The Large Cutting Tools," p. 667.

34. Merlin Donald, *Origins of the Modern Mind: Three Stages in the Evolution of Culture and Cognition* (Cambridge, MA: Harvard University Press, 1991), chs. 5–6, esp. pp. 168ff, 177ff.

35. Merlin Donald, "Preconditions for the Evolution of Protolanguages," in *The Descent of Mind: Psychological Perspectives on Hominid Evolution*, ed. Michael C. Corballis and Stephen E. G. Lea (Oxford: Oxford University Press, 1999), pp. 138–54. For an attempt different from mine to put Donald's mimesis to work in understanding the evolutionary emergence of music, see Elizabeth

Tolbert, "Music and Meaning: An Evolutionary Story," *Psychology of Music* 29 (2001), pp. 84–94.

36. Donald's rehearsal loop is different from the play widespread among mammals and perhaps wider stretches of the animal kingdom. Such play might be regarded as a kind of practice; it is not however subject to much voluntary control but instead guided mainly by instinct. Lion cubs fighting with each other, for example, replicate and perfect effective instinctual patterns of behavior, but their play affords little or no opportunity for reshaping socially transmitted interactions.

37. Donald, "Preconditions," p. 142.

38. Francesco d'Errico, "Palaeolithic Origins of Artificial Memory Systems: An Evolutionary Perspective," in *Cognition and Material Culture: The Archaeology of Symbolic Storage*, ed. Colin Renfrew and Chris Scarre (Cambridge: MacDonald Institute for Archaeological Research, 1999), pp. 19–50; Donald, *Origins of the Modern Mind*, ch. 8; Leroi-Gourhan, *Gesture and Speech*, pp. 252, 115.

39. For a summary and succinct refutation of such views on grounds different from those developed here, see Wynn, "The Evolution of Tools and Symbolic Behavior," pp. 269–71.

40. Martin Clayton, Rebecca Sager, and Udo Will, "In Time with the Music: The Concept of Entrainment and Its Significance for Ethnomusicology," *European Seminar in Ethnomusicology* (Special ESEM CounterPoint Volume) 11 (2005), pp. 3–75. For a general view of entrainment from the vantage of complex systems theory, see Manuel de Landa, "Nonorganic Life," in *Incorporations*, ed. Jonathan Crary and Sanford Kwinter (New York: Zone, 1992), pp. 129–67, esp. pp. 151–53.

41. Joseph E. McGrath and Janice E. Kelly, *Time and Human Interaction: Toward a Social Psychology of Time* (New York: Guilford, 1986), esp. ch. 4.

42. Edward W. Large and Mari Riess Jones, "The Dynamics of Attending: How People Track Time-Varying Events," *Psychological Review* 106 (1999), pp. 119–59; for a brief overview, Mari Riess Jones, "Musical Time," in *The Oxford Handbook of Music Psychology*, ed. Susan Hallam, Ian Cross, and Michael Thaut (Oxford: Oxford University Press, 2009), pp. 81–92.

43. Large and Jones, "The Dynamics of Attending," p. 127; on entrainment and attractors, see de Landa, "Nonorganic Life," pp. 137, 152.

44. Large and Jones, "The Dynamics of Attending"; Mari Riess Jones, Heather Moynihan, Noah MacKenzie, and Jennifer Puente, "Temporal Aspects of Stimulus-Driven Attending in Dynamic Arrays," *Psychological Science* 13 (2002), pp. 313–19; and Mari Riess Jones, Heather Moynihan Johnston, and Jennifer Puente, "Effects of Auditory Pattern Structure on Anticipatory and Reactive Attending," *Cognitive Psychology* 53 (2006), pp. 59–96.

45. See Lawrence M. Ward, "Synchronous Neural Oscillations and Cognitive Processes," *Trends in Cognitive Sciences* 7 (2003), pp. 553–59; Theodore P. Zanto, Joel S. Snyder, and Edward W. Large, "Neural Correlates of Rhythmic Expectancy," *Advances in Cognitive Psychology* 2 (2006), pp. 221–31. For a general review of the idea that phase synchrony among neural networks oscillating at various frequencies is fundamental to cognition, see Francisco Varela, Jean-Philippe Lachaux, Enrico Rodriguez, and Jacques Martinerie, "The Brainweb: Phase Synchronization and Large-Scale Integration," *Nature Reviews Neuroscience* 2 (2001), pp. 229–39.

46. Jessica A. Grahn and Matthew Brett, "Rhythm and Beat Perception in Motor Areas of the Brain," *Journal of Cognitive Neuroscience* 19 (2005), pp. 893–906; also Aniruddh Patel, *Music, Language, and the Brain* (Oxford: Oxford University Press, 2008), pp. 402–11.

47. Music cognitivist Aniruddh Patel agrees. He notes the auditory bias of our entraining capacities—a regular pulse heard will bring us into its tow far more effectively than a regular pulse seen (an isochronous flashing light, for example)—and he sees revealed in this "a tight coupling between auditory input and motor output." *Music, Language, and the Brain*, pp. 410, 404.

48. John Bispham, "Rhythm in Music: What Is It? Who Has It? And Why?" *Music Perception* 24 (2006), pp. 125–34; p. 128.

49. For a productive analysis of musical entrainment emphasizing contemporary cross-species comparison rather than archaeology, see W. Tecumseh Fitch, "The Biology and Evolution of Rhythm: Unravelling a Paradox," in *Language and Music as Cognitive Systems*, ed. Patrick Rebuschat, Martin Rohrmeier, John A. Hawkins, and Ian Cross (Oxford: Oxford University Press, 2012), pp. 73–95. Fitch's argument forms part of his more general rehabilitation of Darwin's ideas on musical and linguistic origins; for consideration of this, see Chapter 3 below.

50. Peter J. Richerson and Robert Boyd, *Not by Genes Alone: How Culture*

Transformed Human Evolution (Chicago: University of Chicago Press, 2005), p. 142.

51. Martin Heidegger, *The Question Concerning Technology and Other Essays*, trans. William Lovitt (New York: Harper & Row, 1977).

52. Heidegger, *The Question Concerning Technology*, p. 13.

53. Stiegler, *Technics and Time, 1*, pt. 1. Stiegler's is a philosophical, not a historical or archaeological project. Viewed from these latter vantage points, it is hampered by an overreliance on the particulars of Leroi-Gourhan's account of hominin evolution, many of which were out of date already by the time Stiegler wrote. We have seen, however, that these superseded particulars do not vitiate all the productive aspects of Leroi-Gourhan's achievement.

54. *Ibid.*, p. 141: "it is the tool...that invents the human, not the human who invents the technical."

55. *Ibid.*, pp. 36, 44–46, and 156–58.

56. For nature vs. nurture, *ibid.*, pp. 154–58; for sedimentation, pp. 140–41.

57. *Ibid.* pp. 136–37. Cf. Derrida, *Of Grammatology*, p. 84: "Leroi-Gourhan no longer describes the unity of man and the human adventure by the simple possibility of the *graphie* in general, but rather as a stage or an articulation in the history of life—of what I have called *différance*.... From 'genetic inscription'... up to the passage beyond alphabetic writing to the orders of the logos and of a certain *Homo sapiens*, the possibility of the *grammè* structures the movement of its history according to rigorously original levels, types, and rhythms" (trans. modified).

58. Stiegler, *Technics and Time*, pp. 153–54, 160.

59. De Landa, "Nonorganic Life."

CHAPTER THREE: 500,000 YEARS AGO

1. *Deixis* refers to elements in utterances that indicate or require contextual information to be fully meaningful. Such elements construct a tight bond between an utterance and its immediate situation; because of this, they often function in a heightened indicative way—e.g., "I want *this* toy, not *that* one"—and often are accompanied by nonlinguistic pointing gestures. Deixis is closely related, thus, to what Charles Sanders Peirce called *indexical* signification, characterized by pointing, proximity, and causal relations of sign to object signified; deictic signs are, in Peirce's famous trio of icon, index, and symbol,

indexes. I return to Peircean semiotics and its implications for hominin evolution in Chapter 5.

2. For the following paragraphs, see Clive Gamble, *The Palaeolithic Societies of Europe* (Cambridge: Cambridge University Press, 1999), esp. ch. 4; and Gamble, *Origins and Revolutions: Human Identity in Earliest Prehistory* (Cambridge: Cambridge University Press, 2007), pp. 211–40. His picture accords in general with other, broader surveys of the behaviors of late Acheulean hominins that take in African and Asian sites; see, for example, Richard G. Klein, *The Human Career: Human Biological and Cultural Origins*, 3rd ed. (Chicago: University of Chicago Press, 2009), pp. 396–424.

3. Gamble, *The Palaeolithic Societies*, pp. 164–72.

4. For such a view, see Eudald Carbonell and Marina Mosquera, "The Emergence of a Symbolic Behavior: The Sepulchral Pit of Sima de los Huesos, Sierra de Atapuerca, Burgos, Spain," *Palevol* 5 (2006), pp. 155–60; more measured is J. M. Bermúdez de Castro, M. Martinón-Torres, et al., "The Atapuerca Sites and Their Contribution to the Knowledge of Human Evolution in Europe," *Evolutionary Anthropology* 13 (2004), pp. 25–41.

5. Chris Stringer has recently argued that the Atapuerca hominins are not examples of *heidelbergensis* at all but early Neandertals, and that the age of the remains may be as recent as 350,000 years—conclusions that might considerably increase the plausibility of some special recognition of the Atapuerca event. See Chris Stringer, "The Status of *Homo heidelbergensis* (Schoetensack 1908)," *Evolutionary Anthropology* 21 (2012), pp. 101–107. For Neandertal cultural attainments, see Chapter 4; for the variety of behaviors that might fall under the general notion of human interment, Chapter 5.

6. See Chris Stringer, "The Changing Landscapes of the Earliest Human Occupation of Britain and Europe," in *The Ancient Human Occupation of Britain*, ed. Nick Ashton, Simon G. Lewis, and Chris Stringer (Amsterdam: Elsevier, 2011), pp. 1–10.

7. Indeed, in a more recent account he describes the "performances" at Boxgrove as creating social *effervescence* (the term is Durkheim's), a "choreography of bodies" bringing "people, things, and place into relationship with one another." Clive Gamble, "When the Words Dry Up: Music and Material Metaphors Half a Million Years Ago," in *Music, Language, and Human Evolution*, ed. Nicholas Bannan (Oxford: Oxford University Press, 2012), pp. 81–106. The

"music" of Gamble's title refers to the place-defining social choreography he describes; he does not infer at Boxgrove musicking in the more modern sense I develop here. I am grateful to him for sharing with me a prepublication copy of this paper.

8. Michael Tomasello, *Origins of Human Communication* (Cambridge, MA: The MIT Press, 2008), pp. 173–80; M. Tomasello, M. Carpenter, J. Call, T. Behne, and H. Moll, "Understanding and Sharing Intentions: The Origins of Cultural Cognition," *Behavioral and Brain Sciences* 28 (2005), pp. 675–735.

9. S.C. Strum and Bruno Latour, "Redefining the Social Link: From Baboons to Humans," *Social Science Information* 26 (1987), pp. 783–802, esp. pp. 790–93. For top-down social ordering, see also Chapters 5 and 7.

10. Gamble, *Palaeolithic Societies*, p. 173.

11. Günther Knoblich and Natalie Sebanz, "Evolving Intentions for Social Interaction: From Entrainment to Joint Action," *Philosophical Transactions of the Royal Society B* 363 (2008), pp. 2021–31.

12. Knoblich and Sebanz, however, would disagree, reserving toolmaking, implausibly, for their fourth and most advanced scenario. The archaeological evidence discussed in Chapter 2, with its semivoluntary *chaîne opératoire* and unconceptualized mimesis, suggests instead that considerable technological complexity and its cultural transmission emerged from relatively simple entrained interactions. The literature on mirror neurons is already vast and in many accounts tends to overreach the evidence for their function, advancing them as the explanation for mimesis, theory of mind, empathy, understanding of intentions, language, even sociality all told. For an overview by proponents of their importance see Giacomo Rizzolatti and Laila Craighero, "The Mirror-Neuron System," *Annual Review of Neuroscience* 27 (2004), pp. 169–92; for well-placed cautions in the face of sweeping claims, Gregory Hickok, "Eight Problems for the Mirror Neuron Theory of Action Understanding in Monkeys and Humans," *Journal of Cognitive Neuroscience* 21 (2008), pp. 1229–43. For recent views and research on bodily actions, tool use, and mirror neurons in relation to language, see "From Action to Language," special issue of *Philosophical Transactions of the Royal Society B* 367 (2012), ed. James Steele, Pier Francesco Ferrari, and Leonardo Fogassi.

13. Tomasello, *Origins*, p. 96; also Michael Tomasello, *The Cultural Origins of Human Communication* (Cambridge, MA: Harvard University Press, 1999),

esp. chs. 1–2. On theory of mind and levels of intentionality, and for a hypothesis as to the chronology of their emergence in hominin evolution, see R. I. M. Dunbar, "The Social Brain: Mind, Language, and Society in Evolutionary Perspective," *Annual Review of Anthropology* 32 (2003), pp. 163–81. For other views of the evolutionary importance of theory of mind, see Peter Carruthers and Peter K. Smith, eds., *Theories of Theories of Mind* (Cambridge: Cambridge University Press, 1996), esp. pt. 4.

14. Tomasello, *Origins*, ch. 3, esp. pp. 73–79, 94–106; and ch. 7, esp. pp. 321–22, 335–37; also 169–73, 191–96; see also the section on protodiscourse that follows later in this chapter.

15. Steven Pinker and Paul Bloom, "Natural Language and Natural Selection," *Behavioral and Brain Sciences* 13 (1990), pp. 707–84.

16. Derek Bickerton, *Language & Species* (Chicago: University of Chicago Press, 1990); for the following paragraphs, see esp. chs. 5–6.

17. See, among other writings: "How Protolanguage Became Language," in *The Evolutionary Emergence of Language: Social Function and the Origins of Linguistic Form*, ed. Chris Knight, Michael Studdert-Kennedy, and James R. Hurford (Cambridge: Cambridge University Press, 2000), pp. 264–84; "Foraging versus Social Intelligence in the Evolution of Protolanguage," in *The Transition to Language*, ed. Alison Wray (Oxford: Oxford University Press, 2002), pp. 207–25; and *Adam's Tongue: How Humans Made Language, How Language Made Humans* (New York: Hill and Wang, 2009).

18. Ray Jackendoff, "Possible Stages in the Evolution of the Language Capacity," *Trends in Cognitive Science* 3 (1999), pp. 272–79, revised and expanded as ch. 8 of Jackendoff, *Foundations of Language: Brain, Meaning, Grammar, Evolution* (Oxford: Oxford University Press, 2002).

19. Wray's general approach to holistic utterances is not new but revives a position elaborated already by Otto Jesperson in the 1920s; see W. Tecumseh Fitch, *The Evolution of Language* (Cambridge: Cambridge University Press, 2010), pp. 496–98.

20. Alison Wray, "Protolanguage as a Holistic System for Social Interaction," *Language & Communication* 18 (1998), pp. 47–67.

21. Mithen, *The Singing Neanderthals*, pp. 3–4, 147–50.

22. See Wray, "Holistic Utterances in Protolanguage: The Link from Primates to Humans," *The Evolutionary Emergence*, ed. Knight et al., pp. 285–302.

23. A somewhat different set of problems in the conceptions of holistic (or "holophrastic") protolanguage of Wray, Mithen, and Michael A. Arbib has been analyzed by Maggie Tallerman, "Holophrastic Protolanguage: Planning, Processing, Storage, and Retrieval," *Interaction Studies* 9 (2008), pp. 84–99. Tallerman argues that modern language is planned and processed in single propositions and the clause-sized units corresponding to them, and that holistic protolanguage—especially as depicted by Mithen and Arbib—would require from our ancestors processing skills implausibly more complex than this. She also takes issue with the "fossils" of protolanguage Wray adduces, idiomatic expressions such as *by and large*. Wray claims that these are processed holistically in modern language, but Tallerman brings other evidence suggesting that they are produced and comprehended as a collection of syntactically governed, discrete lexical items, even when the totality of meaning of these items diverges from what might be expected.

24. Bickerton, *Adam's Tongue*, p. 231, also pp. 65–70; Wray, "Dual Processing in Protolanguage: Performance without Competence," in *The Transition to Language*, ed. Wray, pp. 113–37. Despite these signs of rapprochement, the debate over holistic and compositional protolanguage continues. For a sampling of views see *Interaction Studies* 9:1 (2008), special issue called "Holophrasis and Compositionality in the Emergence of Language," ed. Michael A. Arbib and Derek Bickerton.

25. See, for example, *The Evolutionary Emergence of Language*, ed. Knight et al., which devotes almost 80 percent of its length to questions of contrastive phonology and syntax.

26. Tomasello, *Origins of Human Communication*, esp. chs. 2–3. Tomasello is of course not alone in naming gesture as the source of language; for a recent advocacy of this position see Michael Corballis, *From Hand to Mouth: The Origins of Language* (Princeton: Princeton University Press, 2002). The idea is an ancient one—as is true also of the Bickerton's idea that the first words were onomatopoeic—revived in the early eighteenth century (Vico, Condillac, etc). Tomasello is also not alone in seeing changes in social cognition as the precondition for modern human communication. For related arguments see Robin Dunbar, "Theory of Mind and the Evolution of Language," in *Approaches to the Evolution of Language*, ed. James Hurford, Michael Studdert-Kennedy, and Christopher Knight (Cambridge: Cambridge University Press, 1998), pp.

92–110; Chris Knight, "Language and Revolutionary Consciousness," in *The Transition to Language*, pp. 138–60; and, an important argument taken up in the Excursus that follows this chapter, Dorothy L. Cheney and Robert M. Seyfarth, *Baboon Metaphysics: The Evolution of a Social Mind* (Chicago: University of Chicago Press, 2007).

27. Tomasello, *Origins*, chs. 5–6.

28. Tomasello, *Origins*, pp. 248–49.

29. Jill Bowie, "Proto-discourse and the Emergence of Compositionality," *Interaction Studies* 9 (2008), pp. 18–33; see p. 19.

30. Robbins Burling, "Primate Calls, Human Language, and Nonverbal Communication," *Current Anthropology* 34 (1993), pp. 25–53 (including various responses); Burling, *The Talking Ape: How Language Evolved* (Oxford: Oxford University Press, 2005), chs. 2–3.

31. See Robert Seyfarth, Dorothy Cheney, and Peter Marler, "Monkey Responses to Three Different Alarm Calls: Evidence of Predator Classification and Semantic Communication," *Science* 210 (November 1980), pp. 801–803.

32. The appearance of an enriched range and variety of gesture-calls (and vocalizations in general) might also be connected to the evolutionary lengthening of the hominin vocal tract, involving the descent of the larynx toward its position in modern adult humans. Reconstruction of the vocal tracts of various fossil hominins has accordingly received much attention from paleolinguists and has suggested that a tract like ours was taking shape already by the late Lower Paleolithic era of *Homo heidelbergensis*. Work in this area was spearheaded by Jeffrey T. Laitman and Philip Lieberman; see Jeffrey T. Laitman, "The Anatomy of Human Speech," *Natural History* 93 (1984), pp. 20–27; Laitman, "The Evolution of the Hominid Upper Respiratory System and Implications for the Origins of Speech," in *Glossogenetics: The Origin and Evolution of Language*, ed. E. de Grolier (Paris: Harwood, 1983), pp. 63–90; and Philip Lieberman, *Uniquely Human: The Evolution of Speech, Thought, and Selfless Behavior* (Cambridge, MA: Harvard University Press, 1991), ch. 2. For optimistic overviews of this line of inquiry, Andrew Lock and Charles R. Peters, eds., *Handbook of Human Symbolic Evolution* (Oxford: Oxford University Press, 1996), pp. 116–25; Iain Morley, "Hominin Physiological Evolution and the Emergence of Musical Capacities," in Bannan, *Music, Language, and Human Evolution*, pp. 109–41; and Corballis, *From Hand to Mouth*, pp. 138–44. For

detailed presentation of the case, Iain Morley, *The Prehistory of Music: Human Evolution, Archaeology, & the Origins of Musicality* (Oxford: Oxford University Press, 2013), chs. 5–7. For a recent pessimistic synopsis, casting doubt from several directions on the reliability of correlations of anatomy to flexibility of vocalization, Fitch, *The Evolution of Language*, ch. 8.

33. See Downing Thomas, *Music and the Origins of Language: Theories from the French Enlightenment* (Cambridge: Cambridge University Press, 1995); and Gary Tomlinson, "Vico's Songs: Detours at the Origins of (Ethno)Musicology," *The Musical Quarterly* 83 (1999), pp. 344–77.

34. Charles Darwin, *The Descent of Man, and Selection in Relation to Sex* (facsimile of the 1871 ed., Princeton: Princeton University Press, 1981), pt. 1, p. 56. Further citations in the text.

35. The leading recent proponent of this position is Geoffrey Miller; see "Evolution of Human Music through Sexual Selection," in *The Origins of Music*, ed. Nils L. Wallin, Björn Merker, and Steven Brown (Cambridge, MA: The MIT Press, 2000), pp. 329–60. He goes so far as to offer as evidence for his position Jimi Hendrix's reputedly numerous sexual liaisons.

36. Mithen, *The Singing Neanderthals*, p. 204.

37. Steven Brown, "The 'Musilanguage' Model of Music Evolution," in Wallin et al., *The Origins of Music*, pp. 271–300.

38. Mithen, *The Singing Neanderthals*, ch. 15, esp. pp. 233–37.

39. For this account, see Fitch, *The Evolution of Language*, ch. 4. In another contribution, "The Biology and Evolution of Music: A Comparative Perspective," *Cognition* 100 (2006), pp. 173–215, Fitch advocates the comparative approach and takes on—inconclusively, in my reading—the doubts about comparativism expressed by M. D. Hauser and J. McDermott, "The Evolution of the Music Faculty: A Comparative Perspective," *Nature Neuroscience* 6 (2003), pp. 663–68. Meanwhile, for a comparativist view of musical protolanguage, related to Fitch's, that assigns to *Homo erectus* a vocal learning of "song" akin to that of songbirds, see Björn Merker, "The Vocal Learning Constellation: Imitation, Ritual Culture, Encephalization," in Bannan, *Music, Language, and Human Evolution*, pp. 215–60.

40. For a general survey of affective vocalization across many primate species, Mark D. Hauser, *The Evolution of Communication* (Cambridge, MA: The MIT Press, 1997), esp. pp. 476–90; see also Burling, *The Talking Ape*, p. 102,

and Cheney and Seyfarth, *Baboon Metaphysics*, p. 229.

41. For an introduction to these issues especially focused on linguistic prosody, see Stefanie Shattuck-Hufnagel and Alice E. Turk, "A Prosody Tutorial for Investigators of Auditory Sentence Processing," *Journal of Psycholinguistic Research* 25 (1996), pp. 193–247; for an overview of linguistic thinking and an exploration of musical implications, see Thomas Matthew Pooley, "Melody as Prosody: Toward a Usage-Based Theory of Music" (Ph.D. dissertation, University of Pennsylvania, 2014), esp. chs. 3 and 4.

42. On this "infant directed speech" see Anne Fernald, "Prosody and Focus in Speech to Infants and Adults," *Annals of Child Development* 8 (1991), pp. 43–80; Fernald, "Human Maternal Vocalizations to Infants as Biologically Relevant Signals," in *The Adapted Mind: Evolutionary Psychology and the Generation of Culture*, ed. J. Barkow, L. Cosmides, and J. Tooby (Oxford: Oxford University Press, 1992), pp. 391–428.

43. Aniruddh Patel, *Music, Language, and the Brain* (Oxford: Oxford University Press, 2008), ch. 4, esp. pp. 194–96, 225–38; P. N. Juslin and P. Laukka, "Communication of Emotions in Vocal Expression and Music Performance: Different Channels, Same Code?" *Psychological Bulletin* 129 (2003), pp. 770–814.

44. On melodic contour in general, see Diana Deutsch, "The Processing of Pitch Combinations," in *The Psychology of Music*, ed. Diana Deutsch, 3rd ed. (Amsterdam: Academic Press, 2013), pp. 249–325, esp. pp. 256–58; on the robustness of contour perception and its independence from perception of individual intervals and pitches, see Judy Edworthy, "Interval and Contour in Melody Processing," *Music Perception* 2 (1985), pp. 375–88.

45. See William Forde Thompson, "Intervals and Scales," in *The Psychology of Music*, ed. Deutsch, pp. 107–40, esp. pp. 118–20.

46. For an introduction to the psychology of timbre, see Stephen McAdams and Bruno L. Giordano, "The Perception of Musical Timbre," in *The Oxford Handbook of Music Psychology*, ed. Susan Hallam, Ian Cross, and Michael Thaut (Oxford: Oxford University Press, 2009), pp. 72–80; for a more extensive account, McAdams, "Musical Timbre Perception," in Deutsch, *The Psychology of Music*, pp. 35–67.

47. Patel takes up such processing overlaps in *Music, Language and the Brain*, pp. 282ff.

48. For analyses of the repertoires, see *The Gestural Communication of Apes and Monkeys*, ed. Josep Call and Michael Tomasello (Mahwah, NJ: Psychology Press, 2007).

49. Jackendoff, "Possible Stages," p. 274.

50. Steven Pinker, *How the Mind Works* (New York: Norton, 1997), pp. 528–38; for cheesecake, p. 534.

EXCURSUS

1. See Dorothy L. Cheney and Robert M. Seyfarth, *Baboon Metaphysics: The Evolution of a Social Mind* (Chicago: University of Chicago Press, 2008); further references are given in the text. See also Dorothy L. Cheney and Robert M. Seyfarth, *How Monkeys See the World: Inside the Mind of Another Species* (Chicago: University of Chicago Press, 1992), and Robert M. Seyfarth, Dorothy L. Cheney, and Peter Marler, "Monkey Responses to Three Different Alarm Calls: Evidence of Predator Classification and Semantic Communication," *Science* 210 (14 November 1980), pp. 801–803.

2. Social intelligence was first defined by psychologist Edward Thorndike about 1920; it is known also as "Machiavellian intelligence," following its application to primatology by Franz de Waal, *Chimpanzee Politics: Power and Sex among Apes* (London: Jonathan Cape, 1982).

3. See Kim Sterelny, *Thought in a Hostile World: The Evolution of Human Cognition* (Oxford: Blackwell, 2003), esp. chs. 4, 6, and 7; Kim Sterelny, *The Evolved Apprentice: How Evolution Made Humans Unique* (Cambridge, MA: The MIT Press, 2012), ch. 1.

4. See Leslie C. Aiello and Robin I. M. Dunbar, "Neocortex Size, Group Size, and the Evolution of Language," *Current Anthropology* 34 (1993), pp. 184–93; also Robin Dunbar, *Grooming, Gossip, and the Evolution of Language* (Cambridge, MA: Harvard University Press, 1998). As this synopsis perhaps unfairly suggests, the social intelligence hypothesis can be pressed to explain too much too unilaterally; for an endorsement of it qualified by important views on its limitations, Kay E. Holekamp, "Questioning the Social Intelligence Hypothesis," *Trends in Cognitive Sciences* 11 (2007), pp. 65–69.

5. For their overview of the social intelligence hypothesis, see *Baboon Metaphysics*, pp. 121–29.

6. Here Cheney and Seyfarth's imprecise notion of causality seems to lead

them to an unwarranted leap, for baboons' ability to associate different calls in a sequence with different individuals, whatever its cognitive correlates might be, remains far from grammatical compositionality as linguists discuss and debate it. Cheney and Seyfarth attempt to bolster the case for compositionality by citing instances in which combinations of calls or gestures—a chimpanzee simultaneously drumming and barking—might yield information not conveyed in the gestures separately (pp. 254–56). More convincing is Michael Tomasello's explanation of such cases as additive sequences rather than syntactic wholes: "What seems to happen is that the communicator tries one gesture, monitors the response of the recipient, and, if needed, repeats or tries a different gesture. This...does not show any kind of combinatorial or grammatical capacity." See Michael Tomasello, *Origins of Human Communication* (Cambridge, MA: The MIT Press, 2008), p. 30.

7. See Jerry Fodor, *The Language of Thought* (New York: Thomas Crowell, 1975); also Steven Pinker, *The Language Instinct: How the Mind Creates Language* (New York: Harper & Row, 1995), ch. 3.

8. For a recent overview, James Garson, "Connectionism," *Stanford Encyclopedia of Philosophy*, at http://plato.stanford.edu/entries/connectionism. Two early and important statements on the rapprochement of the opposed views are Kim Sterelny, *The Representational Theory of Mind: An Introduction* (Oxford: Blackwell, 1990), ch. 8, and Tim van Gelder, "Compositionality: A Connectionist Variation on a Classical Theme," *Cognitive Science* 14 (1990), pp. 355–84.

9. See Duane M. Rumbaugh, James E. King, Michael J. Beran, David A. Washburn, and Kristy L. Gould, "A Salience Theory of Learning and Behavior: With Perspectives on Neurobiology and Cognition," *International Journal of Primatology* 28 (2007), pp. 973–96.

10. Lawrence W. Barsalou, "Continuity of the Conceptual System across Species," *Trends in Cognitive Sciences* 9 (2005), 309–11; p. 309. See Cheney and Seyfarth, *Baboon Metaphysics*, p. 243.

11. Giacomo Rizzolatti and Michael A. Arbib, "Language within Our Grasp," *Trends in Neurosciences* 21 (1998), pp. 188–94; further references are given in the text.

12. See Gregory Hickok, "Eight Problems for the Mirror Neuron Theory of Action Understanding in Monkeys and Humans," *Journal of Cognitive Neuroscience* 21 (2008), pp. 1229–43.

CHAPTER FOUR: 250,000 YEARS AGO

1. For the important differences among these examples, see Chapter 5.

2. "There is...a lot less meaning around than there is information. That's because all you need for information is reliable causal covariance.... Information is ubiquitous but not robust; meaning is robust but not ubiquitous." Jerry Fodor, *A Theory of Content and Other Essays* (Cambridge, MA: The MIT Press, 1990), p. 93.

3. Susanne K. Langer, *Philosophy in a New Key* (New York: Mentor, 1951), pp. 192–93.

4. Leonard B. Meyer, *Emotion and Meaning in Music* (Chicago: University of Chicago Press, 1956). Meyer was quick to specify that the "meaning" of his title was not linked to reference or symbolism (p. vii), bringing it in line with Langer's "connotation."

5. John A. Sloboda and Patrik N. Juslin, "Psychological Perspectives on Music and Emotion," in *Music and Emotion: Theory and Research*, ed. Patrik N. Juslin and John A. Sloboda (Oxford: Oxford University Press, 2001), pp. 71–103, esp. pp. 87–93.

6. Eric F. Clarke, *Ways of Listening: An Ecological Approach to the Perception of Musical Meaning* (Oxford: Oxford University Press, 2005); Albert S. Bregman, *Auditory Scene Analysis: The Perceptual Organization of Sound* (Cambridge, MA: The MIT Press, 1990).

7. Hominin taxonomy and speciation is a quickly changing, insecure terrain, echoing with loud debates; for important recent overviews see Richard Klein, *The Human Career: Human Biological and Cultural Origins* 3rd ed. (Chicago: University of Chicago Press, 2009), and Winfried Henke and Ian Tattersall, eds., *Handbook of Paleoanthropology*, 3 vols. (Berlin: Springer Verlag, 2006–2007), vol. 3: *Phylogeny of Hominids*. Just how fluid the situation is was affirmed in the last few years with the discovery of human fossils from a new taxon at Denisova Cave in the Altai Mountains of Siberia; for these "Denisovans" see Chapter 6.

8. See Christopher S. Henshilwood and Curtis W. Marean, "The Origin of Modern Behavior: Critique of the Models and Their Test Implications," *Current Anthropology* 44 (2003), pp. 627–51, esp. pp. 631–32; also John J. Shea, "*Homo sapiens* Is as *Homo sapiens* Was: Behavioral Variability versus 'Behavioral Modernity' in Paleolithic Archaeology," *Current Anthropology* 52 (2011), pp. 1–35.

9. Sally McBrearty and Alison S. Brooks, "The Revolution That Wasn't: A New Interpretation of the Origin of Modern Human Behavior," *Journal of Human Evolution* 39 (2000), pp. 453–563.

10. For general discussion of hypotheses of local, contextual conditions shaping Paleolithic behavior, see Paul Mellars, "The Impossible Coincidence. A Single-Species Model for the Origins of Modern Human Behavior in Europe," *Evolutionary Anthropology* 14 (2005), pp. 12–27, esp. pp. 22–23. For an overview of the emergence of modern behaviors as a "highly variable, historically contingent, polygenetic development," see Nicholas Conard, "Cultural Evolution in Africa and Eurasia during the Middle and Late Pleistocene," in Henke and Tattersall, *Handbook of Paleoanthropology*, pp. 3:2001–37.

11. Geoffrey Pope, "Bamboo and Human Evolution," *Natural History* 10 (1989), pp. 49–56.

12. For a review of the issues, see O. Bar-Yosef, "The Upper Palaeolithic Revolution," *Annual Review of Anthropology* 31 (2002), pp. 363–93; for a more recent, large, and welcome set of revisionist views, Paul Mellars, Katie Boyle, Ofer Bar-Yosef, and Chris Stringer, eds., *Rethinking the Human Revolution* (Cambridge: MacDonald Institute, 2007).

13. Mellars, "The Impossible Coincidence"; on p. 16 he affirms that "many of the most distinctive archeological hallmarks of the classic Middle-Upper Paleolithic transition in Europe can be documented at least 30,000 to 40,000 years earlier in certain parts of Africa than anywhere within Europe itself." See also Mellars, "Introduction: Rethinking the Human Revolution: Eurasian and African Perspectives," in Mellars et al., *Rethinking*, pp. 1–11; and Richard Klein, "Archeology and the Evolution of Human Behavior," *Evolutionary Anthropology* 9 (2000), pp. 17–36. For a general argument advocating basic, long-term continuities instead of revolutionary changes, see Clive Gamble, *Origins and Revolutions: Human Identity in Earliest Prehistory* (Cambridge: Cambridge University Press, 2007). See also ch. 5–6.

14. For an overview of the climatic changes faced by Neandertals, see Clive Gamble, *The Palaeolithic Societies of Europe* (Cambridge: Cambridge University Press, 1999), pp. 174–204; for the Upper Pleistocene (127,000–11,000 years ago), see Chapter 6.

15. See Jean-Jacques Hublin, "Modern-Nonmodern Hominid Interactions: A Mediterranean Perspective," in *The Geography of Neanderthals and Modern*

Humans in Europe and the Greater Mediterranean, ed. Ofer Bar-Yosef and David Pilbeam (Cambridge, MA: Peabody Museum, 2000), pp. 157–82, esp. pp. 161–63; see also Eitan Tchernov, "The Faunal Sequence of the Southwest Asian Middle Paleolithic in Relation to Hominid Dispersal Events," in *Neandertals and Modern Humans in Western Asia*, ed. Takeru Akazawa, Kenichi Aoki, and Ofer Bar-Yosef (New York: Plenum, 1998), pp. 77–90.

16. A general introduction of issues relating to Middle Paleolithic/Middle Stone Age hunting and scavenging, and a strong argument in favor of Neandertal hunting, is Curtis W. Marean and Zelalem Assefa, "Zooarcheological Evidence for the Faunal Exploitation Behavior of Neandertals and Early Modern Humans," *Evolutionary Anthropology* 8 (1999), pp. 22–37; see also Curtis W. Marean and Soo Yeun Kim, "Mousterian Large-Mammal Remains from Kobeh Cave: Behavioral Implications for Neanderthals and Early Modern Humans," *Current Anthropology* 39 (1998), pp. S79–S114.

17. Steven Mithen, *The Prehistory of the Mind: The Cognitive Origins of Art and Science* (London: Thames and Hudson, 1996), chs. 7–8. In the analysis of Terrence Deacon of the emergence of modern human cognition, we will see emphasis of a different kind of cross-domain integration; see Chapter 5.

18. David Lewis-Williams, "Of People and Pictures: The Nexus of Upper Palaeolithic Religion, Social Discrimination, and Art," in *Becoming Human: Innovation in Prehistoric Material and Spiritual Culture*, ed. Colin Renfrew and Iain Morley (Cambridge: Cambridge University Press, 2009), pp. 135–58.

19. Thomas Wynn and Frederick L. Coolidge, "The Expert Neandertal Mind," *Journal of Human Evolution* 46 (2004), 467–87. They pursue the argument, in a broadened context, in *The Rise of Homo sapiens: The Evolution of Modern Thinking* (Chichester, UK: Wiley-Blackwell, 2009).

20. Gamble, *The Palaeolithic Societies of Europe*, ch. 5, esp. pp. 238–67.

21. Michelle C. Langley, Christopher Clarkson, and Sean Ulm, "Behavioral Complexity in Eurasian Neanderthal Populations: A Chronological Examination of the Archaeological Evidence," *Cambridge Archaeological Journal* 18 (2008), pp. 289–307.

22. For the position against acculturation and for the indigeneity of Châtelperronian industries, see Francesco D'Errico, João Zilhão, Michèle Julien, Dominique Baffier, and Jacques Pellegrin, "Neanderthal Acculturation in Western Europe? A Critical Review of the Evidence and Its Interpretation,"

Current Anthropology 39 (1998), pp. S1–S44; Langley and her coauthors, for their part, suggest that the Châtelperronian may be an independent, logical outgrowth of the gradual accumulation of Neandertal behaviors they survey ("Behavioral Complexity," p. 302). Arguing for acculturation—though he questions the appropriateness of the term and allows that cultural exchange between Neandertals and *sapiens* was a two-way street—is Paul Mellars, "The Neanderthal Problem Continued," *Current Anthropology* 40 (1999), pp. 341–64; see also Mellars, "Symbolism, Meaning, and the Neanderthal Mind," *Cambridge Archaeological Journal* 13 (2003), pp. 273–75; and Mellars, "The Impossible Coincidence." Many nuanced positions hover between these extremes, some of them aired in the responses appended to the two *Current Anthropology* articles. Another important participant in the debate, Randall White, sees Neandertals as competent and resourceful in their demanding environments but questions the attribution to them of the most sophisticated artifacts from the crucial, mixed Châtelperronian/Aurignacian site; see "Personal Ornaments from the Grotte du Renne at Arcy-sur-Cure," *Athena Review* 2.4 (2001), pp. 41–46.

23. João Zilhão, "The Emergence of Language, Art, and Symbolic Thinking," in *Homo Symbolicus: The Dawn of Language, Imagination and Spirituality*, ed. Christopher S. Henshilwood and Francesco d'Errico (Amsterdam: John Benjamins, 2011), pp. 111–31; see pp. 119–20.

24. Genetic evidence analyzed about 2000 initially suggested no interbreeding, but newer evidence, gathered as the Neandertal genome has been sequenced by the Neandertal Genome Analysis Consortium, organized by Svante Pääbo of the Max Planck Institute, suggests instead limited genetic exchange, perhaps in the Levant some 50,000–80,000 years ago. See Richard Green et al., "A Draft Sequence of the Neandertal Genome," *Science* 328 (7 May 2010), pp. 710–22.

25. April Nowell, "Defining Behavioral Modernity in the Context of Neandertal and Anatomically Modern Humans," *Annual Review of Anthropology* 39 (2010), pp. 437–52; S. Shennan, "Demography and Cultural Innovation: A Model and its Implications for the Emergence of Modern Human Culture," *Cambridge Archaeological Journal* 11 (2001), pp. 5–16.

26. For Geneste's findings, see Mark White and Nick Ashton, "Lower Palaeolithic Core Technology and the Origins of the Levallois Method in North-Western Europe," *Current Anthropology* 44 (2003), pp. 598–609; see p. 606;

also Gamble, *The Palaeolithic Societies of Europe*, p. 242.

27. Jehanne Féblot-Augustins, "Mobility Strategies in the Late Middle Palaeolithic of Central Europe and Western Europe: Elements of Stability and Variability," *Journal of Anthropological Archaeology* 12 (1993), pp. 211–65, esp. pp. 249–53.

28. For an argument connecting evidence of lengthening material transfers to the emergence of language, for example, see Ben Marwick, "Pleistocene Exchange Networks as Evidence for the Evolution of Language," *Cambridge Archaeological Journal* 13 (2003), pp. 67–81.

29. This problematic term and its archaeological uses are examined in Chapter 5.

30. Francesco d'Errico, Christopher Henshilwood, Graeme Lawson, Marian Vanhaeren, Anne-Marie Tillier, Marie Soressi, Frédérique Bresson, Bruno Maureille, April Nowell, Joseba Lakarra, Lucinda Blackwell, and Michèle Julien, "Archaeological Evidence for the Emergence of Language, Symbolism, and Music—An Alternative Multidisciplinary Perspective," *Journal of World Prehistory* 17 (2003), pp. 1–70; see pp. 36–39.

31. M. J. White and P. B. Pettitt, "Technology of Early Palaeolithic Western Europe: Innovation, Variability, and a Unified Framework," *Lithics* 16 (1995), pp. 27–40.

32. Stephen Kuhn, quoted by Gamble, *The Palaeolithic Societies of Europe*, p. 242.

33. The fact that the spears were fashioned from organic materials is likewise astonishing, but for a different reason: the scarcity of preserved wood from this period. The mainly lithic nature of the archaeological record of early technologies is no doubt due to the differential preservation of stones as opposed to wood, bones, antlers, and so forth; we must suppose that early hominins often seized on hard organic materials as tools, just as chimpanzees in the wild do today. On the spears see esp. Hartmut Thieme, "Lower Palaeolithic Hunting Spears from Germany," *Nature* 385 (1997), pp. 807–10; and Thieme, "The Lower Palaeolithic Art of Hunting: The Case of Schöningen 13 II-4, Lower Saxony, Germany," in *The Hominid Individual in Context: Archaeological Investigations of Lower and Middle Palaeolithic Landscapes, Locales, and Artefacts*, ed. C. Gamble and M. Porr (New York: Routledge, 2005), pp. 115–32. Robin Dennell, "The World's Oldest Spears," *Nature* 385 (27 February 1997), p. 767,

comments: "these hominids were not...acting opportunistically in response to immediate situations. Rather, we see considerable depth of planning, sophistication of design, and patience in carving the wood, all of which have been attributed only to modern humans." For an argument that the makers of the spears were early Neandertals, see Christopher Stringer, "The Status of *Homo heidelbergensis* (Schoetensack 1908)," *Evolutionary Anthropology* 21 (2012), pp. 101–107.

34. See Eric Boëda, J. M. Geneste, C. Griggo, N. Mercier, S. Muhesen, J. L. Reyss, A. Taha, and H. Valladas, "A Levallois Point Embedded in the Vertebra of a Wild Ass (*Equus Africans*): Hafting, Projectiles, and Mousterian Hunting Weapons," *Antiquity* 73 (1999), pp. 394–402; Eric Boëda, Jacques Connan, and Sultan Muhesen, "Bitumen as Hafting Material on Middle Palaeolithic Artifacts from the El Kowm Basin, Syria," in *Neandertals and Modern Humans*, ed. Akazawa, Aoki, and Bar-Yosef, pp. 181–204; Judith M. Grünberg, "Middle Palaeolithic Birch-Bark Pitch," *Antiquity* 76 (2002), pp. 15–16. For an overview of the topic: Dennis M. Sandgathe, *Examining the Levallois Reduction Strategy from a Design Theory Point of View* (Oxford: British Archaeological Reports, 2005), pp. 43–45. Hafting by early *Homo sapiens* in Africa may reach farther back than these Neandertal examples; see Gamble, *Origins and Revolutions*, p. 176, for two possible cases; also Lyn Wadley, "Complex Cognition Required for Compound Adhesive Manufacture in the Middle Stone Age Implies Symbolic Capacity," in Henshilwood and d'Errico, *Homo Symbolicus*, pp. 97–109. Sally McBrearty sees blades and points in east African sites as evidence of composite tools there as much as 285,000 years ago; see McBrearty, "Down with the Revolution," in Mellars et al., *Rethinking*, pp. 133–51.

35. D'Errico et al., "Archaeological Evidence," p. 9.

36. Sonia Ragir has extended the analogy of composite tools and language to discern in the tools a "syntax" manifest in a "semantic" relation of their parts to one another; see "How Is a Stone Tool Like a Sentence?" in *Becoming Loquens: More Studies in Language Origins*, ed. Bernard H. Bichakjian (Frankfurt am Main: Peter Lang, 2000), pp. 49–74. As my distinction of function from semantics suggests, I think this carries the analogy too far.

37. Bordes devised around 1960 an elaborate typology of Paleolithic tools that is still influential; for a brief introduction to his views (and the source of Figure 4.1), see François Bordes, "Mousterian Cultures in France," *Science* 134

(1961), pp. 803–10. For a broad survey of Paleolithic industries, Bordes, *The Old Stone Age*, trans. J. E. Anderson (New York: McGraw-Hill, 1968).

38. Since about 1990 there has been considerable debate among archaeologists concerning how far to extend the term and where to draw the technology's borderlines with other, related lithic industries; for a summary from the midst of these debates, see Michael Chazan, "Redefining Levallois," *Journal of Human Evolution* 33 (1997), pp. 719–35.

39. Beyond Europe, Levallois techniques appear in Africa, where they gradually took shape through the Middle Stone Age, and in southwest Asia. Relatively recent versions of them have been traced as far as Japan; in these many non-European versions, they are obviously not exclusively practiced by Neandertals, but are developed by *Homo sapiens* as well. See McBrearty and Brooks, "The Revolution That Wasn't"; also *The Definition and Interpretation of Levallois Technology*, ed. Harold L. Dibble and Ofer Bar-Yosef (Madison: Prehistory Press, 1995); and Bordes, *The Old Stone Age*, chs. 9–10.

40. Eric Boëda, "Levallois: A Volumetric Construction, Methods, A Technique," in Dibble and Bar-Yosef, *Definition and Interpretation*, pp. 41–68.

41. White and Ashton, "Lower Palaeolithic Core Technology."

42. Recent evidence, in other words, has borne out the insight from 1993 of Chris Stringer and Clive Gamble that "although the Neanderthals were, quite simply, 'not us,' they—or rather their African kin—provided the basis from which we sprang; both they and the early Moderns have a place in our prehistory, whether or not they were our actual lineal ancestors." See Stringer and Gamble, *In Search of the Neanderthals: Solving the Puzzle of Human Origins* (London: Thames and Hudson, 1993), p. 219.

43. See Chapter 2. Carolyn Drake has offered a model of the mental representation of metric music; it involves perception of hierarchic temporal grids and the overlaying on them of experienced groups of events and the articulations separating them; see "Psychological Processes Involved in the Temporal Organization of Complex Auditory Sequences: Universal and Acquired Processes," *Music Perception* 16 (1998), pp. 11–26.

44. For overviews of pitch perception, Andrew J. Oxenham, "The Perception of Musical Tones," in *The Psychology of Music*, ed. Diana Deutsch, 3rd ed. (Amsterdam: Academic Press, 2013), pp. 1–33, esp. 9–18; Rudolf Rasch and Reinier Plomp, "The Perception of Musical Tones," in *The Psychology of Music*,

ed. Diana Deutsch, 2nd ed. (San Diego: Academic Press, 1999), pp. 89–112; and Thomas Stainsby and Ian Cross, "The Perception of Pitch," in *The Oxford Handbook of Music Psychology*, ed. Susan Hallam, Ian Cross, and Michael Thaut (Oxford: Oxford University Press, 2009), pp. 47–58.

45. "Our scene-analysis process is not parsing the parts in a piece of music as wholly distinct auditory objects. Instead it is creating a hierarchical description, marking out the parts as distinct at one level of the hierarchy." Albert S. Bregman, *Auditory Scene Analysis: The Perceptual Organization of Sound* (Cambridge, MA: The MIT Press, 1990), p. 461; see also pp. 203–6, chs. 4–5. For an analysis of the role of memory in musical perception emphasizing both schemas and hierarchy, see Bob Snyder, *Music and Memory: An Introduction* (Cambridge, MA: The MIT Press, 2000).

46. Eugene Narmour, *The Analysis and Cognition of Basic Melodic Structures* (Chicago: University of Chicago Press, 1990), and *The Analysis and Cognition of Melodic Complexity: The Implication-Realization Model* (Chicago: University of Chicago Press, 1992).

47. Fred Lerdahl and Ray Jackendoff, *A Generative Theory of Tonal Music* (Cambridge, MA: The MIT Press, 1983).

48. Ray Jackendoff and Fred Lerdahl, "The Capacity for Music: What Is It, and What's Special About It?" *Cognition* 100 (2006), pp. 33–72.

49. *Sweet Anticipation: Music and the Psychology of Expectation* (Cambridge, MA: The MIT Press, 2007).

50. Still larger groupings, for example the joining of melodies or melodic phrases into higher-level units, are products of more complex, mixed cognition, in which both kinds of hierarchies (here pitch hierarchies and large-scale, rhythmic containment ones) interact, rather than the product of compositional hierarchies alone.

51. For a detailed overview of the issues, Diana Deutsch, "The Processing of Pitch Combinations," in Deutsch, *The Psychology of Music*, pp. 249–325; also Bregman, *Auditory Scene Analysis*, pp. 461–71.

52. On the distinctness in brain processing of general contour mapping and discrete pitch combinatoriality, see Isabelle Peretz, "Music Perception and Recognition," in *The Handbook of Cognitive Neuropsychology*, ed. Bruno Rapp (Philadelphia: Psychology Press, 2001), pp. 519–40.

53. For the artifacts, see Langley et al., "Behavioral Complexity," table 2,

nos. 6–11; for other, more dubious possibilities see table 1; for an illustration of their no. 11, from La Ferrassie, France, see Francesco d'Errico, "Palaeolithic Origins of Artificial Memory Systems: An Evolutionary Perspective," in *Cognition and Material Culture: The Archaeology of Symbolic Storage*, ed. Colin Renfrew and Chris Scarre (Cambridge: Macdonald Institute for Archaeological Research, 1999), pp. 19–50, figure 3.5, no. 12. D'Errico also illustrates two bones with regular notches from a problematic site at the center of Châtelperronian disputes (see above) and argues in favor of their facture by Neandertals and their symbolic implications.

CHAPTER FIVE: 100,000 YEARS AGO

1. Many synoptic projects have featured the revolutionary advent of human symbolism, even while taking care not to locate it only in Europe. Valuable resources among them include Andrew Lock and Charles R. Peters, eds., *Handbook of Human Symbolic Evolution* (Oxford: Clarendon Press, 1996); Steven Mithen, *The Prehistory of the Mind: The Cognitive Origins of Art and Science* (London: Thames and Hudson, 1996); and David Lewis-Williams, *The Mind in the Cave: Consciousness and the Origins of Art* (London: Thames and Hudson, 2002). A beautiful book of a more specific nature about early human representation, which, however, attempts no definition of symbolism, is Randall White, *Prehistoric Art: The Symbolic Journey of Humankind* (New York: Abrams, 2003); a provocative analytic account, again without any definition of symbolism or symbolic cognition, is R. Dale Guthrie, *The Nature of Paleolithic Art* (Chicago: University of Chicago Press, 2005). An important, more technical study is Francesco d'Errico, Christopher Henshilwood, Graeme Lawson, Marian Vanhaeren, Anne-Marie Tillier, Marie Soressi, Frédérique Bresson, Bruno Maureille, April Nowell, Joseba Lakarra, Lucinda Blackwell, and Michèle Julien, "Archaeological Evidence for the Emergence of Language, Symbolism, and Music—An Alternative Multidisciplinary Perspective," *Journal of World Prehistory* 17 (2003), pp. 1–70. Clive Gamble argues against revolutionary models in *The Palaeolithic Societies of Europe* (Cambridge: Cambridge University Press, 1999) and in *Origins and Revolutions: Human Identity in Earliest Prehistory* (Cambridge: Cambridge University Press, 2007).

2. For illustrations see White, *Prehistoric Art*, among many choices.

3. Nicholas Conard, "Cultural Evolution in Africa and Eurasia during the

Middle and Late Pleistocene," in *Handbook of Paleoanthropology*, ed. Winfried Henke and Ian Tattersall (Berlin: Springer Verlag, 2006–2007), pp. 3:2001–37; Nicholas Conard, Maria Malina, and Susanne Münzel, "New Flutes Document the Earliest Musical Tradition in Southwestern Germany," *Nature* 460 (August 2009), pp. 737–40. Wil Roebroeks usefully cautions us that, although the association of early Aurignacian artifacts with modern humans is ubiquitous, it is predicated on their differences from characteristic Neandertal artifacts; there are as yet no early Aurignacian sites combining diagnostic artifacts with fossil human remains. See "Time for the Middle to Upper Paleolithic Transition in Europe," *Journal of Human Evolution* 55 (2008), pp. 918–26, esp. p. 918. For more on Aurignacian humans, see Chapters 6 and 7.

4. Francesco d'Errico and Christopher S. Henshilwood, "The Origin of Symbolically Mediated Behavior: From Antagonistic Scenarios to a Unified Research Strategy," in *Homo Symbolicus: The Dawn of Language, Imagination and Spirituality*, ed. Christopher S. Henshilwood and Francesco d'Errico (Amsterdam: John Benjamins, 2011), pp. 49–73.

5. For the paint pots, see Christopher S. Henshilwood, Francesco d'Errico, Karen L. van Niekerk, Yvan Coquinot, Zenobia Jacobs, Stein-Erik Lauritzen, Michel Menu, and Renata Garcia-Moreno, "A 100,000-Year-Old Ochre-Processing Workshop at Blombos Cave, South Africa," *Science* 334 (14 October 2011), pp. 219–22; for inscribed ochre and ostrich-shell, Christopher S. Henshilwood and Francesco d'Errico, "Middle Stone Age Engravings and Their Significance to the Debate on the Emergence of Symbolic Material Culture," in Henshilwood and d'Errico, *Homo Symbolicus*, pp. 75–96.

6. Whitney Davis, *Replications: Archeology, Art History, Psychoanalysis* (University Park: Pennsylvania State University Press, 1996), chs. 2–3.

7. Merlin Donald, *A Mind So Rare: The Evolution of Human Consciousness* (New York: Norton, 2001), esp. ch. 7 and pp. 152, 252–54.

8. Eva Jablonka and Marion J. Lamb, *Evolution in Four Dimensions: Genetic, Epigenetic, Behavioral, and Symbolic Variation in the History of Life* (Cambridge, MA: The MIT Press, 2005), pp. 193, 199–200.

9. Kim Sterelny, *The Evolved Apprentice: How Evolution Made Humans Unique* (Cambridge, MA: The MIT Press, 2012), ch. 3; for Ferraris, p. 51.

10. Marshall Sahlins, *Culture and Practical Reason* (Chicago: University of Chicago Press, 1976); see p. 169.

11. See also Davis, who defines culture, if not symbolism, in similar terms: "by 'culture' we simply mean socially coordinated replicatory histories"; *Replications*, p. 4.

12. Christopher S. Henshilwood and Curtis W. Marean, "The Origin of Modern Human Behavior: Critique of the Models and Their Test Implications," *Current Anthropology* 44 (2003), pp. 627–51, esp. pp. 635–36.

13. Paul Pettitt, "The Living as Symbols, the Dead as Symbols: Problematising the Scale and Pace of Hominin Symbolic Evolution," in Henshilwood and d'Errico, *Homo Symbolicus*, pp. 141–61.

14. The Deacon dossier is large; see esp. *The Symbolic Species: The Co-evolution of Language and the Human Brain* (London: Penguin, 1997); "The Symbol Concept," in *The Oxford Handbook of Language Evolution*, ed. Maggie Tallerman and Kathleen R. Gibson (Oxford: Oxford University Press, 2012), pp. 393–405; "Beyond the Symbolic Species," *Biosemiotics* 6 (2012), pp. 9–38; "Multilevel Selection in a Complex Adaptive System: The Problem of Language Origins," in *Evolution and Learning: The Baldwin Effect Reconsidered*, ed. Bruce H. Weber and David J. Depew (Cambridge, MA: The MIT Press, 2003), pp. 81–106; and the additional sources cited in the following notes.

15. For these paragraphs, see Deacon, "The Hierarchic Logic of Emergence: Untangling the Interdependence of Evolution and Self-Organization," in Weber and Depew, *Evolution and Learning*, pp. 273–308. Deacon has recently elaborated all of these concepts in an ambitious project to describe the emergent qualities of both life and mind; see *Incomplete Nature: How Mind Emerged from Matter* (New York: Norton, 2012).

16. See, for example, Sandra D. Mitchell, *Unsimple Truths: Science, Complexity, and Policy* (Chicago: University of Chicago Press, 2009), ch. 2.

17. Stuart Kauffman's proposed autocatalytic soups, from which life may have arisen, provide another, more hypothetical example of second-order emergence; see *The Origins of Order: Self-Organization and Selection in Evolution* (Oxford: Oxford University Press, 1993), pt. 2; for a summary statement, Stuart Kauffman, *Investigations* (Oxford: Oxford University Press, 2000), ch. 2.

18. At issue are not merely coded bundles of information but the formal constraints that structure them, for example the Adenine-Thymine and Cytosine-Guanine pairings of DNA molecules. The transmission of this information can be conceived as the historical transformation of constraint into replicator

and hence is dependent on the historicity of second-order emergence; see Deacon, *Incomplete Nature*, esp. chs. 9 and 12; see also "The Hierarchic Logic," pp. 297–301. For a related model of the replication of constraint, see Manuel de Landa's Deleuzian "abstract machine" for the cultural transmission of language, in which specific combinatorial constraints are themselves passed on; *A Thousand Years of Non-Linear History* (New York: Zone Books, 2000), pp. 215–26.

19. Uexküll's *Umwelt* differs in this trans-species inclusiveness from Heidegger's more restricted, humanistic use of the term; for this reason Uexküll's concept has been aggressively revived as a centerpiece of recent posthumanist formulations. See Jakob von Uexküll, *A Foray into the Worlds of Animals and Humans, with A Theory of Meaning* (1934–40), trans. Joseph D. O'Neil (Minneapolis: University of Minnesota Press, 2010).

20. Among Peirce's many, scattered writings on these issues, see Charles Sanders Peirce, *The Essential Peirce: Selected Philosophical Writings*, ed. The Peirce Edition Project (Bloomington: Indiana University Press, 1998), pp. 2:4–11, 161–64, 401–21; Peirce, *Philosophical Writings of Peirce*, ed. Justus Buchler (New York: Dover, 1955), ch. 7 ("Logic as Semiotic: The Theory of Signs"); and Peirce, *Selected Writings*, ed. Philip P. Wiener (New York: Dover, 1966), pp. 381–93.

21. For provocative analysis of these relations-to-relations, Paul Kockelman, "Biosemiosis, Technocognition, and Sociogenesis: Selection and Significance in a Multiverse of Sieving and Serendipity," *Current Anthropology* 52 (2011), pp. 711–39; also Kockelman, *Agent, Person, Subject, Self: A Theory of Ontology, Interaction, and Infrastructure* (Oxford: Oxford University Press, 2013).

22. An early statement of this aspect of Deacon's work is *The Symbolic Species*, ch. 3 ("Symbols Aren't Simple"). It is developed in many of his writings since; see those cited in n. 14, esp. "The Symbol Concept."

23. For example, the famous bonobo Kanzi, an instance Deacon takes up in *The Symbolic Species*, pp. 124–27.

24. It is not sufficient to define symbols negatively by the arbitrariness of the link of sign to object. Deacon positively defines symbolic reference as "reference mediated by a closed system of indexical relations which, taken together, refer holistically to a system of relations in the world"; "The Symbol

Concept," p. 401.

25. A less continuous reading of Deacon's views is that of ethnomusicologist Elizabeth Tolbert, who sees the transition to symbolism as a rupture in which the sign is "decomposed" and a space opened in it where new, non-innate relations of sign and object first appear. For Tolbert, this "decomposability of the sign" marks the birth of human culture, of ideational and linguistic propositionality, and also of the enigmatic nature of musical meaning. Personal communication. See also Tolbert, "The Enigma of Music, the Voice of Reason: 'Music,' 'Language,' and Becoming Human," *New Literary History* 32 (2001), pp. 451–65.

26. See Deacon, "The Symbol Concept," pp. 401–403.

27. This requirement suggests that the debate among protolinguists whether lexicon or syntax developed first, which we reviewed in Chapter 3, might admit a third possibility: neither could appear without the other. The shift from indexical vocalizations with weak, context-bound, deictic referentiality (which I located in a protodiscursive stage) to a syntactic language of symbols may have had the quality of a self-organizing phase transition spawning new, unforeseeable features. Something like this might be modeled in the computer simulations of language emergence of Simon Kirby, "Syntax without Natural Selection: How Compositionality Emerges from Vocabulary in a Population of Learners," in *The Evolutionary Emergence of Language*, ed. Chris Knight, Michael Studdert-Kennedy, and James R. Hurford (Cambridge: Cambridge University Press, 2000), pp. 303–23.

28. For these paragraphs, Terrence Deacon, "The Aesthetic Faculty," in *The Artful Mind: Cognitive Science and the Riddle of Human Creativity*, ed. Mark Turner (Oxford: Oxford University Press, 2006), pp. 21–53; for music, pp. 48–49.

29. This altered coevolution, Deacon argues, reshaped not only phylogeny but also (and through it) ontogeny. The advantages of symbolic communication selected neither for symbols lodged in the brain nor for a Chomskyan universal grammar but instead for a certain *kind* of cognitive ontogeny—for a brain that, through developmental differentiation, would facilitate the learning of all it needed to bring about its own leap into symbolism. See *The Symbolic Species*, ch. 4.

30. Michael Silverstein, "Metapragmatic Discourse and Metapragmatic

Function," in *Reflexive Language: Reported Speech and Metapragmatics*, ed. John A. Lucy (Cambridge: Cambridge University Press, 1993), pp. 33–58; for the quotation, see p. 36; for systematicity and "configuration" of indexes, see pp. 43, 47–48, 54–55; for ritual, see p. 48. For a further developed view of indexical systematicity and ritual metapragmatics, see Silverstein, "Indexical Order and the Dialectics of Sociolinguistic Life," *Language and Communication* 23 (2003), pp. 193–229, esp. pp. 201–204.

31. For an introduction to the importance and puzzles of discrete pitch perception, see *The Psychology of Music*, ed. Diana Deutsch, 3rd ed. (Amsterdam: Academic Press, 2013), esp. ch. 1, Andrew J. Oxenham, "The Perception of Musical Tones," and ch. 3, William Forde Thompson, "Intervals and Scales."

32. See also Chapter 4. Studies of infant perception have suggested that the percept called octave equivalence emerges very early in ontogeny. Sandra Trehub, "Human Processing Predispositions and Musical Universals," in *The Origins of Music*, ed. Nils L. Wallin, Björn Merker, and Steven Brown (Cambridge, MA: The MIT Press, 2000), pp. 427–48; see pp. 431–33. We may share it in the world today with at least a few nonhuman species, though the evidence is sparse and intractable. Rhesus monkeys have been shown to perceive a similarity between instances of a melody played an octave apart; see Aniruddh Patel, *Music, Language, and the Brain* (Oxford: Oxford University Press, 2008), pp. 398–99. Dolphins, also, might spontaneously shift the octaves of sounds they have been trained to produce; see Edward M. Burns, "Intervals, Scales, and Tuning," in *The Psychology of Music*, ed. Diana Deutsch, 2nd ed. (San Diego: Academic Press, 1999), pp. 238–61, esp. p. 253. Starlings, on the other hand, seem to process pitch according to its absolute frequency and do not correlate pitch patterns related in a 2:1 ratio; see *Nature's Music: The Science of Birdsong*, ed. Peter Marler and Hans Slabbekoorn (San Diego: Elsevier, 2004), p. 218.

33. Tonality in this broad sense seems to be related to the hierarchic cognition that underlies pitch combinatoriality also, though its mechanisms remain poorly understood. Isabelle Peretz, "The Nature of Music from a Biological Perspective," *Cognition* 100 (2006), pp. 1–32, esp. pp. 8–10; Ray Jackendoff and Fred Lerdahl, "The Capacity for Music: What Is It, and What's Special about It?" *Cognition* 100 (2006), pp. 33–72, esp. pp. 45–48; Patel, *Music, Language*, pp. 198–203. For a hierarchic, connectionist modeling of tonal perception, see Jamshed J. Bharucha, "Neural Nets, Temporal Composites, and Tonality," in

Deutsch, *The Psychology of Music*, pp. 413–40.

34. Human ontogeny seems in its way to recapitulate this proposed phylogeny, since discrete pitch perception emerges in childhood well after, and seems to be overlaid on, the contour-tracking capacity that is evident already in very young infants. See W. Jay Dowling, "The Development of Music Perception and Cognition," in Deutsch, *The Psychology of Music*, 2nd ed., pp. 603–25, esp. pp. 606–10.

CHAPTER SIX: 100,000–20,000 YEARS AGO, I

1. See Andrew Shryock, Daniel Lord Smail, et al., *Deep History: The Architecture of Past and Present* (Berkeley: University of California Press, 2011), ch. 10.

2. An especially important collection of contributions on these themes is Paul Mellars, Katie Boyle, Ofer Bar-Yosef, and Chris Stringer, eds., *Rethinking the Human Revolution* (Cambridge: MacDonald Institute, 2007), hereafter cited as *Rethinking*.

3. See Chris Stringer, "The Origin and Dispersal of *Homo sapiens*: Our Current State of Knowledge," in *Rethinking*, pp. 15–20, esp. p. 18.

4. J. M. Bermúdez de Castro, M. Martinón-Torres, et al., "The Atapuerca Sites and Their Contribution to the Knowledge of Human Evolution in Europe," *Evolutionary Anthropology* 13 (2004), pp. 25–41, esp. pp. 36–37.

5. John J. Shea, "*Homo sapiens* Is as *Homo sapiens* Was: Behavioral Variability versus 'Behavioral Modernity' in Paleolithic Archaeology," *Current Anthropology* 52 (2011), pp. 1–35; target essay with responses and rebuttal.

6. For a personal account of how the consensus formed and an introduction to the issues facing students of human evolution in its wake, see Chris Stringer, *Lone Survivors: How We Came to Be the Only Humans on Earth* (New York: Times Books, 2012).

7. John J. Shea, "The Boulevard of Broken Dreams: Evolutionary Discontinuity in the Late Pleistocene Levant," in *Rethinking*, pp. 219–32.

8. James F. O'Connell and Jim Allen, "Pre-LGM Sahul (Pleistocene Australia-New Guinea) and the Archaeology of Early Modern Humans," in *Rethinking*, pp. 395–410.

9. Alan R. Templeton, "Out of Africa Again and Again," *Nature* 416 (2002), pp. 45–51.

10. See Richard Green et al., "A Draft Sequence of the Neandertal

Genome," *Science* 328 (7 May 2010), pp. 710-22.

11. See David Reich, Richard E. Green, et al., "Genetic History of an Archaic Hominin Group from Denisova Cave in Siberia," *Nature* 468 (2010), pp. 1053-60; see also Ann Gibbons, "Who Were the Denisovans?" *Science* 333 (2011), pp. 1084-87. The newest analyses by Reich suggest also that Denisovans interbred earlier with another, unidentified hominin species, neither Neandertals nor *sapiens.* See Michael Marshall, "Mystery Human Species Emerges from Denisovan Genome," *New Scientist* 16.39 (November 2013).

12. Michael F. Hammer, August E. Woerner, et al., "Genetic Evidence for Archaic Admixture in Africa," *Proceedings of the Natural Academy of Sciences* 108 (2011), pp. 15,123-28; L. S. Premio and Jean-Jacques Hublin, "Culture, Population Structure, and Low Genetic Diversity in Pleistocene Hominins," *Proceedings of the Natural Academy of Sciences* 106 (2009), pp. 33-37, esp. p. 36.

13. Doron M. Behar, Richard Villems, et al., "The Dawn of Human Matrilineal Diversity," *American Journal of Human Genetics* 82 (2008), pp. 1130-40.

14. See Behar et al., "The Dawn."

15. Paul Mellars, "Why Did Modern Human Populations Disperse from Africa ca. 60,000 Years Ago? A New Model," *Proceedings of the Natural Academy of Sciences* 103 (2006), pp. 9381-86. For another interpretation of genetic evidence not so dependent on a single bottleneck but emphasizing the complexities of population dynamics, see Keith L. Hunley, Meghan E. Healy, and Jeffrey C. Long, "The Global Pattern of Gene Identity Variation Reveals a History of Long-Range Migrations, Bottlenecks, and Local Mate Exchange: Implications for Biological Race," *American Journal of Physical Anthropology* 139(2009), pp. 35-46.

16. Ulrich C. Müller, Jörg Pross, et al., "The Role of Climate in the Spread of Modern Humans into Europe," *Quaternary Science Reviews* 30 (2011), pp. 273-79, presents an alternative view, arguing that the Heinrich Event 48,000 years ago had drastic consequences for Europe, emptying it of archaic human populations; only after it did modern humans move into the area.

17. For these paragraphs, see Stephen Shennan, "Demography and Cultural Innovation: A Model and Its Implications for the Emergence of Modern Human Culture," *Cambridge Archaeological Journal* 11 (2001), pp. 5-16. For modeling of a large population divided into smaller groups in contact with one another, and also for some useful cautions on the limitations of the method, see A. Powell, S.

Shennan, and M. G. Thomas, "Late Pleistocene Demography and the Appearance of Modern Human Behavior," *Science* 324 (2009), pp. 1298–1301.

18. Peter J. Richerson, Robert Boyd, and Robert L. Bettinger, "Cultural Innovations and Demographic Change," *Human Biology* 81 (2009), pp. 211–35, esp. pp. 223–26.

19. Marcel Bradtmöller, Andreas Pastoors, Bernhard Weninger, and Gerd-Christian Weniger, "The Repeated Replacement Model—Rapid Climate Change and Population Dynamics in Late Pleistocene Europe," *Quaternary International* 247 (2012), pp. 38–49. On the limitations of radiocarbon dating of the Middle Paleolithic/Aurignacian border, see the special issue of the *Journal of Human Evolution*, 55.5 (2008); on new analyses that suggest not overlap but hiatus between Neandertal and modern human populations, see two articles there: Olaf Jöris and Martin Street, "At the End of the ^{14}C Time Scale—the Middle to Upper Paleolithic Record of Western Eurasia," pp. 782–802, and Wil Roebroeks, "Time for the Middle to Upper Paleolithic Transition in Europe," pp. 918–26. Roebroeks, however, concludes that the best hypothesis for the extinction of Neandertals remains their disadvantage, compared to sapient humans new to western Europe, in exploiting resources.

20. Brigitte M. Holt and Vincenzo Formicola, "Hunters of the Ice Age: The Biology of Upper Paleolithic People," *Yearbook of Physical Anthropology* 51 (2008), pp. 70–99; see p. 86.

21. Clive Finlayson and José S. Carrión offer another ecological view of Aurignacian cultures, less extreme in its analysis of European climate but agreeing that they represent populations discontinuous with Gravettian settlers, who came later from central Asia; see "Rapid Ecological Turnover and Its Impact on Neanderthal and Other Human Populations," *Trends in Ecology and Evolution* 22 (2007) pp. 213–22; see also Chapter 7.

22. Jirí A. Svoboda, ""On Modern Human Penetration into Northern Eurasia: The Multiple Advances Hypothesis," in *Rethinking*, pp. 329–40.

23. Shea, "The Boulevard of Broken Dreams," pp. 228, 229.

24. R. Nick E. Barton, Abdeljalil Bouzouggar, et al., "Abrupt Climatic Change and Chronology of the Upper Paleolithic in Northern and Eastern Morocco," in *Rethinking*, pp. 177–86.

25. Christopher Stuart Henshilwood, "Fully Symbolic *Sapiens* Behaviour: Innovation in the Middle Stone Age at Blombos Cave, South Africa," in

Rethinking, pp. 123–32; see 128–29.

26. Manuel de Landa, *A Thousand Years of Nonlinear History* (New York: Zone, 1997); see "Conclusions and Speculations" for de Landa's typology of the abstract machines discerned in historical change throughout the book; for passages from which de Landa starts: Deleuze and Guattari, *A Thousand Plateaus: Capitalism and Schizophrenia*, trans. Brian Massumi (Minneapolis: University of Minnesota Press, 1987), pp. 333–37, 510–14.

27. Among the by-now innumerable reproductions of the piece, see the cover of *Rethinking*.

28. Christopher S. Henshilwood, Francesco d'Errico, and Ian Watts, "Engraved Ochres from the Middle Stone Age Levels at Blombos Cave, South Africa," *Journal of Human Evolution* 57 (2009), pp. 27–47; Henshilwood, "Fully Symbolic *Sapiens* Behavior: Innovations in the Middle Stone Age at Blombos Cave, South Africa," in *Rethinking*, pp. 123–32; and Henshilwood and Francesco d'Errico, "Middle Stone Age Engravings and Their Significance to the Debate on the Emergence of Symbolic Material Culture," in *Homo Symbolicus: The Dawn of Language, Imagination and Spirituality* (Amsterdam: John Benjamins, 2011), pp. 75–96.

29. J.-P. Texier, G. Parkington, et al., "A Howiesons Poort Tradition of Engraving Ostrich Eggshell Containers Dated to 60,000 Years Ago at Diepkloof Rock Shelter, South Africa," *Proceedings of the National Academy of Sciences* 107 (2010), pp. 6180–85.

30. For an overview of bead technologies, see Francesco d'Errico and Marian Vanhaeren, "Evolution or Revolution? New Evidence for the Origin of Symbolic Behaviour In and Out of Africa," in *Rethinking*, pp. 275–86; for painstaking study of French Aurignacian beads and important general cautions, Randall White, "Systems of Personal Ornamentation in the Early Upper Palaeolithic: Methodological Challenges and New Observations," in *Rethinking*, pp. 287–302. For the Denisovan possibility, see Gibbons, "Who Were the Denisovans?" p. 1086.

31. For Shryock and Smail, "beads may even suggest the existence of a lingua franca of sorts, though it is not clear how such uniformity was maintained across disparate groups" (*Deep History*, p. 232). The epicyclic attendancy here proposed provides an answer to this question.

32. See D'Errico and Vanhaeren, "Evolution or Revolution?"; White, in

"Systems," pp. 298–300, disagrees.

33. There were no doubt many features by which these materials attained the capacity to signal something that was extraordinary in their contexts of use. For the later end of the period, archaeologist Randall White proposes that a common trait sought in most Aurignacian bead styles was sheen or luster, achieved even by polishing materials that did not naturally show it; see White, "Systems," p. 299.

CHAPTER SEVEN: 100,000–20,000 YEARS AGO, II

1. See Paul Mellars, "Archaeology and the Dispersal of Modern Humans in Europe: Deconstructing the 'Aurignacian,'" *Evolutionary Anthropology* 15 (2006), pp. 167–82.

2. Olaf Jöris and Martin Street, "At the End of the ¹⁴C Time Scale—the Middle to Upper Paleolithic Record of Western Eurasia," *Journal of Human Evolution* 55.5 (2008), pp. 782–802; see p. 797.

3. Thomas Higham, Laura Basell, et al., "Testing Models for the Beginning of the Aurignacian and the Advent of Figurative Art and Music: The Radiocarbon Chronology of Geissenklösterle," *Journal of Human Evolution* 62 (2012), pp. 664–76; see p. 674.

4. Indeed an additional strain of Aurignacian technological transmission, this one represented especially by small "bladelets" probably used in composite tools, seems to extend along the Mediterranean coast and into northern Spain and France; see Mellars, "Archaeology and the Dispersal," p. 169.

5. The nature of the Isturitz excavations makes precision difficult, but there are scant grounds for confidence in the assertion by the original excavators that one of the pipes came from a late Aurignacian layer; see Dominique Buisson, "Les flûtes paléolithiques d'Isturitz (Pyrénées-Atlantiques)," *Bulletin de la Société préhistorique française* 87 (1990), pp. 420–33, esp. p. 421.

6. For meticulous descriptions and an inventory of these pipes, see Iain Morley, *The Prehistory of Music: Human Evolution, Archaeology, & the Origins of Musicality* (Oxford: Oxford University Press, 2013), ch. 3 and appendix.

7. Francesco d'Errico, Christopher Henshilwood, Graeme Lawson, Marian Vanhaeren, Anne-Marie Tillier, Marie Soressi, Frédérique Bresson, Bruno Maureille, April Nowell, Joseba Lakarra, Lucinda Blackwell, and Michèle Julien, "Archaeological Evidence for the Emergence of Language, Symbolism,

and Music—An Alternative Multidisciplinary Perspective," *Journal of World Prehistory* 17 (2003), pp. 1–70; pp. 39–48 of this article summarize the findings of an examination of the Isturitz pipes carried out by d'Errico and Lawson. For the quotation, see p. 45.

8. For a survey of Middle and Upper Paleolithic musical (or putatively musical) artifacts other than pipes, including bullroarers, rasps, percussion instruments, and whistles, see Morley, *The Prehistory of Music*, ch. 4.

9. Personal communication, Elizabeth Blake, PhD candidate, University of Cambridge. Even geofacts may have been pressed into musical service; there is some evidence that stalagmites, stalactites, and other mineral outcroppings in caverns may have been struck, in effect becoming lithic gongs. See Morley, *The Prehistory*, pp. 115–21.

10. On these pipes, see Susanne Münzel, Friedrich Seeberger, and Wulf Hein, "The Geissenklösterle Flute—Discovery, Experiments, Reconstruction," in *Studien zur Musikarchäologie III: The Archaeology of Sound: Origin and Organisation*, ed. E. Hickmann, A. D. Kilmer, and R. Eichmann (Rahden, Germany: Marie Leidorf, 2002), pp. 107–18; Nicholas J. Conard, Maria Malina, and Susanne C. Münzel, "New Flutes Document the Earliest Musical Tradition in Southwestern Germany," *Nature* 460 (2009), pp. 737–40; and Morley, *The Prehistory of Music*, ch. 3 and appendix. The number of pipes unearthed continues to grow, with new fragments discovered at Vogelherd in summer 2014 (personal communication, Nicholas Conard).

11. See d'Errico et al., "Archaeological Evidence," p. 46: "such instruments must, even at around 35,000 years, be several conceptual stages removed from the earliest origins...of instrumental musical expression."

12. *Ibid.*, pp. 43–45; cf. Buisson, "Les flûtes paléolithiques," pp. 427–29.

13. Conard et al., "New Flutes," p. 738.

14. Paleoanthropologist Chris Stringer summed up a similar view of developments in Africa in a *New York Times* interview of July 16, 2012: "different parts of Africa were important at different times, to distinct human species, and this was being controlled by the climate. Africa is a huge place influenced by many different factors: the Mediterranean, the North Atlantic, the South Atlantic, the Southern Ocean, the monsoons coming off the Indian Ocean. At different times this would have produced good areas for humans and bad areas. Populations in different areas would have flourished briefly, developed

new ideas, and then maybe those populations could have died out, even—but not before exchanging genes, tools and behavioral strategies. This kept happening until we get to within the last 100,000 years, and then finally we start to see the modern pattern behaviorally and physically coalescing from these different regions to become what we call modern humans by about 60,000 years ago."

15. D'Errico and Lawson, in their discussion of the Isturitz pipes, are the researchers who have most clearly problematized this aspect of the pipes. "The very need for...multiplication and differentiation of pitches," they write, "would itself rather presuppose an already extant, noninstrumental (probably vocal) pitch-organizing behavior of some kind." In the speculative prehistory they construct of the pipes, they imagine a stage of multiple pipes, each playing a single pitch, fixed together in the manner of raftpipes or "Panpipes"(d'Errico et al., "Archaeological Evidence," pp. 47–48). Though, as we will see, I do not gainsay the sophistication of the arranging of pitches along a pipe, this seems to me improbable, arranging a more elaborate technology prior to a simpler one, as well as superfluous, given the proximity mentioned above of the pipes to other technologies.

16. Andrew Shryock and Daniel Lord Smail, *Deep History: The Architecture of Past and Present* (Berkeley: University of California Press, 2011), p. 233.

17. Bernard Chapais proposes a multistage, incremental, and gradual development of kinship systems encompassing the whole of hominin phylogeny in *Primeval Kinship: How Pair-Bonding Gave Birth to Human Society* (Cambridge, MA: Harvard University Press, 2008). For a summary of his position, see Shryock and Smail, *Deep History*, pp. 173–74.

18. Maurice Bloch, "Why Religion Is Nothing Special but Is Central," *Philosophical Transactions of the Royal Society B* 363 (2008), pp. 2055–61. The essay is reprinted in Bloch, *In and Out of Each Other's Bodies: Theory of Mind, Evolution, Truth, and the Nature of the Social* (London: Paradigm, 2012); see also the preface, ch. 1 ("Durkheimian Anthropology and Religion"), and ch. 5 ("Is There Religion in Çatalhöyük or Just Houses?").

19. See Shryock and Smail, *Deep History*, pp. 174, 268–69.

20. For this description, see esp. Bloch, *In and Out of Each Other's Bodies*, pp. 91–92.

21. Many researchers concerned with the cognitive foundations of religion

have converged on an account of such conceptions similar to this one. See esp. Pascal Boyer, *The Naturalness of Religious Ideas: A Cognitive Theory of Religion* (Berkeley: University of California Press, 1994); Boyer, *Religion Explained: The Evolutionary Origins of Religious Thought* (New York: Basic Books, 2001); Scott Atran, *In Gods We Trust: The Evolutionary Landscape of Religion* (Oxford: Oxford University Press, 2002); and Justin L. Barrett, *Cognitive Science, Religion, and Theology: From Human Minds to Divine Minds* (West Conshohocken, PA: Templeton; 2011). For an overview of this perspective, see Scott Tremlin, *Minds and Gods: The Cognitive Foundations of Religion* (Oxford: Oxford University Press, 2006); for minimal counterintuitions, see ch. 3.

22. The connection is pervasive enough to have featured often in attempts by anthropologists and ethnomusicologists to devise lists of musical universals; see for example Bruno Nettl, "An Ethnomusicologist Contemplates Universals in Musical Sound and Musical Culture," in *The Origins of Music*, ed. Nils L. Wallin, Björn Merker, and Steven Brown (Cambridge, MA: The MIT Press, 2000) pp. 463–72, and Steven Brown and Joseph Jordania, "Universals in the World's Musics," *Psychology of Music* 41 (2011), pp. 229–48. The connection, also, has often been carried over to discussions of Paleolithic practices; for a recent general affirmation, see Iain Morley, "Rituals and Music: Parallels and Practice, and the Palaeolithic," in *Becoming Human: Innovation in Prehistoric Material and Spiritual Culture*, ed. Colin Renfrew and Iain Morley (Cambridge: Cambridge University Press, 2009), pp. 159–78. David Lewis-Williams, *The Mind in the Cave: Consciousness and the Origins of Art* (London: Thames & Hudson, 2002) accords sounds and music an important place in the consciousness-altering, deep-cave rites he hypothesizes, though his primary aim is to explain the role of visual stimuli; see pp. 223–26.

23. Steven Mithen, *The Singing Neanderthals: The Origins of Music, Language, Mind, and Body* (Cambridge, MA: Harvard University Press, 2006), ch. 17.

24. Ian Cross, "Is Music the Most Important Thing We Ever Did? Music, Development, and Evolution," in *Music, Mind, and Science*, ed. S. W. Yi (Seoul: Seoul National University Press, 1999), pp. 10–39. Cross has developed this idea in a number of later essays; see esp. Ian Cross and Ghofur Eliot Woodruff, "Music as Communicative Medium," in *The Prehistory of Language*, ed. Rudolf Botha and Chris Knight (Oxford: Oxford University Press, 2009), pp. 77–98; and Cross, "Music as an Emergent Exaptation," in *Music, Language,*

and Human Evolution, ed. Nicholas Bannan (Oxford: Oxford University Press, 2012), pp. 263–76.

CHAPTER EIGHT: AFTERWARD

1. See Steven Mithen, *After the Ice: A Global Human History 20,000–5000 BC* (Cambridge, MA: Harvard University Press, 2005), p. 506.

2. For many views and reassessments on the beginnings of agriculture, see "The Origins of Agriculture: New Data, New Ideas," special issue of *Current Anthropology* 52 (2011), supp. 4, ed. T. Douglas Price and Ofer Bar-Yosef.

3. Leslie C. Aiello, introduction to "The Origins of Agriculture," p. S171.

4. Andrew Shryock, Daniel Lord Smail, et al., *Deep History: The Architecture of Past and Present* (Berkeley: University of California Press, 2011), pp. 147–48.

5. For a portrait of early Natufian life, Mithen, *After the Ice*, ch. 4.

6. See Olga Soffer, *The Upper Paleolithic of the Central Russian Plain* (San Diego: Academic Press, 1985), chs. 2 and 6.

7. For presentation and critique of Schmidt's interpretation and the revisionist view, see E. B. Banning, "So Fair a House: Göbekli Tepe and the Identification of Temples in the Pre-Pottery Neolithic of the Near East," *Current Anthropology* 52 (2011), pp. 619–60; the target article is followed by responses and a rebuttal.

8. See Chapter 6; also Shryock and Smail, *Deep History*, ch. 10.

9. Notwithstanding these many ingredients, this account remains a fragmentary one. I characterized it at the beginning as a series of snapshots or stills; but how detailed a moving picture can we extrapolate from four, five, or ten stills over a million years? One lacuna that will be obvious to all is my virtual silence on hominin physiological evolution, even concerning the channels of vocalization and audition. If instead I have focused on less palpable features of sociality, behavior, and cognition that can be extrapolated from the archaeological record and conceptualized through coevolutionary argument, it is not merely because these have often been misunderstood in earlier accounts. It is also (and more consequentially) because I believe them to be the aspects that will most directly lead us to the history of the emergence of musicking.

10. Charles Darwin, *The Origin of Species and The Voyage of the* Beagle (New York: Knopf, 2003), p. 913.

EVOLUTION, EMERGENCE, AND HISTORY

1. Hans Jonas, *The Phenomenon of Life: Toward a Philosophical Biology* (Evanston, IL: Northwestern University Press, 2001), p. 45.

Acknowledgments

Many students and colleagues witnessed the development of this book. Four students whose involvement merits special mention are Abigail Fine, Roger Grant, Thomas Pooley, and Gavin Steingo. Among my former music colleagues at Penn and present ones at Yale, Jeffrey Kallberg, Emma Dillon, Brian Kane, and Ellen Rosand all listened, responded, and lifted me at many moments. Colleagues too numerous to name at these and other universities from Cape Town to Oslo to Berkeley heard parts of this work, encouraging, challenging, doubting, always engaging. I would like to thank them all.

An early stage of the project took the form of the Wort Lectures at the University of Cambridge in 2009. I am grateful to Roger Parker for the invitation to deliver them, and to several interlocutors I met there: Ian Cross, Graeme Lawson, Iain Morley, and Elizabeth Blake. Elizabeth provided me with my first lesson in flint-knapping, and she might like to know that I have worked to refine the techniques to which she introduced me—though she would be the first to suspect that I still cannot boast anything approaching Neandertal expertise.

Other personal contacts with humanists from several fields, with anthropologists and archaeologists and with evolutionary, cognitive, and other scientists, have exercised a formative influence on my ideas. They include (in approximate order of their interventions) Stuart Kauffman, Manuel de Landa, Daniel Lord Smail, Robert Seyfarth, Paul Kockelman, Sally McBrearty,

Jamshed Bharucha, Robert Shulman, Terrence Deacon, Richard Prum, Michael Silverstein, Aniruddh Patel, Günter Wagner, Paul Griffiths, Peter Godfrey-Smith, and Stephen Stearns. I am indebted also to Kim Sterelny and Clive Gamble for sharing with me their work in prepublication form, and to the late María Rosa Menocal for welcoming me to Yale by inviting me to offer a seminar at the Whitney Humanities Center in which some of these ideas were elaborated.

Ingrid Monson and Carolyn Abbate both read the manuscript through, the first offering many helpful suggestions, the second page-by-page advice of the sort all writers cherish. The book and I each profited immensely from these readings. The encouragement and suggestions of Zone editor Ramona Naddaff and the expertise of director Meighan Gale and designer Julie Fry have also been invaluable. Professor Nicholas Conard, the archaeologist in charge of Germany's most stunning Paleolithic excavations over the last decade and more, graciously supplied the photographs for the Plates. Virge Kask skillfully drew the other images and diagrams.

Portions of Chapters 1 and 5 revise some sections from my essay "Evolutionary Studies in the Humanities: The Case of Music," *Critical Inquiry* 39 (Summer 2013); I am grateful for the editors' permission to reuse this material. An earlier version of Chapter 2 appeared as "Before *Homo sapiens*: Toward a Deep History of Entrainment," in *Musical Implications: Essays in Honor of Eugene Narmour*, ed. Lawrence F. Bernstein and Alexander Rozin (Pendragon Press, 2013); I am likewise grateful to Pendragon.

Margreta de Grazia and Colin Thubron have long been the most generous of friends and interlocutors, sustaining me, motivating me by example, even rescuing me twice when London's airports shut down. Joseph Kerman talked with me across decades about these matters and many others while collaborating on other projects; he is sorely missed. As I delved ever deeper into the riches of evolutionary theory, my children David, Laura, and Julia, blossoming humanists all, kept me (the lapsing humanist) honest regarding the decisive force of human culture; Laura in particular urged a view of culture extending beyond the human. They appreciate, I know, how proud their father is to be disciplined by them in his enthusiasms—and how much joy and wonderment he gains from watching their own enthusiasms proliferate—and I hope they will find humanism redeemed in a certain way in the final product. My stepson Raymond is a bit young to have thus corrected me, but one correction he would offer, were he to read these notes, would be to include in them our philosophical greyhound Boss.

As to my brilliant and beloved wife, Juliet Fleming, most of what might be said defeats the conventions of acknowledgment, so let this suffice: Whatever this book is, it would have amounted to much less without her.

Index

357

Zone Books series design by Bruce Mau
Typesetting by Meighan Gale
Image placement and production by Julie Fry
Printed and bound by Maple Press